Frank Moore

The patriot preachers of the American Revolution. With

biographical sketches. 1776-1783

Frank Moore

The patriot preachers of the American Revolution. With biographical sketches. 1776-1783

ISBN/EAN: 9783337304904

Printed in Europe, USA, Canada, Australia, Japan

Cover: Foto ©ninafisch / pixelio.de

More available books at **www.hansebooks.com**

THE

PATRIOT PREACHERS

OF THE

AMERICAN REVOLUTION.

WITH BIOGRAPHICAL SKETCHES.

EDITED BY FRANK MOORE.

———

NEW YORK:

CHARLES T. EVANS.

1862.

PREFACE.

It is the purpose of the editor of this volume to present a collection of the most characteristic Sermons, that were preached by the most celebrated divines, who occupied the American pulpits during the period extending from the Repeal of the Stamp Act, in 1766, through the Revolution, to the establishment of peace in 1783. The propriety of the publication of such a collection at the present time must be apparent to readers of all classes. The universal assertion that "the preachers of the Revolution did not hesitate to attack the great political and social evils of their day," demands a support, which nothing but the reproduction of their strong, practical appeals, can afford. As such, this collection is offered.

The brief biographical notices prefixed to each sermon are intended simply to indicate the position and character of their respective writers, and to give a rapid sketch of their lives and services. Those who wish for more particular accounts of them, are referred to the various biographical works already published.

New York, *March*, 1860.

CONTENTS.

PREACHERS OF THE REVOLUTION.

JONATHAN MAYHEW, D. D.

DOCTOR MAYHEW was a descendant from one of the most ancient and honorable families in New England. The first of the name who came to America, was Thomas Mayhew, governor of Martha's Vineyard, who resided at Watertown, Massachusetts, in 1636, and died 1681. The subject of this sketch was the great-grandson of Governor Thomas, and was born in 1720. In 1744, he graduated at Harvard College, and three years after was ordained pastor of the West Church, in Boston. In this charge he continued until his death, "loving his people, and by them beloved;" explaining with manly fortitude, the truths contained in the Bible, however discountenanced; esteeming the approbation of his Father in heaven, far before the applause of the world; inculcating, by his preaching and conduct, the doctrines of grace, as he thought them delivered by our Lord and his apostles, and that religion which is from above, and is full of mercy and good fruits, without partiality and without hypocrisy.

In his early productions, his uncommon talents and
generous independence of spirit, are eminently conspicuous. And though, for his opposition to all priestly
usurpations of authority over the consciences of men,
he had soon to encounter the whole force of enthusiasm and bigotry, his strength of mind, integrity of
soul, and unconquerable resolution in his Master's
service, supported him under every discouragement,
and enabled him to triumph over all his adversaries;
while his respect for and observance of the precepts
of the gospel convinced the world of the sincerity and
uprightness of his heart.   His works will transmit his
name to posterity, under the endearing character of a
steady and able advocate for religious and civil
liberty, and of a firm believer and constant practiser
of pure and undefiled religion. If at any time, through
the warmth of his feelings, his zeal in the cause of
religion and truth, and his aversion to the commands
of man in the Church of Christ, he was hurried beyond
the bounds of moderation, his many virtues and great
services toward establishing Christianity on the most
enlarged foundation, abundantly atone for such defects.
Indeed, the natural keenness and poignancy of his wit,
whetted often by cruel and unchristian usage, must
palliate his severest strokes of satire.   Nor will these
light objections depreciate his general reputation, if it
be remembered, that in his most social hours he inva-
riably sustained the united character of a Christian and
a gentleman.

The following sermon was the latest publication

made by Doctor Mayhew. It was published shortly after its delivery in 1766, and was dedicated to the Honorable William Pitt. Doctor Mayhew died, at the age of forty-six, on the eighth day of July, 1766.

REPEAL OF THE STAMP-ACT.

Our soul is escaped as a bird from the snare of the fowlers; the snare is broken, and we are escaped.
Our help is in the name of the Lord, who made heaven and earth.

PSALM cxxiv. 7, 8.

THE late gracious appearance of divine Providence for us, in the day of our trouble, seemed so seasonable, so signal, so important; in a word, so interesting to the present and future generations, that we of this society thought it expedient to agree among ourselves upon a day, in order to take a particular religious notice of it; and to praise the name of the Lord, in whom is our help.

If there had been any probability of our being called together for this end by proclamation, as upon some less memorable occasions, we should not have been desirous to anticipate the day; which might have had the appearance of ostentation. But of that, so far as I have heard, there was very little, if any, prospect. By this perfectly voluntary, and free-will offering, I hope we shall render to God, in some poor measure, the glory due to his name; and that He will graciously accept it through our Lord Jesus Christ the
1*

righteous, our mediator and advocate with the Father. At the same time it is supposed that, in proceeding thus, we give no just ground of offence to Jew or Gentile, or to the church of God; which we would by no means do. We only exercise that liberty wherewith Christ hath made us free, being desirous that all other persons and churches should do the same; and not choosing that either they or we should be "entangled with any yoke of bondage."

Having rendered our devout thanks to God, whose kingdom ruleth over all, and sung his high praises, permit me now, my friends and brethren, with unfeigned love to my country, to congratulate you on that interesting event which is the special occasion of this solemnity; an event, as I humbly conceive, of the utmost importance to the whole British empire, whose peace and prosperity we ought ardently to desire; and one very peculiarly affecting the welfare of these colonies. Believe me, I lately took no inconsiderable part with you in your grief and gloomy apprehensions, on account of a certain parliamentary act, which you supposed ruinous in its tendency to the American plantations, and, eventually, to Great Britain. I now partake no less in your common joy, on account of the repeal of that act; whereby these colonies are emancipated from a slavish, inglorious bondage; are reinstated in the enjoyment of their ancient rights and privileges, and a foundation is laid for lasting harmony between Great Britain and them, to their mutual advantage.

But when you requested me to preach a sermon on this joyful occasion, I concluded it was neither your expectation nor desire, that I should enter very particularly into a political consideration of the affair. Had I not conceived this to have been your intention, I must, though with reluctance, have given you a refusal; partly from a conviction of the impropriety of minutely discussing points of this nature in the pulpit, and partly from a sense of my own inability to do it as it ought to be done. I suppose I shall best answer your expectation, as well as most gratify my own inclination, by waiving political controversy, and giving you such counsels and exhortations respecting your duty to God and man, as are agreeable to the sacred oracles, to the dictates of sober reason, and adapted to the occasion.

This is therefore, what I chiefly purpose to do in the ensuing discourse, as God shall enable me. And may the Father of lights teach me to speak, and you to hear in such a manner, that our assembling together at this time, out of the ordinary course, may be to his honor, and to Christian edification. However, if my discourse is to be particularly adapted to this great occasion, instead of being so general, as to be almost as suitable to any other, you are sensible it is necessary that the occasion itself should be kept in view. I shall therefore briefly premise a few things relative thereto, by way of introduction to the main design: such things, I mean, as shall now be taken for granted. In mentioning which, my aim will be to express, in brief, what I take to be the general sense of these colonies, rather than to explain my own. For it is on such commonly received opinions, that my exhortations and cautions will be grounded; leaving the particular discussion of them to others, who are better qualified for it, and to whom it more properly belongs. And if I should be mistaken in any of these particulars, it is hoped candor will excuse it; seeing these are matters out of the way of my profession.

In pursuance of this plan, it shall now be taken for granted, that as we were free-born, never made slaves by the right of conquest in war, if there be indeed any such right, nor sold as slaves in any open lawful market, for money, so we have a natural right to our own, till we have freely consented to part with it, either in person, or by those whom we have appointed to represent, and to act for us. It shall be taken for granted that this natural right is declared, affirmed, and secured to us, as we are British subjects, by Magna Charta; all acts contrary to which are said to be *ipso facto*, null and void : and, that this natural constitutional right has been further confirmed to most of the plantations by particular subsequent royal charters, taken in their obvious sense; the legality and authority of which charters were never once denied by either house of Parliament; but implicitly, at least, acknowledged, ever since they were respectively granted, till very lately. It is taken for granted also, that the right of trial by juries, is a constitutional one with respect to all British subjects in general, particularly to the colonists ; and that the plantations in which civil government has been established, have all along, till of late, been in the uninterrupted enjoyment of both the rights aforesaid, which are of the utmost importance, being essential to liberty.

It shall, therefore, be taken for granted, that the colonies had great reason to petition and remonstrate against a late act of Parliament, as being an infraction of these rights, and tending directly to reduce us to a state of slavery. It is, moreover, taken for granted, whatever becomes of this question about rights, that an act of that sort was very hard, and justly grievous, not to say oppressive; as the colonies are poor, as most of them were originally settled at the sole and great expense of the adventurers—the expense of their money, their toil, their blood; as they have expended a great deal from time to time in their wars with their French and savage neighbors, and in the support of his majesty's government here; as they have, moreover, been ever ready to grant such aids of men and money to the crown, for the common cause, as they were able to give—by which means a great load of debt still lies on several of them; and as Great Britain has drawn vast emolument from them in the way of commerce, over and above all that she has ever expended for them, either in peace or war; so that she is, beyond all comparison, richer, more powerful and respectable now, than she would have been if our fathers had never emigrated; and both they and their posterity have, in effect, been laboring from first to last, for the aggrandizement of the mother country. In this light that share of common sense which the .colonists have, be it more or less, leads them to consider things.

It is taken for granted, that as the surprising unexampled growth of these colonies, to the extension of his majesty's dominion, and prodigious advantage of Britain in many respects, has been chiefly owing, under God, to the liberty enjoyed here; so the infraction thereof in two such capital points as those before referred to, would undoubtedly discourage the trade, industry and population of the colonies, by rendering property insecure and precarious; would soon drain them of all their little circulating money; would put it absolutely out of their power to purchase British commodities, force them into manufactures of their own, and terminate, if not in the ruin, yet in the very essential detriment of the mother country. It shall therefore, also, be taken for granted, that although the colonies could not justly claim an exclusive right of taxing themselves, and the right of being tried by juries, yet they had great reason to remonstrate against the act aforesaid on the footing of inexpedience, the great hardship, and destructive tendency of it, as a measure big with mischief to Britain as well as to themselves; and promoted at first, perhaps, only by persons who were real friends to neither.

But as to any methods of opposition to that measure, on the part of the colonies, besides those of humble petitioning, and other strictly legal ones, it will not, I conclude, be supposed, that I appear in this place as an advocate for them, whatever the general sense of the colonists may be concerning this point. And I take for granted, that we are all perfectly agreed in condemning the riotous and felonious proceedings of certain men of Belial,* as they have been justly called, who had the effrontery to cloak their rapacious violences with the pretext of zeal for liberty; which is so far from being a new thing under the sun, that even Great Britain can furnish us with many, and much more flagrant examples of it.

But, my brethren, however unconstitutional, oppressive, grievous or ruinous the aforesaid act was in its nature, and fatal in its tendency, his majesty and

---

* The Book of America, chap. ii. v. 13.

the Parliament have been pleased to hearken to the just complaints of the colonies, seconded and enforced by the prudent, spirited conduct of our merchants ; by certain noble and ever-honored patriots in Great Britain, espousing our cause with all the force of reason and eloquence, and by the general voice of the nation ; so that a total repeal of that dreadful act is now obtained. His majesty and the Parliament were far too wise, just and good, to persist in a measure after they were convinced it was wrong; or to consider it as any point of honor, to enforce an act so grievous to three million good subjects, so contrary to the interest of the British merchants and manufacturers, and to the general sense of the nation. They have been pleased, in the act of repeal itself, greatly to their honor, implicitly to acknowledge their fallibility and erroneous judgment in the other act, by saying, that " The continuance of the said act would be attended with many inconveniences, and might be productive of consequences greatly detrimental to the commercial interests of these kingdoms."

These being the reasons asssigned for the repeal, we may justly conclude, that if these many inconveniences and detrimental consequences could have been foreseen, the act complained of would never have been passed. And as the same reasons will doubtless operate at least as strongly, probably much more strongly hereafter, in proportion to the growth of the colonies, than they do at present, we may naturally conclude also, that an act of the like nature will never again be heard of. Thus " our soul is escaped as a bird from the snare of the fowlers; the snare is broken, and we are escaped," though not without much struggling in the snare, before it gave way and set us at liberty again.

But when I speak of that pernicious act as a snare, and those who prepared it for us as fowlers, greedy of their prey, let it be particularly observed, that I intend not the least reflection on our gracious sovereign or the Parliament; who must not be supposed to have any evil designs against the colonies, which are so necessary to Great Britain, and by which so many thousands of her manufacturers are supported, who, but for them, must actually starve, emigrate, or do what I choose to forbear mentioning. No! I apply this, as I conclude you will, only to some evil-minded individuals in Britain, who are true friends neither to her nor us; and who, accordingly, spared no wicked arts, no deceitful, no dishonorable, no dishonest means to push on and obtain, as it were by surprise, an act so prejudicial to both; and. in some sort, to the ensnaring of his majesty and the Parliament, as well as the good people of America; being, not improbably, in the interests of the houses of Bourbon and the Pretender, whose cause they meant to serve, by bringing about an open rupture between Great Britain and her colonies! These, these men, my brethren, are the cunning fowlers, these the ensnarers, from whose teeth "our soul is escaped as a bird." And such traitors will, doubtless, ere long be caught in another snare, suitable for them, to the satisfaction of the king's good subjects on both sides the Atlantic, if his majesty and the Parliament should judge it necessary for the vindication of their own honor, or for the public good, to bring them to condign punishment.

Let me just add here, that according to our latest

and best advices, the king, his truly patriotic ministry
and Parliament, have the interest, particularly the
commercial interest of the colonies much at heart;
being now disposed even to enlarge, instead of curtail-
ing their privileges, and to grant us every indulgence,
consistent with the common good of the British empire. More than which we cannot reasonably, and,
I am persuaded, do not desire.

These things being premised, let me now proceed
to those reflections, exhortations and cautions relative
to them, which were the chief design of this discourse.
And the present occasion being a very peculiar one,
such as never before occurred in America, and, I hope
in God, never will again, I shall crave your indulgence if I am considerably longer than is customary
on other occasions, which are less out of the ordinary
course.

In the first place, then, it is evident from the preceding view of things, that we have the greatest cause
for thankfulness to Almighty God, who doeth his will
among the inhabitants of the earth, as well as in the
armies of heaven. He, in whose hands are the hearts
of all men, not excepting those of kings; so that he
turneth them whithersoever he will, as the rivers of
water, hath inspired the people of America with a
noble spirit of liberty, and remarkably united them in
standing up for that invaluable blessing. He hath
raised us up friends of the greatest eminence in Britain, in our perilous circumstances. He hath united
the hearts of almost all wise and good men there, to
plead our cause and their own successfully. He hath
blessed the king with an upright ministry, zealous for
the public good, and knowing wherein it consists. He

hath given the king wisdom to discern, and integrity
to pursue, the interests of his people, at the late alarming crisis, when so much depended on the measures
that were then speedily to be taken. He hath changed
his royal purpose, and that of his Parliament, in a
matter which nearly and essentially concerned at least
our temporal happiness—disposing them to take off
from our necks that grievous and heavy burden, which,
to be sure, was not put upon us but with reluctance,
and through the dishonest artifices of certain wicked
men who, perhaps, intended, if possible, entirely to
alienate the affections of the colonists from their common father the king, and from their mother country.
O execrable design! to the accomplishment of which,
the pernicious measure aforesaid apparently tended.
But blessed be He who governeth among the nations,
that he hath confounded the devices of such treacherous men.

To allude to the psalm, a part of which I mentioned
as my text; "If it had not been the Lord who was on
our side, when men rose up against us, and if they
could have had their wicked will, then they had
swallowed us up quick—then the waters had overwhelmed us, the stream had gone over our soul; then
the proud waters had gone over our soul. Blessed be
the Lord, who hath not given us as a prey to their teeth;"
the ravening teeth of those cunning fowlers, from
whose treacherous snare we have just escaped; our
help being in the name of the Lord, who made heaven
and earth. To Him, therefore, we justly owe the un-
dissembled gratitude of our hearts, as well as the joyful praises of our lips. For I take it for granted, that
you all firmly believe, that He who made the world,

exercises a providential government over it; so that the very hairs of our head are all numbered by, and that a sparrow doth not fall to the ground without Him. How much more then, is his providence to be acknowledged in the rise, in the preservation, in the great events, the revolutions, or the fall of mighty states and kingdoms?

To excite our gratitude to God the more effectually, let us consider the greatness of our late danger and of our deliverance; let us take a brief retrospective view of the perplexed, wretched state, in which these colonies were, a few months ago, compared with the joyful and happy condition in which they are at present, by the removal of their chief grievances.

We have never known so quick and general a transition from the depth of sorrow to the height of joy, as on this occasion; nor, indeed, so great and universal a flow of either, on any other occasion whatever. It is very true, we have heretofore seen times of great adversity. We have known seasons of drought, dearth, and spreading mortal diseases; the pestilence walking in darkness, and the destruction wasting at noon-day. We have seen wide devastations, made by fire; and amazing tempests, the heavens on flame, the winds and the waters roaring. We have known repeated earthquakes, threatening us with speedy destruction. We have been under great apprehensions by reason of formidable fleets of an enemy on our coasts, menacing fire and sword to all our maritime towns. We have known times when the French and savage armies made terrible havock on our frontiers, carrying all before them for a while; when we were not without fear, that some capital towns in the colonies would fall

into their merciless hands. Such times as these we
have known; at some of which almost every face
gathered paleness, and the knees of all but the good
and brave waxed feeble. But never have we known
a season of such universal consternation and anxiety
among people of all ranks and ages, in these colonies,
as was occasioned by that parliamentary procedure,
which threatened us and our posterity with perpetual
bondage and slavery. For they, as we generally suppose, are really slaves to all intents and purposes, who
are obliged to labor and toil only for the benefit of
others; or, which comes to the same thing, the fruit
of whose labor and industry may be lawfully taken
from them without their consent, and they justly
punished if they refuse to surrender it on demand, or
apply it to other purposes than those which their
masters, of their mere grace and pleasure, see fit to
allow.

Nor are there many American understandings acute
enough to distinguish any material difference between
this being done by a single person, under the title of
an absolute monarch, and done by a far distant legislature, consisting of many persons, in which they are
not represented; and the members whereof, instead of
feeling, and sharing equally with them in the burden
thus imposed, are eased of their own in proportion to
the greatness and weight of it. It may be questioned
whether the ancient Greeks or Romans, or any other
nation in which slavery was allowed, carried their idea
of it much further than this. So that our late apprehensions, and universal consternation, on account of
ourselves and posterity, were far, very far indeed,
from being groundless. For what is there in this

world more wretched than for those who were born free, and have a right to continue so, to be made slaves themselves, and to think of leaving a race of slaves behind them—even though it be to masters, confessedly the most humane and generous in the world? Or what wonder is it, if, after groaning with a low voice for a while, to no purpose, we at length groaned so loudly, as to be heard more than three thousand miles; and to be pitied throughout Europe, wherever it is not hazardous to mention even the name of liberty, unless it be to reproach it as only another name for sedition, faction, or rebellion?

On the other hand, never did the tide of joy swell so high, or roll so rapidly through the bosoms and veins of the people in general, on any public occasion, as on the news of the repeal. "Then was our mouth filled with laughter, and our tongue with singing," when the Lord turned our captivity; this was received as an emancipation indeed, from unmerited slavery. Nor were there ever before so great external demonstrations of joy among the people of America; not even when all Canada was reduced, or when it was secured to the crown of England by treaty, and our apprehensions of coming under the yoke of France were vanished away. And some there are, who suppose that France would not have hesitated at allowing such a number of flourishing colonies the exclusive right of taxing themselves, for the sake of a free trade with them, could they have been prevailed on, by violating their allegiance, to put themselves under her protection; as I am fully persuaded these colonies would not do, for all that France has to give. In my poor opinion, we never had so much real occasion for joy, on any temporal account, as when we were thus emancipated, and our soul escaped as a bird from the dreadful snare.   And I am persuaded it would rejoice the generous and royal heart of his majesty, if he knew that by a single turn of the sceptre, when he assented to the repeal, he had given more pleasure to three million good subjects, than ever he and his royal grandfather gave them by all the triumphs of their arms, from Lake Superior eastward to the isles of Manilla; though so numerous, so great, so illustrious; and though we partook so largely in the national joy on those occasions.   A pepper-corn* a year added to his majesty's exchequer, would not surely ——! But I forbear.

If you please, we will now descend to some farther particulars, relative to our late unhappy and present joyful circumstances, in order to excite our thankfulness to God, for so memorable a deliverance.   This continent, from Canada to Florida, and the West-India islands, most of them at least, have exhibited a dismal mixed scene of murmuring despondence, tumult and outrage; courts of justice shut up, with custom-houses and ports ; private jealousies and animosities, evil surmisings, whisperings and backbitings, mutual reproaches, open railing, and many other evils, since the time in which the grievous act aforesaid was to have taken place.   Almost every British American, as was before observed, considered it as an infraction of their rights, or their dearly purchased privileges, call them which you will; and the sad earnest of such a galling yoke to be laid on our necks, already some-

* See Lord Clare's ever-memorable speech in an august assembly.

what sore by preceding grievances, as neither we nor our fathers were able to bear; or rather, as being itself such a yoke, and likely to grow heavier by length of time, without any increase either of ability or patience to endure it.

The uneasiness was, therefore, just and universal, except, perhaps, among a few individuals, who either did not attend to consequences, or who expected to find their private account in the public calamity, by exercising the gainful, the invidious, and not very reputable office of taskmasters over their groaning countrymen and brethren; even our bought negro slaves apparently shared in the common distress—for which one cannot easily account, except by supposing that even some of them saw, that if the act took place, their masters might soon be too poor to provide them suitable food and raiment; and thought it would be more ignominious and wretched to be the servants of servants, than of freemen.

But to return. The general discontent operated very differently upon the minds of different people, according to the diversity of their natural tempers and constitutions, their education, religious principles, or the prudential maxims which they had espoused. Some at once grew melancholy, sitting down in a kind of lethargic, dull desperation of relief, by any means whatever. Others were thrown in a sort of consternation, not unlike to a frenzy occasioned by a raging fever; being ready to do any thing or every thing, to obtain relief; but yet, unhappily, not knowing what, when, where, how; nor having any two rational and consistent ideas about the matter; scarce more than a person in a delirium has of the nature of, or proper method of curing the fever which is the cause of his madness. Some few were, I believe, upon the principles of Sibthrop, Manwaring, Filmer, and that goodly tribe, determined to go no farther in order to obtain redress, than in the way of petition and remonstrance; and this, even though they had been sure of success in some hardy enterprise. Others, who had no religious scruples of this kind, yet thought it extremely imprudent and hazardous to oppose a superior power in such a manner as might, perhaps, draw the whole weight of its resentment on the colonies, to their destruction. But the greater part, as I conceive, though I may be mistaken in this, were firmly united in a consistent, however imprudent or desperate a plan, to run all risks, to tempt all hazards, to go all lengths, if things were driven to extremity, rather than to submit; preferring death itself to what they esteemed so wretched and inglorious a servitude. And even of devout women not a few were, I imagine, so far metamorphosed into men on this sad occasion, that they would have declined hardly any kind of manly exertions, rather than live to propagate a race of slaves, or to be so themselves. In short such was the danger, and in their opinion, so great and glorious the cause, that the spirit of the Roman matrons in the time of the commonwealth, seemed to be now equalled by the fairer daughters of America.

The uneasiness of some persons was much increased by an imagination, that the money to be raised by the duty on stamps would partly be applied to pay certain civil officers' salaries; whereby they would become more entirely and absolutely dependent on the crown, less on the people, and consequently, as was supposed, more arbitrary and insolent. Others were anxious, because they imagined, with how much or how little reason you will best judge, that the money was to be chiefly applied toward maintaining a standing army in America; not so much to defend and secure the colonies from enemies, of whom they had none, except the aforesaid fowlers, as to awe the colonies themselves into an implicit obedience to ministerial measures, however unjust or execrable in their nature.

There is no end, you know, to people's fears and jealousies, when once they are thoroughly alarmed. And so some suspected, that this money was partly intended to maintain a standing army of bishops, and other ecclesiastics, to propagate the importance of certain rites and ceremonies, to which they had an aversion—the divine right of diocesan episcopacy and tithes, with many et ceteras of the like sacred and interesting importance. These strange notions and fears prevailed very much among certain odd people, who liked their old religion, and were not able to see the reasonableness of their paying for the support of any other.

I am not accountable for other people's whimsical apprehensions; I am here only representing the perplexity into which people's minds were thrown by the novel taxation, according to their different views of it —a taxation which was probably never thought of till a few years ago, when it was proposed to a great and good secretary of state, who was far too friendly to the colonies, as well as too wise, to burn his fingers with an American stamp-act. This diversity of humors, sentiments, and opinions among the colonists,

2

of which I have been speaking, naturally occasioned great animosities, mutual censures and reproaches, insomuch that it was hardly safe for any man to speak his thoughts on the times, unless he could patiently bear to lie under the imputation of being a coward, an incendiary, rebel, or enemy to his country ; or to have some other odium cast upon him.

In the mean time, most of the courts were shut up, and almost all business brought to a stand ; and, in some colonies, wide breaches were made between their several governors and houses of assembly ; those governors thinking it their duty to push the execution of the stamp-act ; and some of them trying to prevent the assemblies petitioning, in the joint manner proposed. In this state of general disorder, approaching so near to anarchy, some profligate people, in different parts of the continent, took an opportunity to gratify their private resentments, and to get money in an easier and more expeditious way than that of labor ; committing abominable excesses and outrages on the persons or property of others. What a dreadful scene was this ! Who can take a cursory review of it even now, without horror, unless he is lost to all sense of religion, virtue, and good order ? These were some of the bitter, and in a good measure, the natural fruits of that unhappy measure which preceded them.

Nor were we wholly unapprehensive of something still worse ; of having a more dreadful scene, even a scene of blood and slaughter opened ! I will not be particular here ; but ask you what you think of British subjects making war upon British subjects on this continent ! What might this have terminated in ? Perhaps in nothing less than the ruin of the colonies, and the downfall of a certain great kingdom, which has long been the support of other states, the terror of her enemies, and the envy and glory of Europe! If I had myself, once, some apprehensions of this kind, as I confess I had, I was very far from being singular therein.

One of the best judges of such matters, that any nation or age ever offered, as well as one of the best men, and most accomplished orators, speaking on this point, in a certain august assembly, is reported to have expressed himself thus: "On a good, on a sound bottom, the force of this country can crush America to atoms. I know the valor of your troops; I know the skill of your officers. But on this ground, on the stamp-act, when so many here will think it a crying injustice, I am one that will lift up my hand against it. In such a cause your success may be hazardous. America, if she falls, would fall like a strong man, would embrace the pillars of state, and pull down the constitution along with her." Thus the great patron of America.*

Even the remotest apprehensions of this kind, must give a very sensible pain to any American, who at once sincerely loves his own country, and wishes that the happy civil constitution, the strength and glory of Great Britain, may be as lasting as the world, and

---

* The Right Hon. William Pitt.—But the author thinks it a piece of justice due to so great and respectable a name, to acknowledge that he has no better authority for mentioning it on this particular occasion, than that of the public prints, lately spread all over America; giving an account of some debates in the honorable House of Commons. He also acknowledges that this is all the authority he has for citing some other passages afterward as from the same illustrious patriot.

still increasing; as God is my witness, I both wish
and pray. If Britain, which has long been the principal support of liberty in Europe, and is, at least was,
the chief bulwark against that most execrable of all
tyrannies, Popery, should in destroying her colonies
destroy herself (heaven forbid it!) what would become of those few states which are now free? what of
the Protestant religion? The former might, not improbably, fall before the *grand monarch* on this side
the Alps; the latter before the successor of the apostle Judas and grand vicar of Satan, beyond them, and
so, at length, one universal despotism swallow up
all!

Some of us had, lately, painful apprehensions of
this kind, when there was talk of a great military force
coming to stamp America into a particular kind of
subjection, to which most people here have an invincible aversion. It would doubtless, have been a noble
effort of genius and humanity in the—what shall I
call them? fowlers or financiers?—to extort a little
money from the poor colonies by force of arms, at the
risk of so much mischief to America, to Britain, to
Europe, to the world. And the golden temptation, it
is said, took with too many, for a while. A Pandora's
box, or Trojan horse, indeed!

> O miseri, quæ tanta insania, cives!
> Creditis avectos hostes! aut ulla putatis
> Dona carere dolis Danaûm? sic notus?*

But not to digress. I have now briefly reminded
you of our late sad, perplexed, alarming circumstances;

---

* Æn. II.

not for the sake of reproaching those who brought us into them, but to excite your gratitude to God, for our deliverance out of them, and for our present happy condition. The repeal, the repeal has at once, in a good measure, restored things to order, and composed our minds, by removing the chief ground of our fears. The course of justice between man and man is no longer obstructed; commerce lifts up her head, adorned with golden tresses, pearls and precious stones. All things that went on right before, are returning gradually to their former course; those that did not, we have reason to hope, will go on better now; almost every person you meet, wears the smiles of contentment and joy; and even our slaves rejoice, as though they had received their manumission. Indeed, all the lovers of liberty in Europe, in the world, have reason to rejoice; the cause is in some measure common to them and us. Blessed revolution! glorious change! How great are our obligations for it to the supreme Governor of the world? He hath given us beauty for ashes, and the oil of gladness for the spirit of heaviness. He hath turned our groans into songs, our mourning into dancing. He hath put off our sackcloth, and girded us with gladness, to the end that our tongues, our glory may sing praises to him. Let us all then rejoice in the Lord, and give honor to him; not forgetting to add the obedience of our lives, as the best sacrifice that we can offer to heaven; and which, if neglected, will prove all our other sacrifices have been but ostentation and hypocrisy, which are an abomination to the Lord.

The apostle Peter makes a natural transition from fearing God to honoring the king. Let me, accordingly, in the next place, exhort you, my friends and brethren, to a respectful, loyal and dutiful manner of speech and conduct, respecting his majesty and his government; thereby making a suitable return to him for the redress of our late grievances. I am, indeed, well apprised of the firm attachment of these colonies in general, and of our own province in particular, to the king's person, and to the Protestant succession in his illustrious house, for the preservation of which, there is hardly a native of New England who would not, upon constitutional principles, which are those of liberty, cheerfully hazard his life, or even more lives than one, if he had them, to lay down in so good a cause. I have not the least suspicion of any disaffection in you to his majesty; but yet the duty of subjects to kings, and to all that are in authority, is frequently to be inculcated by the ministers of the gospel, if they will follow the example of the apostles in this respect. And the present occasion seems particularly proper to remind you of that important duty, since we have now before us a recent and memorable proof of his majesty's moderation, his attention to the welfare of his people, and readiness, so far as in him lies, according to the constitution, to redress their grievances, on reasonable and humble complaint. If any persons among us have taken it unkindly, that his majesty should have given his royal assent to an act, which they think was an infraction of those liberties and privileges to which they were justly entitled; and if the usual tide and fervor of their loyal affection is in any degree abated on that account, yet, surely, the readiness which his majesty has shown to hear and redress his people's wrongs, ought to give a new spring and additional vigor to their loyalty and obedience.

Natural parents, through human frailty, and mistakes about facts and circumstances, sometimes provoke their children to wrath, though they tenderly love them, and sincerely desire their good. But what affectionate and dutiful child ever harbored resentment on any such account, if the grievance was removed, on a dutiful representation of it? Hardly any thing operates so strongly on ingenuous minds, though, perhaps of quick resentment, as the mild condescension of a superior to the force of reason and right on the part of the inferior. I shall make no application of this any farther, than to remind you that British kings are the political fathers of their people, and the people their children. The former are not tyrants, or even masters; the latter are not slaves, or even servants.

Let me farther exhort you to pay due respect in all things to the British Parliament; the lords and commons being two branches of the supreme legislative over all his majesty's dominions. The right of Parliament to superintend the general affairs of the colonies, to direct, check or control them, seems to be supposed in their charters; all which, I think, while they grant the power of legislation, limit the exercise of it to the enacting such laws as are not contrary to the laws of England or Great Britain; so that our several legislatures are subordinate to that of the mother country, which extends to and over all the king's dominions, at least so far as to prevent any parts of them from doing what would be either destructive to each other, or manifestly to the ruin of Britain.

It might be of the most dangerous consequences to the mother country, to relinquish this supposed authority or right, which, certainly, has all along been recognized by the colonies; or to leave them dependent on the crown only, since, probably, within a century, the subjects in them will be more than thrice as numerous as those of Great Britain and Ireland. And, indeed, if the colonies are properly parts of the British empire, as it is both their interest and honor to be, it seems absurd to deny, that they are subjects to the highest authority therein, or not bound to yield obedience to it. I hope there are very few people, if any, in the colonies, who have the least inclination to renounce the general jurisdiction of Parliament over them, whatever we may think of the particular right of taxation. If in any particular cases, we should think ourselves hardly treated, laid under needless and unreasonable restrictions, or curtailed of any liberties or privileges, which other of our fellow subjects in common enjoy, we have an undoubted right to complain, and, by humble and respectful, though not abject and servile petitions, to seek the redress of such supposed grievances.

The colonists are men, and need not be afraid to assert the natural rights of men; they are British subjects, and may justly claim the common rights, and all the privileges of such, with plainness and freedom. And from what has lately occurred, there is reason to hope, the Parliament will ever hereafter be willing to hear and grant our just requests; especially if any grievances should take place, so great, so general and alarming, as to unite all the colonies in petitioning for redress, as with one voice. The humble united prayers

of three or four million loyal subjects, so connected
with Great Britain, will not be thought unworthy of a
serious attention, especially when seconded by such
spirited resolutions and conduct of the American Merchants, as they have lately given an example of.
Humble petitions, so enforced, always carry great
weight with them; and, if just and reasonable, will
doubtless meet with a suitable return, as in the late
instance; since Great Britain can scarce subsist without the trade of her colonies, which will be still increasing. And an equitable, kind treatment of them,
on her part, will firmly bind them to her by the three-
fold cord of duty, interest and filial affection; such a
one, as the wise man says, is not easily broken. This
would do more, far more to retain the colonies in due
subjection, than all the fleets or troops she would think
proper to send for that purpose.

But to return; we ought, in honor to ourselves, as
well as duty to the king and Parliament, to frustrate
the malicious prophecies, if not the hopes, of some persons in Britain, who have predicted the most ungrateful and indecent returns from us to our mother country, for deliverance from the late grievances. It has
been foretold that, in consequence thereof, the colonies would grow insolent and assuming; that they
would affect a kind of triumph over the authority of
Parliament; that they would little or nothing regard
it hereafter, in other cases; that they would give some
broad intimations of their opinion, that it was not for
want of inclination, but of power, that the late grievous
act was not enforced; that they would treat their
brethren in Britain in an unworthy, disrespectful manner; and the like. Such things as these have been

2*

predicted, and, probably, by those very fowlers who
contrived the snare, from which, to their great mortification, our soul is now escaped as a bird. Let us,
my brethren (for it is in our power, and it is our duty),
make such men false prophets, by a contrary behavior : "prophets of the deceit of their own hearts."
This might, probably, vex them sorely, since it is
likely their chief aim is, to bring about a fixed, confirmed disaffection on our part, and a severe resentment on the other, while the jealous enemies of the
growing power of Britain, wag their ever-plotting and
enterprising heads, saying, "Aha! so we would have
it." Let us highly reverence the supreme authority of
the British empire, which to us is the highest, under
that of heaven. Let us, as much as in us lies, cultivate harmony and brotherly love between our fellow
subjects in Britain and ourselves. We shall doubtless
find our account in this at last, much more than in a
contrary way of proceeding. There are no other
people on earth that "naturally care for us." We
are connected with them by the strongest ties ; in
some measure by blood ; for look but a century or
two back, and you will find their ancestors and ours
in a great measure the same persons, though their
posterity is now so divided. We are strongly connected with them by a great commercial intercourse,
by our common language, by our common religion as
Protestants, and by being subjects of the same king,
whom God long preserve and prosper, while his enemies are clothed with shame. If we consider things
properly, it is indeed our great felicity, our best
security, and highest glory in this world, to stand in
such a relation as we do, to so powerful an empire ;

one which rules the ocean, and wherein the principles
of liberty are in general predominant. It would be our
misery, if not our ruin, to be cast off by Great Britain,
as unworthy her farther regards. What then would
it be, in any supposable way, to draw upon ourselves
the whole weight of her just resentment! What are we
in the hands of that nation, which so lately triumphed
over the united powers of France and Spain? Though
it must, indeed, be acknowledged, that she did this,
in a great measure, by means of her commercial intercourse with, and aids from the colonies—without
which she must probably have made a more inglorious
figure at the end, than she did at the beginning of the
last war; even though Mr. Pitt himself had had the
sole direction of it under his majesty.

Consider how many millions of people there are in
other countries, groaning in vain under the iron sceptre of merciless despotism, who, if they were but im-
perfectly apprised of the happiness we enjoy, would
most ardently desire to be in our situation, and to
stand in the like relation to Great Britain. Let us not
be insensible of our own felicity in this respect; let us
not entertain a thought of novelties or innovations, or
be given to change. Let us not indulge to any groundless jealousies of ill intentions toward us in our mother-
country, whatever there may be in some designing individuals, who do the devil's work, by sowing discord.

It is for the interest of Britain, as she well knows, to
retain the affection of these growing colonies, and to
treat them kindly to that end. And this bond of
interest on her part, is the strongest security to us,
which we can have in any political relation whatever.
We are bound, in honor to the king and Parliament,

to suppose, that it was not for want of ability to enforce a late act, and to crush us, that it was repealed;
but from a conviction of the inexpediency, the dangerous consequences, and many inconveniences of continuing it. And the like reasons will probably operate
forever against any act of the same nature, and grow
stronger and stronger. It can answer no valuable
end, for us to harbor grudges or secret resentment
on account of redressed and past grievances; no good
end wantonly and grossly to insult, and thereby to
incense any particular powerful persons on the other
side of the water, as the supposed enemies of the colonies. To me this seems impolitic at least; as it may
perhaps make such persons our enemies, if they were
not so before; or, if they were, fix their enmity; and
make them more industrious than ever in seeking opportunities to do us mischief. Much less can it answer
any good end, to affect to triumph over the power of
Parliament. This would, in short, appear equally
insolent, disloyal and ridiculous, in the eyes of all
sober, unprejudiced men.

May God give us the wisdom to behave ourselves
with humility and moderation, on the happy success
of our late remonstrances and struggles! . . . We are
bound in honor so to behave, not only that we may
frustrate the malignant predictions before referred to,
but that we may answer the just expectation of our
friends in Britain, who so nobly espoused our cause,
and, as it were, pawned their own honor (how great
and sacred a pledge!) for our good conduct, if our
grievances were removed. By such an engagement
they did us honor, as it manifested their candid and
kind sentiments concerning us. This lays us under an

additional obligation, in point of gratitude, to that good behavior, which would have been our duty without it.

I cannot but here remind you particularly of the words of that immortal patriot in Parliament, who has now a second time been the principal means of saving Britain and her colonies from impending ruin.* "Say, said he, the Americans have not in all things acted with prudence and temper ; they have been wronged ; they have been driven to madness by injustice. Will you now punish them for the madness you have occasioned ? Rather let prudence and temper come first from this side ; I will undertake for America that she will follow the example." What son, either of America or Liberty, is there, that has the least spark of ingenuousness, who can help being touched and penetrated to the inmost recesses of the heart by such magnanimous and generous expressions in behalf of the colonies ? Who is there, that would not almost as willingly die, as that that illustrious patron of America should ever have occasion to be ashamed of espousing its cause, and making himself answerable for us ?

We had other advocates of distinguished eminence and worth, who generously came under similar engagements for us. God forbid, my brethren, that any one of them should ever have the least reason to blush for his ill-placed confidence in us; as all of them will, if we show any unworthy behavior toward the king, the Parliament, or our mother country, after this proof of their moderation and regard for us. And if they, our friends, should have cause to blush for us in

---

* The Right Hon. Mr. Pitt.

this respect, what must we do for ourselves! Where shall we find caverns far enough removed from the light of day, in which to hide our heads! or what reason shall we have to expect friends, advocates and sponsors again, how much soever we may need them, if we have no more regard for the honor of those who appeared for us at the late alarming crisis; when it was accounted almost criminal to say any thing in our behalf?

Let me subjoin, that as the good people of this province had the honor to lead in a spirited, though decent and respectful application for the redress of our late grievances; methinks they should now be ambitious to have the honor of leading in a prudent, temperate, wise behavior, in consequence of the success; and, if need be, as I hope there is not, ambitious of setting an example of moderation and discretion to other colonies. This honor would be equal to the first mentioned; and would probably recommend us greatly to those, whom it will always be our interest and duty to please; so long, at least, as we can do it without renouncing our birthright. It will contribute to remove any impressions that may have been made of late, to our disadvantage. It will at once gratify our best friends, and falsify the slanders of our enemies, who delight in representing us as a seditious, factious and turbulent sort of people, who cannot endure the wholesome and necessary restraints of government. May God rebuke them for, and forgive them this wrong!

Let none suspect that, because I thus urge the duty of cultivating a close harmony with our mother country, and a dutiful submission to the king and

Parliament, our chief grievances being redressed, I mean to dissuade people from having a just concern for their own rights, or legal, constitutional privileges. History, one may presume to say, affords no example of any nation, country or people, long free, who did not take some care of themselves; and endeavor to guard and secure their own liberties. Power is of a grasping, encroaching nature, in all beings, except in Him to whom it emphatically "belongeth;" and who is the only king that, in a religious or moral sense, "can do no wrong." Power aims at extending itself, and operating according to mere will, wherever it meets with no balance, check, control or opposition of any kind. For which reason it will always be necessary, as was said before, for those who would preserve and perpetuate their liberties, to guard them with a wakeful attention; and in all righteous, just and prudent ways, to oppose the first encroachments on them. " *Obsta principiis.*" After a while it will be too late. For in the states and kingdoms of this world, it happens as it does in the field or church, according to the well-known parable, to this purpose— that while men sleep, then the enemy cometh and soweth tares, which cannot be rooted out again till the end of the world, without rooting out the wheat with them.

If I may be indulged here in saying a few words more, respecting my notions of liberty in general, such as they are, it shall be as follows. Having been initiated, in youth, in the doctrines of civil liberty, as they were taught by such men as Plato, Demosthenes, Cicero and other renowned persons among the ancients; and such as Sidney and Milton, Locke and Hoadley,

among the moderns, I liked them; they seemed rational.
Having earlier still learned from the Holy Scriptures
that wise, brave and virtuous men were always friends
to liberty; that God gave the Israelites a king (or absolute monarch) in his anger, because they had not
sense and virtue enough to like a free commonwealth,
and to have himself for their king; that the Son of
God came down from heaven to make us "free indeed," and that where the spirit of the Lord is, there
is liberty; this made me conclude, that freedom was a
great blessing. Having, also, from my childhood up,
by the kind providence of my God, and the tender
care of a good parent now at rest with Him, been
educated to the love of liberty, though not of licentiousness, which chaste and virtuous passion was still
increased in me as I advanced toward and into manhood; I would not, I cannot now, though past middle
age, relinquish the fair object of my youthful affections,
Liberty; whose charms, instead of decaying with time
in my eyes, have daily captivated me more and more.
I was, accordingly, penetrated with the most sensible
grief, when, about the first of November last, that day
of darkness, a day hardly to be numbered with the
other days of the year, she seemed about to take her
final departure from America, and to leave that ugly
hag slavery, the deformed child of Satan, in her room.
I am now filled with a proportionable degree of joy
in God, on occasion of her speedy return, with new
smiles on her face, with augmented beauty and splendor. Once more then, hail! celestial maid, the
daughter of God, and, excepting his Son, the first-
born of heaven! Welcome to these shores again;
welcome to every expanding heart! Long mayest

thou reside among us, the delight of the wise, good and brave; the protectress of innocence from wrongs and oppression, the patroness of learning, arts, eloquence, virtue, rational loyalty, religion! And if any miserable people on the continent or isles of Europe, after being weakened by luxury, debauchery, venality, intestine quarrels, or other vices, should, in the rude collisions, or now uncertain revolutions of kingdoms, be driven, in their extremity, to seek a safe retreat from slavery in some far distant climate, let them find, O let them find one in America under thy brooding, sacred wings, where our oppressed fathers once found it, and we now enjoy it, by the favor of Him, whose service is the most glorious freedom! Never, O never, may He permit thee to forsake us, for our unworthiness to enjoy thy enlivening presence! By His high permission, attend us through life and death to the regions of the blessed, thy original abode, there to enjoy forever the glorious liberty of the sons of God!

But I forget myself; whither have I been hurried by this enthusiasm, or whatever else you will please to call it? I hope your candor will forgive this odd excursion, for which I hardly know how to account myself.

There were two or three things more which I intended to say relative to this joyful occasion. To go on, then, these colonies are better than ever apprised of their own weight and consequence, when united in a legal opposition to any unconstitutional, hard and grievous treatment, which may be an advantage to them. God often bringeth good out of evil; or what is intended for evil by men, is by him meant for good. So it was particularly in the memorable case

of Joseph, whom his hard-hearted, envious brethren
sold as a slave into Egypt. There he became great,
and his father and brethren were at length obliged to
have recourse to him, to keep them and theirs from
perishing. And thus, not improbably, may good come
out of our late troubles, as well as out of those oppressions which occasioned the flight of our forefathers
into the deserts of America. The great shock which
was lately given to our liberties, may end in the con-
firmation and enlargement of them. As it is said, the
stately oaks of the forest take the deeper root, extend
their arms the farther, and exalt their venerable heads
the higher, for being agitated by storms and tempests,
provided they are not actually torn up, rent in pieces,
or quite blasted by the lightning of heaven. And
who knows, our liberties being thus established, but
that on some future occasion, when the kingdoms of
the earth are moved, and roughly dashed one against
another by Him that taketh up the isles as a very little
thing, we, or our posterity, may even have the great
felicity and honor to " save much people alive," and
keep Britain herself from ruin. I hope she will never
put it out of our power by destroying us; or out of
the inclination of any, by attempting it. It is to be
hoped, the colonies will ·never abuse or misapply any
influence which they may have, when united as aforesaid; or discover a spirit of murmuring, discontent of
impatience under the government of Great Britain,
so long as they are justly and kindly treated. On the
other hand, it is to be hoped they will never lose a
just sense of liberty, or what they may reasonably
expect from the mother country. These things they
will keep in mind if they are wise, and cultivate a

firm friendship and union with each other upon equal terms, as far as distance and other circumstances will allow. And if ever there should be occasion, as I sincerely hope and pray there may not, their late experience and success will teach them how to act, in order to obtain the redress of grievances. I mean by joint, manly and spirited, but yet respectful and loyal petitioning, setting aside some excesses and outrages, which all sober men join in condemning.

I believe history affords few examples of a more general, generous and just sense of liberty in any country, than has appeared in America within the year past. In which time the mercantile part in particular have done themselves much honor, and had a great share in preserving the liberties of the plantations, when in the most imminent danger—though this is not said with the least thought of reflecting on any other body or order of men, as wanting in their endeavors to the same noble end. Had we patiently received the yoke, no one can tell when, or whether ever it would have been taken off. And if there be some animals adapted by nature to bear heavy burdens submissively—one of which, however, is said, on a certain occasion, to have had the gift of speech, and expostulated with his master for unjustly smiting him —I hope the Americans will never be reckoned as belonging to that spiritless, slavish kind, though their "powers of speech"* should not, in the opinion of some nameless, heroic pamphleteer-scoffers in Britain, exceed those of the other, however defective they may be in point of "eloquence."* I thank God they

---

* An abusive superficial pamphlet in favor of the measures of the late ministry.

can at least feel, and complain so as to be tolerably understood.

If your patience will hold out, I will add a few words further, by way of advice, and so conclude. While we endeavor to cultivate harmony and union with our mother country and our sister colonies, in all generous and manly ways, we should not, surely, neglect to cultivate the same among ourselves. There have, I am sorry to say it, but really there have lately been many unwarrantable jealousies, and bitter mutual reproaches among the people of this town and province, occasioned by that unhappy measure which has been so often referred to. Even wise and good men, though all equally against that measure, could not, however, agree what was to be done, upon the maxims of prudence, though alike concerned for the public welfare. Accordingly, some were blamed as too warm and sanguine, others as too phlegmatic and indifferent, in the common and noble cause of liberty. Many were censured, and some, I am well assured, very unjustly, as being friends to, and encouragers of the fatal measure aforesaid. But how far these accusations were just or unjust on either side, I will not take upon me particularly to determine. Be that as it may, is it not best, my brethren, to let these contentions subside, now the end is obtained, and we have so fair a prospect before us? Are there any valuable ends to be answered by perpetuating these disputes? I cannot readily conceive any. Perhaps it is, because I have less penetration than most others. Be it as it will, I know One, and One whom we all profess to reverence, who hath said: "Blessed are the peacemakers, for they shall be called the children of God." And, "Let us study the

things that make for peace," said he that was not behind the chief of the apostles, and the things wherewith one may edify another.

These sayings may apologize for me, if I am wrong
in preaching peace at this time. And if none will
be offended with me for speaking plainly as to this
matter, to me it really seems most prudent, most
Christian, to bury in oblivion what is past; to begin
our civil, political life anew, as it were, from this joyful era of restored and confirmed liberty; to be at
union among ourselves; to abstain from all party
names and national reflections, respecting any of our
fellow-subjects; and to exert ourselves, in our several
stations, to promote the common good, by love serving one another. Let us make allowances mutually
for human frailty, for our different views and concep-
tions of things, which may be in a great measure un-
avoidable; for difference of natural constitution, an
unequal flow of animal spirits, or strength of nerves.
Let no one censure another more hardly, if at all,
than the necessity of the case plainly requires.

I hope these counsels of peace will not be dis-
relished by any " son of peace," or any wise and good
man, that does me the honor to be my auditor on this
occasion ; for I mean not to give offence, but only to
do good. Such counsels as they are, I humbly com-
mend them to the God of love and peace, to whose
holy will I believe them agreeable, for his blessing;
that they may have their just influence on all that
hear them. And you will not forget, that we must
all one day give an account to him ; so that it nearly
concerns us to have our ways, motives, and all our
doings approved by him.

In fine, let us all apply ourselves with diligence and in the fear of God, to the duties of our respective stations. There has been a general dissipation among us for a long time; a great neglect and stagnation of business. Even the poor and laboring part of the community, whom I am very far from despising, have had so much to say about government and politics, in the late times of danger, tumult, and confusion, that many of them seemed to forget they had any thing to do. Methinks, it would now be expedient for them, and perhaps for most of us, to do something more, and talk something less; every one studying to be quiet, and to do his own business; letting things return peaceably into their old channels, and natural courses, after so long an interruption.

My immediate aim in what I now say being only to recommend industry, good order, and harmony, I will not meddle with the thorny question, whether, or how far, it may be justifiable for private men, at certain extraordinary conjunctures, to take the administration of government in some respects into their own hands. Self-preservation being a great and primary law of nature, and antecedent to all civil laws and institutions, which are subordinate and subservient to the other; the right of so doing, in some circumstances, cannot well be denied. But certainly, there is no plausible pretence for such a conduct among us now. That which may be excusable, and perhaps laudable, on some very singular emergencies, would at other times be pragmatical, seditious, and high-handed presumption. Let all, therefore, now join with heart and hand in supporting the lawful, constitutional government over us, in its just dignity and vigor; in supporting his majesty's representatives, the civil magistrates, and all persons in authority, in the lawful exercise of their several offices. No true friend of liberty can reasonably object against this; and if any persons should, it would show that while they speak great swelling words of vanity, making liberty the pretext, they themselves are the servants of corruption, the ignoble slaves of sin.

Without this due regard to government and laws, we shall still be miserable, my friends, notwithstanding all that God and the king have done to make us happy. If one had wings like a dove, it were better to fly far away, and remain alone in the wilderness, where he might be at rest, than to live in a society where there is no order, no subordination; but anarchy and confusion reign. Of these we have surely had enough already; though at the same time I bless God that there has not been much more, considering the great danger in which we have been, with the general alarm and consternation by reason of that which is said to make even a wise man mad, and much more the rash and indiscreet, of whom there is a great proportion in all communities; considering also the absolute necessity there was, or at least seemed to be, of some very uncommon struggles and exertions, in order to break the snare and the natural impetuosity of many people's tempers. So important a change in the situation of public affairs, so great a deliverance, has, perhaps, seldom been brought about in any country, with so little criminal excess, unless it were done by God alone, without the instrumentality or agency of men, by nature liable to so many errors and infirmities. But whatever there has been of this kind, ought to be, and I hope is, lamented by all good men.

May that God, in whom our help has been, continue to protect us, our rights and privileges! May he direct our paths through this uncertain life, and all the changes of it; and, of his infinite mercy in Jesus Christ, finally bring us all to those peaceful and glorious regions where no evil spirits, no wicked fowlers will come—where no snares will be spread for us, no proud waters to go over our soul! And if we hope for admission into those eternal mansions of joy, let every one of us, as the apostle Peter exhorts, "honor all men, love the brotherhood, fear God, honor the king." AMEN.

THIS eminent man, celebrated alike for his piety and sterling patriotism, was born at Boston, Massachusetts. Through the exertions of his friends, who discovered in him a desire to obtain a liberal education, he was entered at Harvard College, from which institution he graduated with credit in 1740. From college he went to Portsmouth, in New Hampshire, where he was employed to take charge of a grammar-school until 1745, at which time he was invited to preach in the First Church, as assistant to Mr. Fitch. Two years after, he was ordained, and from this time until the commencement of the difficulties between England and her colonies, he continued an active laborer for the cause of the church.

Dr. Langdon was a very zealous whig. His bold and open opposition to the measures of the British government, rendered him highly acceptable to the patriots of New England, and through the influence of John Hancock and others, he was, in 1774, installed as successor of Mr. Locke in the presidency of Harvard College. When he took the chair it gave great delight to the sons of liberty; and in 1775, a month after the commencement of the war, he was chosen to preach the election sermon. This effort will be found in the following pages.

3

President Langdon's connection with the college did not prove of the most satisfactory character. His administration was a perpetual struggle with difficulties and embarrassments, amid the dangers of civil war and the excitement of a political revolution. He wanted judgment, and had no spirit of government. He did not receive that respect and kindness from the students and others connected with the college, that were due his character as a scholar and a Christian. Under these circumstances he resigned the presidency, and in 1781, became the pastor of a church at Hampton Falls, near Portsmouth, New Hampshire. In 1788 he preached the election sermon at Concord, and the same year occupied a seat in the New Hampshire Convention, in which body he took an active part, and had an extensive influence in removing the prejudices which prevailed against the Federal Constitution. At the age of seventy-four, on the twenty-ninth of November, 1794, he closed a life well spent, beloved for his piety, hospitality, and good-will to his fellow-men.

GOVERNMENT CORRUPTED BY VICE.

And I will restore thy judges as at the first, and thy counsellors as at the beginning: afterward thou shalt be called the city of righteousness, the faithful city.—ISAIAH, i. 26.

SHALL we rejoice, my fathers and brethren, or shall we weep together, on the return of this anniversary,

which from the first settlement of this colony has
been sacred to liberty, to perpetuate that invaluable
privilege of choosing, from among ourselves, wise
men, fearing God, and hating covetousness, to be
honorable counsellors, to constitute one essential
branch of that happy government which was established on the faith of royal charters?

On this day, the people have from year to year assembled, from all our towns, in a vast congregation,
with gladness and festivity, with every ensign of joy
displayed in our metropolis, which now, alas! is made
a garrison of mercenary troops, the stronghold of despotism. But how shall I now address you from this
desk, remote from the capital,* and remind you of the
important business which distinguished this day in
our calendar, without spreading a gloom over this
assembly, by exhibiting the melancholy change made
in the face of our public affairs?

We have lived to see the time when British liberty
is just ready to expire; when that constitution of
government which has so long been the glory and
strength of the English nation, is deeply undermined
and ready to tumble into ruins;—when America is
threatened with cruel oppression, and the arm of
power is stretched out against New England, and
especially against this colony, to compel us to submit
to the arbitary acts of legislators who are not our representatives, and who will not themselves bear the
least part of the burdens which, without mercy, they
are laying upon us. The most formal and solemn

---

* This sermon was preached at Watertown, Mass,

grants of kings to our ancestors are deemed by our oppressors as of little value, and they have mutilated the charter of this colony in the most essential parts, upon false representations, and new invented maxims of policy, without the least regard to any legal process. We are no longer permitted to fix our eyes on the faithful of the land, and trust in the wisdom of their counsels, and the equity of their judgment; but men in whom we can have no confidence, whose principles are subversive of our liberties, whose aim is to exercise lordship over us, and share among themselves the public wealth; men who are ready to serve any master, and execute the most unrighteous decrees for high wages, whose faces we never saw before, and whose interests and connections may be far divided from us by the wide Atlantic, are to be set over us as counsellors and judges, at the pleasure of those who have the riches and power of the nation in their hands, and whose noblest plan is to subjugate the colonies first, and then the whole nation to their will.

That we might not have it in our power to refuse the most absolute submission to their unlimited claims of authority, they have not only endeavored to terrify us with fleets and armies sent to our capital, and distressed and put an end to our trade, particularly that important branch of it, the fishery, but at length attempted, by a sudden march of a body of troops in the night, to seize and destroy one of our magazines, formed by the people merely for their own security; if, as after such formidable military preparation on the other side, matters should not be pushed to an extremity. By this, as might well be expected, a skirmish was brought on; and it is most evident, from a variety of concurring circumstances, as well as numerous depositions, both of the prisoners taken by us at that time, and our men then on the spot only as spectators, that the fire began first on the side of the king's troops. At least five or six of our inhabitants were murderously killed by the regulars at Lexington, before any man attempted to return the fire, and when they were actually complying with the command to disperse; and two more of our brethren were likewise killed at Concord Bridge by a fire from the king's soldiers, before the engagement began on our side. But whatever credit falsehoods transmitted to Great Britain from the other side may gain, the matter may be rested entirely on this—that he that arms himself to commit a robbery, and demands the traveller's purse, by the terror of instant death, is the first aggressor, though the other should take the advantage of discharging his pistol first and killing the robber.

The alarm was sudden; but in a very short time spread far and wide; the nearest neighbors in haste ran together to assist their brethren, and save their country. Not more than three or four hundred met in season, and bravely attacked and repulsed the enemies of liberty, who retreated with great precipitation. But by the help of a strong reinforcement, notwithstanding a close pursuit, and continual loss on their side, they acted the part of robbers and savages, by burning, plundering, and damaging almost every house in their way, to the utmost of their power, murdering the unarmed and helpless, and not regarding the weakness of the tender sex, until they had

secured themselves beyond the reach of our terrifying
arms.*

That ever-memorable day, the nineteenth of April,
is the date of an unhappy war openly begun, by the
ministers of the king of Great Britain, against his good
subjects in this colony, and implicitly against all the
colonies. But for what? Because they have made a
noble stand for their natural and constitutional rights,
in opposition to the machinations of wicked men, who
are betraying their royal master, establishing Popery
in the British dominions, and aiming to enslave and
ruin the whole nation, that they may enrich themselves and their vile dependents with the public treasures, and the spoils of America.

We have used our utmost endeavors, by repeated
humble petitions and remonstrances—by a series of
unanswerable reasonings published from the press, in
which the dispute has been fairly stated, and the
justice of our opposition clearly demonstrated—and
by the mediation of some of the noblest and most
faithful friends of the British constitution, who have
powerfully pleaded our cause in Parliament—to prevent such measures as may soon reduce the body

---

* Near the meeting-house in Menotomy two aged helpless men,
who had not been out in the action, and were found unarmed in a
house where the regulars entered, were murdered without mercy. In
another house in that neighborhood, a woman in bed with a new-born
infant—about a week old—was forced by the threats of the soldiery to
escape almost naked to an open outhouse; her house was then set on
fire, but was soon extinguished by one of the children which had lain
concealed till the enemy was gone. In Cambridge a man of weak mental powers, who went out to gaze at the regular army as they passed,
without arms, or thought of danger, was wantonly shot at, and killed by
those inhuman butchers, as he sat on a fence.

politic to a miserable, dismembered, dying trunk,
though lately the terror of all Europe. But our king,
as if impelled by some strange fatality, is resolved to
reason with us only by the roar of his cannon, and the
pointed arguments of muskets and bayonets. Because
we refuse submission to the despotic power of a
ministerial Parliament, our own sovereign, to whom
we have been always ready to swear true allegiance—
whose authority we never meant to cast off—who
might have continued happy in cheerful obedience,
as faithful subjects as any in his dominions—has
given us up to the rage of his ministers, to be seized
at sea by the rapacious commanders of every little
sloop of war and piratical cutter, and to be plundered
and massacred by land by mercenary troops, who
know no distinction betwixt an enemy and a brother,
between right and wrong; but only, like brutal pur-
suers, to hunt and seize the prey pointed out by their
masters.

We must keep our eyes fixed on the supreme government of the ETERNAL KING, as directing all
events, setting up or pulling down the kings of the
earth at his pleasure, suffering the best forms of human
government to degenerate and go to ruin by corruption; or restoring the decayed constitutions of kingdoms and states, by reviving public virtue and religion, and granting the favorable interpositions of his
providence. To this our text leads us; and though I
hope to be excused on this occasion from a formal discourse on the words in a doctrinal way, yet I must
not wholly pass over the religious instruction contained in them.

Let us consider—that for the sins of a people God

may suffer the best government to be corrupted, or
entirely dissolved; and that nothing but a general reformation can give ground to hope that the public
happiness will be restored, by the recovery of the
strength and perfection of the state, and that divine
Providence will interpose to fill every department
with wise and good men.

Isaiah prophesied about the time of the captivity
of the ten tribes of Israel, and about a century before
the captivity of Judah.   The kingdom of Israel was
brought to destruction, because its iniquities were full;
its counsellors and judges were wholly taken away,
because there remained no hope of reformation.   But
the sceptre did not entirely depart from Judah, nor
a lawgiver from between his feet, till the Messiah
came; yet greater and greater changes took place in
their political affairs; their government degenerated
in proportion as their vices increased, till few faithful
men were left in any public offices; and, at length,
when they were delivered up for seventy years into
the hands of the king of Babylon, scarce any remains
of their original excellent civil polity appeared among
them.

The Jewish government, according to the original
constitution which was divinely established, if considered merely in a civil view, was a perfect republic.
The heads of their tribes, and elders of their cities,
were their counsellors and judges.· They called the
people together in more general or particular assemblies, took their opinions, gave advice, and managed
the public affairs according to the general voice.
Counsellors and judges comprehend all the powers
of that government, for there was no such thing as

legislative authority belonging to it, their complete
code of laws being given immediately from God by
the hand of Moses.   And let them who cry up *the
divine right of kings* consider, that the only form
of government which had a proper claim to a divine
establishment, was so far from including the idea of
a king, that it was a high crime for Israel to ask to be
in this respect like other nations; and when they were
thus gratified, it was rather as a just punishment of
their folly, that they might feel the burdens of court
pageantry, of which they were warned by a very
striking description, than as a divine recommendation
of kingly authority.

Every nation, when able and agreed, has a right to
set up over itself any form of government which to it
may appear most conducive to its common welfare.
The civil polity of Israel is doubtless an excellent
general model, allowing for some peculiarities; at
least some principal laws and orders of it may be
copied, to great advantage, in more modern establishments.

When a government is in its prime, the public good
engages the attention of the whole; the strictest regard
is paid to the qualifications of those who hold the
offices of the state; virtue prevails—every thing is
managed with justice, prudence, and frugality; the
laws are founded on principles of equity rather than
mere policy, and all the people are happy.   But vice
will increase with the riches and glory of an empire;
and this gradually tends to corrupt the constitution,
and in time bring on its dissolution.   This may be
considered not only as the natural effect of vice, but a
righteous judgment of heaven, especially upon a na-
 3*

tion which has been favored with the blessing of re
gion and liberty, and is guilty of undervaluing them;
and eagerly going into the gratification of every lust.

In this chapter the prophet describes the very corrupt state of Judah in his day, both as to religion
and common morality ; and looks forward to that
increase of wickedness which would bring on their
desolation and captivity. They were *a sinful nation,
a people laden with iniquity, a seed of evil-doers, children that were corrupters, who had forsaken the Lord,
and provoked the Holy One of Israel to anger.* The
whole body of the nation, from head to foot, was full
of moral and political disorders, without any remaining soundness. Their religion was all mere ceremony
and hypocrisy ; and even the laws of common justice
and humanity were disregarded in their public courts.
They had counsellors and judges, but very different
from those at the beginning of the commonwealth.
Their princes were rebellious against God, and the
constitution of their country, and companions of
thieves, giving countenance to every artifice for seiz-
ing the property of the subjects in their own hands,
and robbing the public treasury. Every one loved
gifts, and followed after rewards ; they regarded the
perquisites more than the duties of their office ; the
general aim was at profitable places and pensions
they were influenced in every thing by bribery ; and
their avarice and luxury were never satisfied, but hurried them on to all kinds of oppression and violence,
so that they even justified and encouraged the murder
of innocent persons to support their lawless power,
and increase their wealth. And God, in righteous
judgment, left them to run into all this excess of vice

to their own destruction, because they had forsaken him, and were guilty of wilful inattention to the most essential parts of that religion which had been given them by a well-attested revelation from heaven.

The Jewish nation could not but see and feel the unhappy consequences of so great a corruption of the state. Doubtless, they complained much of men in power, and very heartily and liberally reproached them for their notorious misconduct. The public greatly suffered, and the people groaned, and wished for better rulers and better management. But in vain they hoped for a change of men and measures and better times, when the spirit of religion was gone, and the infection of vice was become universal. The whole body being so corrupted, there could be no rational prospect of any great reformation in the state, but rather of its ruin ; which accordingly came on in Jeremiah's time. Yet if a general reformation of religion and morals had taken place, and they had turned to God from all their sins—if they had again recovered the true spirit of their religion, God, by the gracious interpositions of his providence, would soon have found out methods to restore the former virtue of the state, and again have given them men of wisdom and integrity, according to their utmost wish, to be counsellors and judges. This was verified in fact, after the nation had been purged by a long captivity, and returned to their own land humbled, and filled with zeal for God and his law.

By all this we may be led to consider the true cause of the present remarkable troubles which are come upon Great Britain and these colonies; and the only effectual remedy.

We have rebelled against God. We have lost the true spirit of Christianity, though we retain the outward profession and form of it. We have neglected and set light by the glorious gospel of our Lord Jesus Christ, and his holy commands and institutions. The worship of many is but mere compliment to the Deity, while their hearts are far from him. By many the gospel is corrupted into a superficial system of moral philosophy, little better than ancient Platonism. And after all the pretended refinements of moderns in the theory of Christianity, very little of the pure practice of it is to be found among those who once stood foremost in the profession of the gospel. In a general view of the present moral state of Great Britain it may be said : *There is no truth, nor mercy, nor knowledge of God in the land. By swearing, and lying, and killing, and stealing, and committing adultery,* their wickedness breaks out; and one murder after another is committed, under the connivance and encouragement even of that authority by which such crimes ought to be punished, that the purposes of oppression and despotism may be answered. As they have increased, so have they sinned, therefore God is changing their glory into shame. The general prevalence of vice has changed the whole face of things in the British government.

The excellency of the constitution has been the boast of Great Britain, and the envy of neighboring nations. In former times the great departments of the state, and the various places of trust and authority, were filled with men of wisdom, honesty and religion, who employed all their powers, and were ready to risk their fortunes and their lives for the public

good. They were faithful counsellors to kings; directed
their authority and majesty to the happiness of the
nation; and opposed every step by which despotism
endeavored to advance. They were fathers of the
people, and sought the welfare and prosperity of the
whole body. They did not exhaust the national wealth
by luxury and bribery, or convert it to their own
private benefit, or the maintenance of idle useless
officers and dependents; but improved it faithfully for
the proper purposes, for the necessary support of government, and defence of the kingdom. Their laws
were dictated by wisdom and equity; and justice was
administered with impartiality. Religion discovered
its general influence among all ranks, and kept out
great corruptions from places of power.

But in what does the British nation now glory? In
a mere shadow of its ancient political system? In
titles of dignity without virtue? In vast public
treasures continually lavished in corruption, till every
fund is exhausted, notwithstanding the mighty streams
perpetually flowing in? In the many artifices to
stretch the prerogatives of the crown beyond all constitutional bounds, and make the king an absolute
monarch, while the people are deluded with a mere
phantom of liberty? What idea must we entertain
of that government, if such an one can be found, which
pretends to have made an exact counterbalance of
power between the sovereign, the nobles, and the commons, so that the three branches shall be an effectual
check upon each other, and the united wisdom of the
whole shall conspire to promote the national felicity;
but which in reality is reduced to such a situation that
it may be managed at the sole will of one court favor-

ite? What difference is there betwixt one man s *choosing*, at his own pleasure, by his single vote, the majority of those who are to represent the people; and his *purchasing in* such a majority, according to his own nomination, with money out of the public treasury, or other effectual methods of influencing elections? And what shall we say, if in the same manner, by places, pensions, and other bribes, a minister of state can at any time gain over a *nobler majority* likewise, to be entirely subservient to his purposes, and moreover persuade his *royal master* to resign himself up wholly to the direction of his counsels? If this should be the case of any nation from one seven years' end to another, the bargain and sale being made sure for such a period, would they still have reason to boast of their excellent constitution? Ought they not rather to think it high time to restore the corrupted dying state to its original perfection? I will apply this to the Roman senate under Julius Cæsar, which retained all its ancient formalities, but voted always only as Cæsar dictated. If the decrees of such a senate were urged on the Romans as fraught with all the blessings of Roman liberty, we must suppose them strangely deluded, if they were persuaded to believe it.

The pretence for taxing America has been that the nation contracted an immense debt for the defence of the American colonies; and that as they are now able to contribute some proportion toward the discharge of this debt, and must be considered as part of the nation, it is reasonable they should be taxed; and the Parliament has a right to tax and govern them in all cases whatever by its own supreme authority.

Enough has been already published on this grand controversy, which now threatens a final separation of the colonies from Great Britain. But can the amazing national debt be paid by a little trifling sum squeezed from year to year out of America, which is continually drained of all its cash by a restricted trade with the parent country, and which in this way is taxed to the government of Britain in a very large proportion? Would it not be much superior wisdom and sounder policy for a distressed kingdom to retrench the vast unnecessary expenses continually incurred by its enormous vices? To stop the prodigious sums paid in pensions, and to numberless officers, without the least advantage to the public? To reduce the number of devouring servants in the great family? To turn their minds from the pursuit of pleasure and the boundless luxuries of life, to the important interests of their country and the salvation of the commonwealth? Would not a reverend regard to the authority of divine revelation, a hearty belief of the gospel of the grace of God, and a general reformation of all those vices which bring misery and ruin upon individuals, families, and kingdoms, and which have provoked heaven to bring the nation into such perplexed and dangerous circumstances, be the surest way to recover the sinking state, and make it again rich and flourishing? Millions might annually be saved, if the kingdom were generally and thoroughly reformed; and the public debt, great as it is, might in a few years be cancelled by a growing revenue, which now amounts to full ten millions per annum, without laying additional burdens on any of the subjects. But the demands of corruption are constantly increasing, and will forever exceed all the resources of wealth which the wit of man can invent or tyranny impose.

Into what fatal policy has the nation been impelled by its public vices! To wage a cruel war with its own children in these colonies, only to gratify the lust of power, and the demands of extravagance! May God in his mercy recover Great Britain from this fatal infatuation; show them their errors, and give them a spirit of reformation, before it is too late to avert impending destruction. May the eyes of the king be opened to see the ruinous tendency of the measures into which he has been led, and his heart inclined to treat his American subjects with justice and clemency, instead of forcing them still farther to the last extremities! God grant some method may be found out to effect a happy reconciliation, so that the colonies may again enjoy the protection of their sovereign, with perfect security of all their natural rights, and civil and religious liberties.

But, alas! have not the sins of America, and of New England in particular, had a hand in bringing down upon us the righteous judgments of Heaven? Wherefore is all this evil come upon us? Is it not because we have forsaken the Lord? Can we say we are innocent of crimes against God?—No, surely; it becomes us to humble ourselves under his mighty hand, that he may exalt us in due time. However unjustly and cruelly we have been treated by man, we certainly deserve, at the hand of God, all the calamities in which we are now involved. Have we not lost much of that spirit of genuine Christianity which so remarkably appeared in our ancestors, for which God distinguished them with the signal favors

of providence, when they fled from tyranny and persecution into this western desert? Have we not departed
from their virtues? Though I hope and am confident
that as much true religion, agreeable to the purity and
simplicity of the gospel, remains among us as among
any people in the world, yet in the midst of the present great apostasy of the nations professing Christianity, have not we likewise been guilty of departing
from the living God? Have we not made light of
the gospel of salvation, and too much affected the
cold, formal, fashionable religion of countries grown
old in vice and overspread with infidelity? Do not
our follies and iniquities testify against us? Have
we not, especially in our seaports, gone much too far
into the pride and luxuries of life? Is it not a fact
open to common observation, that profaneness, intem-
perance, unchastity, the love of pleasure, fraud, avarice, and other vices, are increasing among us from
year to year? And have not even these young governments been in some measure infected with the corruptions of European courts? Has there been no
flattery, no bribery, no artifices practiced, to get into
places of honor and profit, or carry a vote to serve a
particular interest, without regard to right or wrong?
Have our statesmen always acted with integrity? and
every judge with impartiality, in the fear of God?

In short, have all ranks of men showed regard to
the divine commands, and joined to promote the Redeemer's kingdom and the public welfare? I wish
we could more fully justify ourselves in all these respects. If such sins have not been so notorious
among us as in older countries, we must, nevertheless,
remember, that the sins of a people who have been

remarkable for the profession of godliness, are more aggravated by all the advantages and favors they have enjoyed, and will receive more speedy and signal punishment; as God says of Israel: "*You only have I known of all the families of the earth, therefore will I punish you for all your iniquities.*"

The judgments now come upon us are very heavy and distressing, and have fallen with peculiar weight on our capital; where, notwithstanding the plighted honor of the chief commander of the hostile troops, many of our brethren are still detained as if they were captives; and those that have been released have left the principal part of their substance, which is withheld by arbitrary orders, contrary to an express treaty, to be plundered by the army.*

Let me address you in the words of the prophet—

---

* Soon after the battle of Lexington, General Gage stipulated with the select-men of Boston, that if the inhabitants would deliver up their arms, to be deposited in Faneuil Hall, and returned when circumstances would permit, they should have liberty to quit the town, and take with them all their effects. They readily complied; but soon found themselves abused. With great difficulty, and very slowly they obtain passes; but are forbidden to carry out any thing besides household furniture and wearing apparel. Merchants and shopkeepers are obliged to leave behind all their merchandise, and even their cash is detained. Mechanics are not allowed to bring out the most necessary tools for their work. Not only their family stores of provisions are stopped, but it has been repeatedly and credibly affirmed, that poor women and children have had the very smallest articles of this kind taken from them, which were necessary for their refreshment while they travelled a few miles to their friends; and that even from young children, in their mothers' arms, the cruel soldiery have taken the morsel of bread given to prevent them from crying, and thrown it away. How much better for the inhabitants to have resolved, at all hazards, to defend themselves by their arms against such an enemy, than suffer such shameful abuse!

"O Israel, *return unto the Lord thy God, for thou hast fallen by thine iniquity.*" My brethren, let us repent and implore the divine mercy. Let us amend our ways and our doings ; reform every thing which has been provoking to the Most High, and thus endeavor to obtain the gracious interpositions of Providence for our deliverence.

If true religion is revived by means of these public calamities, and again prevails among us ; if it appears in our religious assemblies, in the conduct of our civil affairs, in our armies, in our families, in all our business and conversation, we may hope for the direction and blessing of the Most High, while we are using our best endeavors to preserve and restore the civil government of this colony, and defend America from slavery.

Our late happy government is changed into the terrors of military execution. Our firm opposition to the establishment of an arbitary system is called *rebellion*, and we are to expect no mercy but by yielding property and life at discretion. This we are resolved at all events not to do ; and therefore, we have taken arms in our own defence, and all the colonies are united in the great cause of liberty.

But how shall we live while civil government is dissolved? What shall we do without *counsellors* and *judges?* A state of absolute anarchy is dreadful. Submission to the tyranny of hundreds of imperious masters, firmly embodied against us, and united in the same cruel design of disposing of our substance and lives at their pleasure, and making their own will our law in all cases whatever, is the vilest slavery, and worse than death.

Thanks be to God, that he has given us, as men, natural rights, independent of all human laws whatever; and these rights are recognized by the grand charter of British liberties. By the *law of nature* any body of people, destitute of order and government, may form themselves into a civil society according to their best prudence, and so provide for their common safety and advantage. When one form is found, by the majority, not to answer the grand purpose in any tolerable degree, they may by common consent put an end to it, and set up another; only as all such great changes are attended with difficulty, and danger of confusion, they ought not to be attempted without urgent necessity, which will be determined always by the general voice of the wisest and best members of the community. If the great servants of the public forget their duty, betray their trust and sell their country, or make war against the most valuable rights and privileges of the people; reason and justice require that they should be discarded, and others appointed in their room, without any regard to formal resignations of their forfeited power.

It must be ascribed to some supernatural influence on the minds of the main body of the people through this extensive continent, that they have so universally adopted the method of managing the important matters necessary to preserve among them a free government, by corresponding committees and congresses, consisting of the wisest and most disinterested patriots in America, chosen by the unbiased suffrages of the people assembled for that purpose, in their several towns, counties, and provinces. So general agreement, through so many provinces of so large a country, in one mode of self-preservation, is unexampled in any history; and the effect has exceeded our most sanguine expectations. Universal tumults, and all the irregularities and violence of mobbish factions, naturally arise when legal authority ceases. But how little of this has appeared in the midst of the late obstructions of civil government! Nothing more than what has often happened in Great Britain and Ireland, in the face of the civil powers in all their strength— nothing more than what is frequently seen in the midst of the perfect regulations of the great city of London; and, may I not add, nothing more than has been absolutely necessary to carry into execution the spirited resolutions of a people too sensible to deliver themselves up to oppression and slavery. The judgment and advice of the continental assembly of delegates have been as readily obeyed as if they were authentic acts of a long-established Parliament. And in every colony the votes of a congress have had equal effect with the laws of great and general courts.

It is now ten months since Massachusetts has been deprived of the benefit of that government which was so long enjoyed by charter. They have had no general assembly for matters of legislation and the public revenue. The courts of justice have been shut up; and almost the whole executive power has ceased to act. Yet order among the people has been remarkably preserved; few crimes have been committed punishable by the judge; even former contentions betwixt one neighbor and another have ceased; nor have fraud and rapine taken advantage of the imbecility of the civil powers.

The necessary preparations for the defence of our liberties required not only the collected wisdom and strength of the colony, but an immediate cheerful application of the wealth of individuals to the public service, in due proportion; or a taxation which depended on general consent. Where was the authority to vote, collect, or receive the large sums required, and make provision for the utmost extremities? A *Congress* succeeded to the honors of a *General Assembly* as soon as the latter was crushed by the hand of power. It gained all the confidence of the people. Wisdom and prudence secured all that the laws of the former constitution could have given. And we now observe, with astonishment, an army of many thousands of well-disciplined troops suddenly assembled, and abundantly furnished with all the necessary supplies, in defence of the liberties of America.

But is it proper or safe for the colony to continue much longer in such imperfect order? Must it not appear rational and necessary, to every man that understands the various movements requisite to good government, that the many parts should be properly settled, and every branch of the legislative and executive authority restored to that order and vigor on which the life and health of the body politic depend? To the honorable gentlemen, now met in this new congress as the fathers of the people, this weighty matter must be referred. Who knows but in the midst of all the distresses of the present war to defeat the attempts of arbitrary power, God may in mercy restore to us our judges as at first, and our counsellors as at the beginning.

On your wisdom, religion, and public spirit, honored gentlemen, we depend, to determine what may be done as to the important matter of reviving the form of government, and settling all the necessary affairs relating to it in the present critical state of things, that we may again have law and justice, and avoid the danger of anarchy and confusion. May GOD be with you, and by the influences of his spirit direct all your counsels and resolutions for the glory of his name, and the safety and happiness of this colony. We have great reason to acknowledge with thankfulness the evident tokens of the divine presence with the former congress; that they were led to foresee present exigencies, and make such effectual provision for them. It is our earnest prayer to the Father of lights, that he would irradiate your minds, make all your way plain, and grant you may be happy instruments of many and great blessings to the people by whom you are constituted, to New England, and all the united colonies.

Let us praise our God for the advantages already given us over the enemies of liberty; particularly, that they have been so dispirited by repeated experience of the efficiency of our arms; and that in the late action at Chelsea,* when several hundreds of our soldiery, the greater part open to the fire of so many cannon, swivels, and muskets from a battery advantageously situated, from two armed cutters, and many barges full of marines, and from ships of the line in the harbor, not one man on our side was killed, and

---

* This action was in the night following the 27th current, after our soldiery had been taking off the cattle from some islands in Boston harbor. By the best information we have been able to procure, about one hundred and five of the king's troops were killed, and one hundred and sixty wounded, in the engagement.

but two or three wounded; when, by the best intelligence, a great number were killed and wounded on the other side, and one of their cutters was taken and burnt, the other narrowly escaping with great damage.

If God be for us, who can be against us? The enemy has reproached us for calling on his name, and professing our trust in him. They have made a mock of our solemn fasts, and every appearance of serious Christianity in the land. On this account, by way of contempt, they call us *saints;* and, that they themselves may keep at the greatest distance from this character, their mouths are full of horrid blasphemies, cursing and bitterness, and vent all the rage of malice, and barbarity. And may we not be confident that the Most High, who regards these things, will vindicate his own honor, and plead our righteous cause against such enemies to his government, as well as our liberties. Oh, may our camp be free from every accursed thing! May our land be purged from all its sins! May we be truly a holy people, and all our towns cities of righteousness! Then the Lord will be our refuge and strength, a very present help in trouble; and we shall have no reason to be afraid though thousands of enemies set themselves against us round about, though all nature should be thrown into tumults and convulsions. He can command the stars in their courses to fight his battles, and all the elements to wage war with his enemies. He can destroy them with innumerable plagues, or send faintness into their hearts, so that the men of might shall not find their hands. In a variety of methods he can work salvation for us, as he did for his people in ancient days, and according to the many remarkable deliverances granted in former times to Great Britain and New England, when popish machinations threatened both countries with civil and ecclesiastical tyrany.*

May the Lord hear us in this day of trouble, and the name of the God of Jacob defend us; send us help from his sanctuary; and strengthen us out of Zion. We will rejoice in his salvation, and in the name of our God we will set up our banners; let us look to Him to fulfil all our petitions.

---

* When we consider the late Canada Bill; which implies not merely a *toleration* of the Roman Catholic religion (which would be just and liberal) but a *firm establishment* of it through that extensive province, now greatly enlarged to serve political purposes; by which means multitudes of people, subjects of Great Britain, which may hereafter settle that vast country, will be tempted, by all the attachments arising from an establishment, to profess that religion, or be discouraged from any endeavors to propagate reformed principles; have we not great reason to suspect, that all late measures respecting the colonies have originated from popish schemes of men who would gladly restore the race of Stuart, and who look on popery as a religion most favorable to arbitrary power? It is plain fact, that *despotism has an establishment* in that province equally with the Roman Catholic Church. The governor, with a council very much under his power, has by his commission almost unlimited authority, free from the clog of representatives of the people. However agreeable this may be to the genius of the French, English subjects there will be discouraged from continuing in a country, where both they and their posterity will be deprived of the greatest privileges of the British constitution, and in many respects feel the effects of absolute monarchy.

Lord Littleton, in his defence of this detestable statute, frankly concedes, that it is an *establishment* of the Roman Catholic religion, and that part of the policy of it was to provide a check upon the New England colonies. And the writer of an address of the people of Great Britain to the inhabitants of America just published, expresses himself with great precision when he says, that statute gave toleration to ENGLISH subjects.

4

THIS gentleman is celebrated as the divine who opened with prayer the Continental Congress of 1774. He was born in Philadelphia about the year 1730, and after receiving a liberal education, became rector of the Episcopal church in his native city. While in this position, he not only won a wide reputation as a preacher, but gained some eminence in the field of letters. In 1771 he published a series of letters under the signature of *Tamoc Caspipina*, bearing particularly upon the English politics of the day. At a late period they were collected in a volume and passed through several editions. In 1776, he was appointed Chaplain to the Congress, and while in the occupancy of that office, he gave the salary incident to it, for the relief of the families of Pennsylvanians killed in battle. At an early stage of the war, however, he manifested a decided opposition to independence, and in a long letter endeavored to dissuade Washington from continuing in the cause of the patriots. This act deprived him of the confidence of his fellow-men, and soon after he went to England, where he died in 1798. He is spoken of by his cotemporaries as a man of brilliant talents, and an interesting orator, possessed of fine poetical taste. His sermon given in

the present collection, is an excellent specimen of his
rhetoric. It was preached in Christ Church, in Philadelphia, on the seventh of July, 1775, and dedicated
to General Washington.

THE DUTY OF STANDING FAST IN OUR LIBERTIES.

Stand fast, therefore, in the liberty wherewith Christ hath made us free.
GALATIANS, v. 1.

GENTLEMEN OF THE FIRST BATTALION OF THE CITY
AND LIBERTIES OF PHILADELPHIA :—Though I readily
accepted of the invitation with which you were
pleased to honor me, and am fully satisfied that there
can be no impropriety in complying with your request,
yet I confess, that I now feel such an uncommon degree of diffidence, as nothing but a sense of duty, and
a sincere sympathy with you in your present trying
circumstances could enable me to overcome. The occasion is of the first importance; the subject in a great
measure new to me—throwing myself, therefore, upon
your candor and indulgence, considering myself under
the twofold character of a minister of Jesus Christ,
and a fellow-citizen of the same state, and involved in
the same public calamity with yourselves, and looking
up for counsel and direction to the source of all wisdom, " who giveth liberally to those that ask it," I
have made choice of a passage of Scripture, which will
give me an opportunity of addressing myself to you as
freemen, both in the spiritual and temporal sense of

the word, and of suggesting to you such a mode of conduct, as will be most likely, under the blessing of Heaven, to insure to you the enjoyment of these two kinds of liberty. " Stand fast, therefore, in the liberty wherewith Christ hath made us free."

The inspired author of this excellent admonition was so sensible of the invaluable blessings and comforts that resulted from that free spirit, with which Jesus Christ, through his ministry, had established his Gala-tian converts, that he was jealous of the least attempt to destroy or even obstruct in them its life-giving operation. He could not brook the narrow spirit of those Judaizing Christians, who, from the most selfish and illiberal motives, sought to force a yoke upon the necks of their Gentile brethren, which neither they themselves, nor their fathers had been able to bear. These Gentiles, too, he severely reproves for not main-taining their ground, and asserting their gospel free-dom against the insidious devices of their brethren, who only wanted to bring them into servitude, " that they might glory in their flesh."—" O foolish Galatians! who hath bewitched you?" He ascribes their blind-ness and infatuation to some diabolical charm, which had locked up the powers of their freeborn spirits, and made them tamely submit to slavish carnal ordi-nances, which the gospel of Jesus had entirely ex-ploded and abolished. He reminds them, by a spirited explication of a most striking allegory, that they were not " children of the bond-woman, but of the free ;" that their observance of the ceremonial law was a tribute, which they were not bound to pay ; or, if they should be so weak as to submit to it, that it could not emancipate them from the bondage of earth and hell; but that their real freedom, their full and complete justification, their happiness, temporal and eternal, were only to be acquired by a vigorous exertion of those spiritual powers within themselves, which through the riches of God's free grace in Jesus Christ, had been communicated to their souls. He concludes this part of his address with the truly noble and apostolic precept of my text: "Stand fast, therefore, in the liberty wherewith Christ hath made us free."

Having thus briefly opened the occasion and meaning of the words, I shall proceed to show, in the first place, what we are to understand by that spiritual liberty "wherewith Christ hath made us free," and what kind of conduct that must be which is here expressed by the words "stand fast."

I. However severe, my dear brethren, the loss of our temporal liberties may be, there is certainly a bondage far more severe than this; yea, far more cruel, than that of Israel under their their Egyptian taskmasters—a bondage not only to men, but to the fallen spirits of darkness, seeking to exercise over us a joint power and dominion with our own irregular and corrupt passions—a bondage universal, from which no son of Adam hath ever been exempt—a tyranny whose baleful influences have been felt, from the fall of man down to this very day. It has seized not only upon the body, but upon the soul. It has erected its throne in the heart, and from thence imposes its arbitrary decrees. It is confined to no age or sex, no state or condition of human life. High and low, learned and unlearned, the savage and the sage, are alike victims of this despotic power—alike slaves by nature under this bondage of corruption.

It is perpetually manifesting itself under a variety of forms, according to our prevailing desires and pursuits. It follows us into the sanctuary of God. It steals into our private devotions. It gives a pharisaical tincture to our best good-works. It reigns as a master and absolute sovereign in the wicked and unregenerate. Yea, it frequently enters the most spiritual and regenerate hearts in hostile form, and seeks to shake their confidence in the goodness of their true and rightful Sovereign, and their humble hope of deliverance through the redeeming power of his ever-blessed Son.

Now, who would not wish to be delivered from such a bondage as this? And yet, my brethren, such a wish cannot be formed till, by divine grace, the free-born powers of the soul are brought to be sensible of their burden, and to groan beneath the weight of oppression. "The whole (or they that think themselves whole) need not a physician, but they that are sick." The madman hugs his chains, as if they were ensigns of royalty. Insensible of his calamity, he cannot even wish for relief.

But no sooner does the child of grace, the offspring of heaven, come to feel the bondage of the infernal usurper; no sooner does he find himself harrassed and oppressed by the obedience which he exacts to his unrighteous laws; no sooner is he convinced that such an obedience must terminate in everlasting slavery and wretchedness, than he awakens from his sleep of security, and turns to and avails himself of that light and strength, and spiritual courage and constancy, which his Redeemer is ever at hand to impart, and without which he feels himself absolutely unequal to the conflict, and incapable of extricating himself from the ignoble servitude.

From hence, then, it appears that the liberty with which Christ hath made us free, is nothing less than such a release from the arbitrary power of sin, such an enlargement of the soul by the efficacy of divine grace, and such a total surrender of the will and affections to the influence and guidance of the divine spirit ("for we are made a willing people in the day of God's power"), as will enable us to live in the habitual cheerful practice of every grace and virtue here, and qualify us for the free, full and uninterrupted enjoyment of heavenly life and liberty hereafter.

These glorious privileges being once obtained, the sinner being once justified and adopted into the family of God, and having received the seal of his heavenly citizenship, the conduct recommended to him in my text as the most effectual for the preservation of these privileges, is here expressed by the words, "stand fast;" that is to say, maintain, firm and unshaken, the ground which Christ hath given you. Be ever vigilant and prepared, against the open or insidious attacks of your adversary.

He is not commanded to march upon the devil's ground, to seek out the tempter or the temptation, in order to make a trial of his strength, or merely that he may have the honor of a victory, but only to "stand fast," to act upon the defensive, and armed at all points with a celestial panoply, to be ready to resist and repel the most daring attempts of his perfidious foe; as well knowing, that if he suffers himself to be taken captive, slavery and woe must be his everlasting portion; but, if he comes off conqueror from the conflict, that the life, liberty, and joys of heaven will be his everlasting reward. Thus far have I travelled in a well-known path, and spoken a language familiar to most of you, and which you have long been accustomed to hear from this pulpit.

II. I am now to strike into another path, which, though it may not always terminate in such glorious scenes of never-ending felicity as the former, yet, if steadfastly pursued, will conduct the sons of men to a happiness, of an inferior kind indeed, but highly necessary to their present temporary state of existence in this world.

If *spiritual liberty* calls upon its pious votaries to extend their views far forward to a glorious hereafter, *civil liberty* must at least be allowed to secure in a considerable degree our well-being here. And I believe it will be no difficult matter to prove that the latter is as much the gift of God in Christ Jesus as the former, and consequently, that we are bound to stand fast in our civil as well as our spiritual freedom.

From what hath been said under my first head of discourse, I think it must appear, that liberty, traced to her true source, is of heavenly extraction, that divine virtue is her illustrious parent, that from eternity to eternity they have been and must be inseparable companions, and that the hearts of all intelligent beings are the living temples, in which they ought to be jointly worshipped.

We have the authority of divine revelation to assert, that this globe of earth was once the favored spot on which she was sent to reside, and that the first man felt and enjoyed her divine influence within and around him. But the same revelation tells us, what our own experience cannot but confirm, that when man lost his virtue, he lost his liberty too; and from that fatal period became subject to the bondage of corruption, the slave of irregular passions, at war with himself and his own species, an alien from his native country, a sorrowful stranger and a weary pilgrim in this world of woe.

It was not only to put him into a capacity of regaining his forfeited heavenly bliss, but to mitigate, likewise, the sorrows of his earthly sojourn, that the everlasting Jesus, in and by whom God originally created man, vouchsafed to communicate to him when fallen, a ray of hope, a spark of heavenly light, wisdom, power, and goodness, by which, through the effectual workings of his grace, he might in future time inspire him and his helpless posterity with such principles as would lead them to know, contend for, and enjoy, liberty, in its largest and noblest extent.

Whatever of order, truth, equity and good government is to be found among the sons of men, they are solely indebted for to this everlasting Counsellor, this Prince of Peace. By nature surrounded with innumerable wants, which his own single, unassisted hand could by no means supply, exposed to innumerable dangers, which his utmost strength and sharpest foresight could not possibly ward off, it must surely have been this wisdom of the Father that first taught man, by social compact, to secure to himself the possession of those necessaries and comforts which are so dear and valuable to his natural life. And though no particular mode of government is pointed out to us in His holy gospel, yet the benevolent spirit of that gospel is directly opposed to every other form than such as

4*

has the common good of mankind for its end and aim.

Now this common good is matter of common feeling. And hence it is, that our best writers, moral and political, as well clergy as laity, have asserted, that true government can have no other foundation than common consent. 'Tis the power, the wisdom, the majesty of the people committed to one, to a few, or to many—yea, in some hitherto favored states, the one, the few, and the many, have been entrusted together, that they might mutually control and be controlled by each other.

Inasmuch, therefore, as this solemn delegation was intended for the good of the whole; inasmuch as all rulers are in fact the servants of the public, and appointed for no other purpose than to be " a terror to evil-doers, and a praise to them that do well;" whenever this divine order is inverted, whenever these rulers abuse their sacred trust, by unrighteous attempts to injure, oppress, and enslave those very persons, from whom alone, under God, their power is derived—does not humanity, does not reason, does not Scripture, call upon the man, the citizen, the Christian of such a community, to " stand fast in that liberty wherewith Christ (in their very birth, as well as by succeeding appointments of his Providence) hath made them free !"

The apostle enjoins us to " submit to every ordinance of man for the Lord's sake." But surely a submission to the unrighteous ordinances of unrighteous men, cannot be "for the Lord's sake:" for " He loveth righteousness, and his countenance beholds the things that are just."

Possessed, therefore, of these principles—principles upon which the present constitution of Britain was happily settled at one of her most glorious and memorable eras, and upon which alone it can still be supported; possessed of these principles, I trust it will be no difficult matter to satisfy your consciences with respect to the righteousness of the cause in which you are now engaged.

The struggle, 'tis true, is an unnatural one. The hard necessity of standing upon our defence against our brethren, children of the same family, educated in the same manners, the same religion with ourselves, bound together by a long reciprocation of endearing offices, by a long participation of common blessings, and of common dangers and distresses, mutually protecting and protected by each other. The hard necessity, I say, of defending ourselves, our just and undoubted rights, against such unnatural adversaries, (though sadly to be lamented, as one of the heaviest judgments with which heaven could visit us for our iniquities) ought not, however, to make us surrender at discretion, or discourage us from "standing fast in that liberty wherewith Christ (as the great providential governor of the world) hath made us free!"

We venerate the parent land from whence our progenitors came. We wish to look up to her as the guardian, not the invader of her children's rights. We glory in the name of children. But then we wish to be treated as children. And children, too, that have arrived at years of discretion. But, if we are to judge from the late ungenerous and ill-digested plans of policy, which have been adopted by those whom she hath entrusted with the powers of administration, we cannot but think, that they began to be jealous of our rising glory, and from an ill-grounded apprehension of our aiming at independency, were desirous of checking our growth.

Yet why this unreasonable and unrighteous jealousy? —We wish not to interfere with that commercial system which they have hitherto pursued. We have not even stretched our expectations beyond the line which they themselves had drawn. We wish not to possess the golden groves of Asia, to sparkle in the public eye with jewels torn from the brows of weeping nabobs, or to riot on the spoils of plundered provinces.* We rather tremble for the parent state, and

---

* Here perhaps it may be objected, that the Americans do with a very ill grace censure their English brethren, either for their iniquitous conquests in Asia, or for the luxuries thereby introduced among them, whilst they themselves are rioting upon the labor of thousands of their own species, torn away from their native retreats, from their dearest relations and friends, and doomed to a most abject and perpetual slavery. In answer to this objection it may be asked—where did this infamous commerce originate? And where is it still carried on with all the eagerness which avarice can inspire? Where, but in England?—By what means can it be abolished? Surely by that power alone, which America acknowledges the parent state may justly exercise over all her dominions, viz., the power of regulating their trade.—Is it not well known, that the legislatures of some of the colonies have done what they could to put a stop to the importation of African slaves, by loading it with the heaviest duties? and that others, having attempted the total abolition of it by acts of assembly, which their governor refused to pass, have then petitioned the parent state for new instructions to their governors on this head, and after all, have failed of success?

It is, however, devoutly to be wished, that when a happy reconciliation once takes place, this poisonous branch may entirely be shut out, before our great commercial stream becomes so infected by the contagion as to endanger the health and security of the whole empire.

would fain keep off from our own borders those luxuries, which may perhaps already have impaired her constitutional vigor. We only wish, that what we have, we may be able to call our own ; that those fruits of honest industry, which our ancestors had acquired, or those which have been, or may be added to them by the sweat of our own brows, should not be wrested from us by the hand of violence, but left to our own free disposal; satisfied as we are in our consciences, that when constitutionally called upon, we shall not give "grudgingly or of necessity," but cheerfully and liberally.

And as to any pretensions to, or even desire of, independency, have we not openly disavowed them in all our petitions, representations, and remonstrances? Have we not repeatedly and solemnly professed an inviolable loyalty to the person, power, and dignity of our sovereign, and unanimously declared, that it is not with him we contend, but with an envious cloud of false witnesses, that surround his throne, and intercept the sunshine of his favor from our oppressed land ?

If, notwithstanding all this, Britain, or rather some degenerate sons of Britain, and enemies to our common liberty, still persist in embracing *delusion*, and believing a lie—if the sword is still unsheathed against us, and *submit or perish* is the sanguinary decree— why then——. I cannot close the sentence——. Indulge a minister of Jesus! My soul shrinks back with horror from the tragic scene of fraternal slaughter— and the free spirit of the citizen is arrested by the tenderness of gospel love. Gracious God! stop the precious effusion of British and American blood—too precious to be spared in any other cause than the joint interest of both against a common foe!

Pained as I am at this melancholy prospect, I mean not, however, to decline addressing you in your military capacity, and suggesting such a conduct for the preservation of your temporal rights as, by the blessing of heaven, will be most likely to insure you success.

"Stand fast," then.

I. "Stand fast" by a strong faith and dependence upon Jesus Christ, the great Captain of your salvation. Enlist under the banner of his cross. And let this motto be written upon your hearts: "*In hoc signo vinces*," "Under this standard thou shalt overcome."

II. "Stand fast" by a virtuous and unshaken unanimity. Of such a unanimity you have a most striking example now before your eyes—three millions of people, or a vast majority of them, bound by no other ties than those of honor and public virtue, voluntarily submitting to the wise political determinations of an honorable council of delegates assembled by their own free and unbiased choice. Avail yourselves of this illustrious example. Be unanimous in your particular department. And as one refractory spirit may defeat the best-devised plan of operations, and throw your whole corps into confusion, see that this unanimity be productive of a just and becoming subordination.

Remember, the gentlemen who command you are your neighbors, friends and fellow-citizens, who have their all at stake as well as you. Their authority has not been imposed upon you. They were invested with it by yourselves. 'Tis surely your part, then, to sup-

port them in the just execution of it, not doubting
but that on their part they will always consider that
they are not called to lord it over mercenaries, but
affectionately to command freemen and fellow-suf-
ferers. Accustom yourselves, therefore, to discipline
now, or else when the day of trial comes (which
Heaven avert!) you will too late lament your unhappy neglect.

III. "Stand fast" by an undaunted courage and
magnanimity. And here give me leave to remind
you that there is a kind of courage which seems to
be merely animal or constitutional. This may stand
a soldier in good stead, perhaps, for a few moments,
amid the heat and fury of a battle, when his blood
and spirits are set on fire by the warlike sound of
drums and trumpets. But I would have you possessed of more than this, even a courage that will
prove you to be good Christians as well as good soldiers; a firm, invincible fortitude of soul, founded
upon religion and the glorious hope of a better world;
a courage that will enable you not only to withstand
an armed phalanx, to pierce a squadron, or force an
intrenchment, when the cause of virtue and your
country calls you to such a service, but will support
you likewise against the principalities and powers of
darkness, will stand by you under the assaults of pain
and sickness, and give you firmness and consolation
amid all the horrors of a death-bed scene.

Such a courage as this, too, will always be tempered
with prudence, humanity, and greatness of soul. It
will never degenerate into savage cruelty and barbarity. If to spread undistinguishing ruin and devastation through a country—if, with more than Gothic rage

to break into the sweet retreats of domestic felicity, and drive the aged and the helpless from their once quiet habitations—O my God! if this be heroism, if this be military virtue, suffer not our people to learn the destructive art. Let them rather continue to be injured and oppressed themselves, than taught thus wantonly to injure and oppress others. This caution, however, is unnecessary to you. Permit me, then, only to observe, that in our present circumstances we contend not for victory but for liberty and peace.

Nor let me dismiss this head of advice without reminding you of the glorious stand that hath been already made for us by our northern brethren, and calling upon you to thank Heaven for his great and gracious interposition. Surely "the Lord of Hosts was with them;" surely "the God of Jacob was their refuge." Drop a pious tear to the memory of the illustrious slain, and let them yet live in the annals of American freedom.

Lastly, "stand fast" by a steady constancy and perseverance. Difficulties unlooked for may yet arise, and trials present themselves sufficient to shake the utmost firmness of human fortitude. Be prepared, therefore, for the worst. Suffer not your spirits to evaporate by too violent an ebullition now. Be not too eager to bring matters to an extremity; lest you should be wearied out by a continual exertion, and your constancy should fail you at the most important crisis. Coolly and deliberately wait for those events which are in the hands of Providence, and depend upon him alone for strength and expedients suited to your necessities.

In a word, my brethren, though the worst should

come—though we should be deprived of all the conveniences and elegancies of life—though we should be cut off from all our usual sources of commerce, and constrained, as many of our poor brethren have already been, to abandon our present comfortable habitations—let us, nevertheless, "stand fast" as the guardians of Liberty. And though we should not be able to entertain the heaven-born maid with such affluence and splendor as we have hitherto done, let us still keep close to her side, as our inseparable companion, preserve her from the violence of her adversaries, and, if at last necessary, be content to retire with her to those peaceful though homely retreats of rural life in which she was first entertained by our venerable ancestors—determined to contend to the very last for such an illustrious prize, and never to part with her but for the more sure and complete enjoyment of her blessings in a world of glory.

"Now, therefore, be strong, O Zerubbabel, and be strong, O Joshua, the son of Josedech the high-priest, and be strong, O ye counsellors, generals, and people of the land; for I am with you, saith the Lord of hosts. Look unto me, and be saved, all ye ends of the earth!" Even so grant, thou great and glorious God, that to thee only we may look, and from thee experience that deliverance which we ask, not for any merits of our own, but for the sake and through the merits of the dear Son of thy love, Christ Jesus our Lord! To whom, with thee, O Father, and thee, O blessed Spirit! three persons in one eternal God, be ascribed all honor, praise, and dominion, now, henceforth, and forever!

WILLIAM SMITH, D. D.

DOCTOR SMITH was a native of Scotland, and graduated at Aberdeen, in 1747. After his arrival in America, he was for two years employed as a tutor in the family of Colonel Martin, on Long Island. Revisiting England, he received regular ordination in the Episcopal Church, and in the month of May, 1754, was placed at the head of the University of Penn sylvania, and constituted its first Provost. Under his administration, the institution rapidly grew into fame, continuing in advancement, until the period of the revolution. At that time, being suspected of views unfavorable to a separation from Great Britain, and being strongly attached to the Church of England, the more ardent whigs, and some of the Presbyterians, who were whigs to a man, determined to remove him from office, much against the judgment of the friends of the institution. The old provincial charter was abrogated, a new institution was chartered by the state legislature in 1779, and endowed with the property of the old college, and the confiscated property of the tories. Ten years after, Doctor Smith and his friends procured a restitution of the property of the college to the trustees, and in 1791 an act of the legislature was passed consolidating the two institutions. At this time, Doctor Smith retired permanently from the college, carrying with him the respect and admiration of his fellow-men. He died at Philadelphia, on the 14th of May, 1803, leaving a collection of writings, which were published soon after. The sermon which succeeds this sketch, was preached in Christ Church, on the twenty-third of June, 1775. In the Preface, the learned author says, it " was drawn up on a few days' notice, and without any view to the press, at the request of some of the author's worthy friends, to whom he could refuse nothing of this kind. At their request, it is now likewise submitted to the public, as it was preached, without varying or suppressing a single sentiment or material expression; and with the addition only of a few lines, and three or four explanatory notes. The author considered that, although he was called to this office by a particular body, yet he was to address a great and mixed assembly of his fellow-citizens, and a number of the first characters in America, now met in consultation, at a most alarming crisis. Animated with the purest zeal for the mutual interests of Great Britain and the colonies; ardently panting for the return of those halcyon days of harmony during which both countries so long flourished together, as the glory and wonder of the world; he thought it his duty, with the utmost impartiality, to attempt a statement of the unhappy controversy that now rends the empire in pieces; and to show, if peradventure he might be permitted to vouch for his fellow-citizens, so far as he has been conversant among them, that the idea of an independence upon the parent country, or the least licentious opposition to its just interests, is utterly foreign to their thoughts; that they contend only for the sanctity of charters and laws, together with the right of granting their own money; and that our rightful sovereign has nowhere more loyal subjects, or more zealously attached to those principles of government under which his family inherits the throne. These, with a few things which seemed necessary respecting the church at this time, are the topics handled in the following sermon. If the principles it contains are but thoroughly felt, the reader will not regret that the limits of a single discourse would not allow a particular application of them."

THE CRISIS OF AMERICAN AFFAIRS.

The Lord God of gods; the Lord God of gods, he knoweth, and Israel he shall know, if it be in rebellion, or if in transgression against the Lord, save us not this day.—JOSHUA, xxii. 22.

THESE words, my brethren, will lead us into a train of reflections wholly suitable to the design of our present meeting; and I must beg your indulgence till I explain, as briefly as possible, the solemn occasion on which they were first delivered, hoping the application I may afterward make of them, may fully reward your attention.

The two tribes of Reuben and of Gad, and the half-tribe of Manasseh, had chosen their inheritance on the eastern side of Jordan, opposite to the other tribes of Israel. And although they knew that this situation would deprive them of some privileges which remained with their brethren on the other side, and particularly that great privilege of having the place of the altar and tabernacle of God among them ; yet, as the land of Canaan was judged too small for all the twelve tribes, they were contented with the possessions they had chosen. And thus they spoke to Moses : " It is a land of cattle, and thy servants have much cattle, wherefore, if we have found grace in thy sight, let this land be given to us for a possession, and we will build sheepfolds here for our cattle, and cities for our little ones; and we ourselves will go ready armed before our brethren, the children of Israel—and will not return into our houses, until we have inherited every man his inheritance." And Moses said unto them : " If you will do this thing, and will go all of you armed over Jordan before the Lord, until he have driven out his enemies from before him ; and the land (of Canaan) be subdued (for your brethren); then afterward ye shall return, and this land (of Gilead) shall be your possession before the Lord."*

This, then, was the great original contract, under which these two tribes and a half were allowed to separate from the rest, and to dwell on the other side of Jordan. They were to assist their brethren in their necessary wars, and to continue under one government with them, even that of the great Jehovah him-

---

* Numbers, xxxii.

self, erecting no separate altar, but coming to perform their sacrifices at that one altar of Shiloh, where the Lord had vouchsafed to promise his special presence.

Though this subjected them to inconveniences, yet, as uniformity of worship and the nature of their theocracy required it, they adhered faithfully to their contract.

In the fear of God, they bowed themselves at his altar, although not placed in their own land, and, in love to their brethren, they supported them in their wars, "till there stood not a man of all their enemies before them;" and at last Joshua, their great leader, having no farther need of their assistance, gave them this noble testimony—that they had in all things obeyed his voice as their general, and faithfully performed all that they had promised to Moses the servant of God. Wherefore he blessed them, and dismissed them to return to their own land "with much riches, and with cattle, and with silver, and with gold, and with much raiment."

No sooner, therefore, had they entered their own country, than in the fulness of gratitude, on the banks of Jordan, at the common passage, over against Canaan, they built a *high* or *great altar*, that it might remain an eternal monument of their being of one stock, and entitled to the same civil and religious privileges with their brethren of the other tribes.

But this their work of piety and love, was directly misconstrued. The cry was immediately raised against them. The zealots of that day scrupled not to declare them rebels against the living God, violators of his sacred laws and theocracy, in setting up an altar against his holy altar; and therefore the whole congregations of the brother-tribes that dwelt in Canaan, gathered themselves together, to go up to war against their own flesh and blood ; in a blind transport of unrighteous zeal, purposing to extirpate them from the face of the earth, as enemies to God and the commonwealth of Israel !

In that awful and important moment (and oh, my God, that the example could be copied among the brother-tribes of our Israel in the parent land!) I say, in that awful and important moment, some milder and more benevolent men that were, whose zeal did not so far transport them, but that, before they unsheathed the sword to plunge it with unhallowed hand into the bowels of their brethren, they thought it justice first to inquire into the truth of the charge against them. And, for the glory of Israel, this peaceable and prudent council prevailed.

A most solemn embassy was prepared, at the head of which was a man of sacred character and venerable authority, breathing the dictates of religion and humanity—Phineas, the son of Eleazer the high-priest, accompanied with ten other chiefs or princes, one from each of the nine tribes as well as from the remaining half tribe of Manasseh.

Great was the astonishment of the Gileadites* on receiving this embassy, and hearing the charge against them. But the power of conscious innocence is above all fear, and the language of an upright heart superior to all eloquence. By a solemn appeal to Heaven for the rectitude of their intentions, unpremeditated and

---

* The two tribes and a half are here briefly and generally denominated Gileadites, from the name of the land they had chosen.

vehement, in the words of my text, they disarmed
their brethren of every suspicion—"The Lord God
of gods," say they (in the fervency of truth, repeating
the invocation)—"the Lord God of gods"—he that
made the heavens and the earth—who searcheth the
hearts, and is acquainted with the most secret thoughts
of all men—"He knoweth, and all Israel shall know,"
by our constancy in the religion of our fathers, that
this charge against us is utterly false.

Then, turning from their brethren, with unspeakable
dignity of soul and clearness of conscience, they address the Almighty Jehovah himself—"O thou
Sovereign Ruler of the universe, our God and our
fathers' God. if it be in rebellion or in transgression
against thee that we have raised this monument of our
zeal for the commonwealth of Israel, save us not this
day! If the most distant thought has entered our
hearts of erecting an *independent altar ;* if we have
sought, in one instance, to derogate from the glory of
that sacred altar which thou hast placed among our
brethren beyond Jordan, as the common bond of
union and worship among all the tribes of Israel, let
not this day's sun descend upon us, till thou hast
made us a monument of thine avenging justice, in the
sight of the surrounding worlds!"

After this astonishing appeal to the great God of
heaven and earth, they proceed to reason with their
brethren ; and tell them that, so far from intending a
separation either in government or religion. this altar
was built with a direct contrary purpose—"That it
might be a witness between us and you, and our generations after us ; that your children may not say to
our children in time to come, ye have no part in the

Lord." We were afraid lest in some future age, when our posterity may cross Jordan, to offer sacrifices in the place appointed, your posterity may thrust them from the altar, and tell them, that because they live not in the land where the Lord's tabernacle dwelleth, they are not of his people nor entitled to the Jewish privileges.

But while this altar stands, they shall always have an answer ready. They will be able to say: "Behold the pattern of the altar of the Lord which our fathers made." If our fathers had not been of the seed of Israel, they would not have fondly copied your customs and models. You would not have beheld in Gilead, an altar in all things an imitation of the true altar of God, which is in Shiloh; except only that ours is an high "or great altar to see" from far. And this may convince you that it was not intended as an altar of sacrifice (for then it would have been but three cubits in height, as our law directs), but as a monumental altar, to instruct our generations forever, that they are of the same pedigree with yourselves, and entitled to the same civil and religious privileges.

This noble defence wrought an immediate reconciliation among the discordant tribes. "The words (when reported) pleased the children of Israel—they blessed God together" for preventing the effusion of kindred blood, "and did not go up to destroy the land where their brethren, the children of Reuben* and Gad dwelt."

---

* Though for brevity, the sacred text in this and other places, only mentions Reuben and Gad, yet the half-tribe of Manasseh is also supposed to be included.

5

The whole history of the Bible cannot furnish a passage more instructive than this to the members of a great empire, whose dreadful misfortune it is to have the evil demon of civil or religious discord gone forth among them. And would to God, that the application I am now to make of it could be delivered in accents louder than thunder, till they have pierced the ear of every Briton; and especially their ears who have meditated war and destruction against their brother tribes of Reuben and Gad, in this our *American Gilead*. And let me add—would to God too, that we, who this day consider ourselves in the place of those tribes, may, like them, be still able to lay our hands on our hearts in a solemn appeal to the God of gods, for the rectitude of our intentions toward the whole commonwealth of our *British Israel*. For, called to this sacred place on this great occasion, I know it is your wish that I should stand superior to all partial motives, and be found alike unbiased by favor or by fear. And happy it is that the parallel now to be drawn, requires not the least sacrifice either of truth or virtue.

Like the tribes of Reuben and Gad, we have chosen our inheritances in a land separated from that of our fathers and brethren, not indeed by a small river, but an immense ocean. This inheritance we likewise hold by a plain original contract, entitling us to all the natural and improvable advantages of our situation, and to a community of privileges with our brethren, in every civil and religious aspect; except in this, that the throne or seat of empire, that great altar at which the men of this world bow, was to remain among them.

Regardless of this local inconvenience, uncankered by jealousy, undepressed by fear, and cemented by mutual love and mutual benefits, we trod the path of glory with our brethren for a hundred years and more—enjoying a length of felicity scarce ever experienced by any other people. Mindful of the hands that protected us in our youth, and submitting to every just regulation for appropriating to them the benefit of our trade—our wealth was poured in upon them from ten thousand channels, widening as they flowed, and making their poor to sing, and industry to smile, through every corner of their land. And as often as dangers threatened, and the voice of the British Israel called our brethren to the field, we left them not alone, but shared their toils, and fought by their side, " till there stood not a man of all their enemies before them." Nay, they themselves testified on our behalf, that in all things we not only did our part, but more than our part, for the common good, and they dismissed us home loaded with silver and with gold* in recompense for our extraordinary services.

So far you see the parallel holds good. But what high altars have we built to alarm our British Israel; and why have the congregations of our brethren gathered themselves together against us? Why do their embattled hosts already cover our plains? Will they not examine our case, and listen to our plea?

" The Lord God of gods—he knows," and the whole

---

* The parliamentary reimbursements for our exertions in the French war; similar to what Joshua gave the two tribes and half on the close of his wars.

surrounding world shall yet know, that whatever
American altars we have built, far from intending to
dishonor, have been raised with an express view to
perpetuate, the name and glory of that sacred altar,
and seat of empire and liberty, which we left behind
us, and wish to remain eternal among our brethren, in
the parent land.

Esteeming our relation to them our greatest felicity;
adoring the Providence that gave us the same progenitors; glorying in this, that when the new world
was to be portioned out among the kingdoms of the
old, the most important part of this continent fell to
the sons of a Protestant and free nation; desirous
of worshipping forever at the same altar with them;
fond of their manners, even to excess; enthusiasts to
that sacred plan of civil and religious happiness, for
the preservation of which they have sacrificed from
age to age; maintaining, and always ready to maintain, at the risk of every thing that is dear to us, the
most unshaken fidelity to our common sovereign, as
the great centre of our union, and guardian of our
mutual rights; I say, with these principles and these
views, we thought it our duty, to build up American
altars, or constitutions, as nearly as we could, upon
the great British model.

Having never sold our birthright, we considered
ourselves entitled to the privileges of our father's
house—"to enjoy peace, liberty and safety;" to be
governed, like our brethren, by our own laws, in all
matters properly affecting ourselves, and to offer up
our own sacrifices at the altar of British empire;
contending that a forced devotion is idolatry, and
that no power on earth has a right to come in between

us and a gracious sovereign, to measure forth our loyalty, or to grant our property, *without our consent*.

These are the principles we inherited from Britons themselves. Could we depart from them, we should be deemed bastards and not sons, aliens and not brethren.

The altars, therefore, which we have built are not* high or rival altars to create jealousy, but humble monuments of our union and love, intended to bring millions yet unborn from every corner of this vast continent, to bend at the great parent-altar of British liberty, venerating the country from which they sprung, and pouring their gifts into her lap when their countless thousands shall far exceed hers.

It was our wish that there should be an eternal " witness between our brethren and us," that if at any future period, amid the shifting scenes of human interests and human affections, their children should say to our children: " Ye have no portion in the birth-right of Britons," and so seek to push them from the common shrine of freedom, when they come to pay their homage there; they might always have an answer ready : " Behold the pattern of the altar which our fathers built; behold your own religious and civil institutions, and then examine the frames of government and systems of laws raised by our fathers in

---

* In this respect our plea is even stronger than that of the two tribes and a half. For, till an explanation was given, the height of their altar, like those of the heathen, who loved to sacrifice on lofty places, might create a suspicion of their lapsing into idolatry; either intending to worship other gods, or the God of Israel in an unlawful place and manner.—*Bishop Patrick*.

every part of America!" Could these have been such exact copies of your own, if they had not inherited the same spirit and sprung from the same stock with yourselves?

Thus far you see the parallel yet holds good, and I think, cannot be called a perversion of my text; if you will allow that the supreme power of an empire, whether theocratical, monarchical, or howsoever distributed, may be represented under the figure of one common altar, at which the just devotion of all the subjects is to be paid. But it is said that we have of late departed from our former line of duty, and refused our homage at the great altar of British empire. And to this it has been replied that the very refusal is the strongest evidence of our veneration for the altar itself. Nay, it is contended by those charged with this breach of devotion, that when, in the shape of unconstitutional exactions, violated rights and mutilated charters, they were called to worship idols instead of the true divinity, it was in a transport of holy jealousy that they dashed them to pieces, or whelmed them to the bottom of the ocean.

This is, in brief, the state of the argument on each side. And hence, at this dreadful moment, ancient friends and brethren stand prepared for events of the most tragic nature.

Here the weight of my subject almost overcomes me; but think not that I am going to damp that noble ardor which at this instant glows in every bosom present. Nevertheless, as from an early acquaintance with many of you, I know that your principles are pure, and your humanity only equalled by your transcendent love of your country, I am sure you will indulge the passing tear, which a preacher of the gospel of love must now shed over the scenes that lie before us. Great and deep distress about to pervade every corner of our land! millions to be called from their peaceful labors by the sound of the trumpet, and the alarm of war! Garments rolled in blood, and even victory itself only yielding an occasion to weep over friends and relatives slain! These are melancholy prospects; and therefore you will feel with me the difficulties I now labor under—forsaken by my text, and left to lament alone, that in the parent land no Phineas has prevailed; no embassy* of great or good men has been raised, to stay the sword of destruction, to examine into the truth of our case, and save the effusion of kindred blood. I am left to lament that, in this sad instance, Jewish tenderness has put Christian benevolence to shame. "Our brethren, the house of our fathers, even they have called a multitude against us. Had an enemy thus reproached us, then perhaps we might have borne it. But it was you, men our equals, our guides, our acquaintance, with whom we took sweet council, and walked together unto the house of God." Or had it been for any essential benefit to the commonwealth at large, we would have laid our hands on our mouths, and bowed obedience with our usual silence. But for dignity and supremacy! What

---

* It is acknowledged with gratitude that many great and exalted characters have plead the cause of America; and, previous to all coercive measures, advised an inquiry or hearing, similar to that for which Phineas was appointed. What is here lamented, and will be long lamented, is that this council could not take place. If brethren could come together in such a temper as this, the issue could not fail to be for their mutual glory and mutual happiness.

are they when set in opposition to common utility, common justice, and the whole faith and spirit of the constitution? True dignity is to govern freemen, not slaves; and true supremacy is to excel in doing good.

It is time, and, indeed, more than time, for a great and enlightened people to make *names* bend to *things*, and *ideal honor* to *practical safety*. Precedents and indefinite claims are surely things too nugatory to convulse a mighty empire. Is there no wisdom, no great and liberal plan of policy to reunite its members, as the sole bulwark of liberty and Protestantism; rather than by their deadly strife to increase the importance of those states that are foes to freedom, truth and humanity? To devise such a plan, and to behold British colonies spreading over this immense continent, rejoicing in the common rights of freemen, and imitating the parent state in every excellence, is more glory than to hold lawless dominion over all the nations on the face of the earth.

But I will weary you no longer with fruitless lamentations concerning things that might be done. The question now is—since they are not done, must we tamely surrender any part of our birthright, or of that great charter of privileges, which we not only claim by inheritance, but by the express terms of our colonization? I say, God forbid! For here, in particular, I wish to speak so plain that neither my own principles nor those of the church to which I belong may be misunderstood.

Although, in the beginning of this great contest, we thought it not our duty to be forward in widening the breach, or spreading discontent—although it be our fervent desire to heal the wounds of the public, and to show, by our temper, that we seek not to distress, but to give the parent states an opportunity of saving themselves, and saving us before it be too late; nevertheless, as we know that our civil and religious rights are linked together in one indissoluble bond, we neither have, nor seek to have, any interest separate from that of our country; nor can we advise a desertion of its cause. Religion and liberty must flourish or fall together in America. We pray that both may be perpetual.

A continued submission to violence is no tenet of our church. When her brightest luminaries, near a century past, were called to propagate the court doctrine of a *dispensing power above law*, did they treacherously cry, "Peace, peace, when there was no peace?" Did they not magnanimously set their foot upon the line of the constitution, and tell majesty to its face, that "they could not betray the public liberty," and that the monarch's only safety consisted in "governing according to the laws?" Did not their example, and consequent sufferings, kindle a flame that illuminated the land, and introduced that noble system of public and personal liberty secured by the revolution? Since that period, have not the avowed principles of our greatest divines been against raising the church above the state—jealous of the national rights, resolute for the Protestant succession, favorable to the reformed religion, and desirous to maintain the faith of toleration? If exceptions have happened, let no society of Christians stand answerable for the deviations or corruptions of individuals.

The doctrine of absolute non-resistance has been fully exploded among every virtuous people. The

5*

freeborn soul revolts against it, and must have been long debased, and have drank in the last dregs of corruption, before it can brook the idea "that a whole people injured may, in no case, recognize their trampled majesty." But to draw the line, and say where submission ends and resistance begins, is not the province of the ministers of Christ, who has given no* rule in this matter, but left it to the feelings and consciences of the injured. For when pressures and sufferings come, when the weight of power grows intolerable, a people will fly to the constitution for shelter; and, if able, will resume that power which they never surrendered, except as far as it might be exercised for the common safety. Pulpit casuistry is too feeble to direct or control here. God, in his own government of the world, never violates freedom; and his Scriptures themselves would be disregarded, or considered as perverted, if brought to belie his voice, speaking in the hearts of men.

The application of these principles, my brethren, is

---

* Doctor Smith, in a sermon first published in 1755, on 1 Peter, ii. 17, delivered his sentiments fully on this point—in the following words, viz.: "It would be absurd to argue, as some have done, that the apostle here meant to enjoin a continued submission to violence. The love of mankind, and the fear of God, those very principles from which we trace the divine original of just government, will lead us, by all probable means, to resist every attempt to enslave the freeborn soul, and oppose the righteous will of God by defeating the happiness of men. Resistance, however, is to be a last resource, and none but the majority of a whole people, can determine in what cases it is necessary. In the Scriptures, therefore, obedience is rightly inculcated in general terms. For a people may sometimes imagine grievances they do not feel, but will never miss to feel and complain of them where they really are, unless their minds have been gradually prepared for slavery by absurd tenets."

now easy, and must be left to your own consciences and feelings. You are now engaged in one of the grandest struggles to which freemen can be called. You are contending for what you conceive to be your constitutional rights, and for a final settlement of the terms upon which this country may be perpetually united to the parent state.

Look back, therefore, with reverence look back, to the times of ancient virtue and renown. Look back to the mighty purposes which your fathers had in view when they traversed a vast ocean and planted this land. Recall to your minds their labors, their toils, their perseverance, and let their divine spirit animate you in all your actions.

Look forward also to distant posterity. Figure to yourselves millions and millions to spring from your loins, who may be born *freemen* or *slaves*, as Heaven shall now approve or reject your councils. Think that on you it may depend, whether this great country, in ages hence, shall be filled and adorned with a virtuous and enlightened people ; enjoying liberty and all its concomitant blessings, together with the religion of Jesus, as it flows uncorrupted from his holy oracles ; or covered with a race of men more contemptible than the savages that roam the wilderness, because they once knew the things which belonged to their happiness and peace, but suffered them to be "hid from their eyes."

And while you thus look back to the past, and forward to the future, fail not, I beseech you, to look up to the God of gods—the rock of your salvation. As the clay in the potter's hands, so are the nations in the hands of him, the everlasting Jehovah! He lifteth up, and he casteth down—he resisteth the proud, and giveth grace to the humble—he will keep the feet of his saints—the wicked shall be silent in darkness, and by strength shall no man prevail.

The bright prospects of the gospel; a thorough veneration of the Saviour of the world; a conscientious obedience to his divine laws; faith in his promises; and the steadfast hope of immortal life through him; these only can support a man in all times of adversity as well as prosperity. You might more easily " strike fire out of ice," than stability or magnanimity out of crimes. But the good man, he who is at peace with the God of all peace, will know no fear but that of offending him, whose hand can cover the righteous, " so that he needs not fear the arrow that flieth by night nor the destruction that wasteth at noonday; for a thousand shall fall beside him, and ten thousand at his right hand, but it shall not come nigh to him; for he shall give his angels charge over him to keep him in all his ways."

On the omnipotent God, therefore, through his blessed Son, let your strong confidence be placed; but do not vainly expect that every day will be to you a day of prosperity or triumph. The ways of Providence lie through mazes too intricate for human penetration. Mercies may often be held forth to us in the shape of sufferings; and the vicissitudes of our fortune, in building up this American fabric of happiness and glory, may be various and checkered.

But let not this discourage you, yea, rather let it animate you with a holy fervor, a divine enthusiasm, ever persuading yourselves that the cause of *virtue* and *freedom* is the cause of God upon earth; and that the whole theatre of human nature does not exhibit a more august spectacle than a number of freemen in dependence upon Heaven, mutually binding themselves to encounter every difficulty and danger in support of their native and constitutional rights, and for transmitting them holy and unviolated to their posterity.

It was this principle that inspired the heroes of ancient times; that raised their names to the summit of renown, and filled all succeeding ages with their unspotted praise. It is this principle too that must animate your conduct, if you wish your names to reach future generations, conspicuous in the roll of glory; and so far as this principle leads you, be prepared to follow, whether to life or to death.

While you profess yourselves contending for liberty, let it be with the temper and dignity of freemen, undaunted and firm, but without wrath or vengeance, so far as grace may be obtained to assist the weakness of nature. Consider it as a happy circumstance, if such a struggle must have happened, that God hath been pleased to postpone it to a period when our country is adorned with men of enlightened zeal; when the arts and sciences are planted among us to secure a succession of such men—when our morals are not far tainted by luxury, profusion or dissipation—when the principles that withstood oppression in the brightest era of the English history, are ours as it were by peculiar inheritance; and when we stand upon our own ground, with all that is dear around us animating us to every patriotic exertion. Under such circumstances and upon such principles, what wonders, what achievements of true glory, have not been performed?

For my part, I have long been possessed with a strong
and even enthusiastic persuasion, that Heaven has
great and gracious purposes toward this continent,
which no human power or human device shall be able
finally to frustrate. Illiberal or mistaken plans of
policy may distress us for a while, and perhaps sorely
check our growth; but if we maintain our own virtue;
if we cultivate the spirit of liberty among our children;
if we guard against the snares of luxury, venality and
corruption, the genius of America will still rise triumphant, and that with a power at last too mighty for opposition. This country will be free—nay, for ages to
come a chosen seat of freedom, arts, and heavenly
knowledge, which are now either drooping or dead in
most countries of the old world.

To conclude, since the strength of all public bodies,
under God, consists in their union; bear with each
other's infirmities, and even varieties of sentiments, in
things not essential to the main point. The tempers
of men are cast in various moulds. Some are quick
and feelingly alive in all their mental operations, especially those which relate to their country's weal, and
are therefore ready to burst forth into flame upon
every alarm. Others again, with intentions alike
pure, and a clear unquenchable love of their country,
too steadfast to be damped by the mists of prejudice, or,
worked into conflagration by the rude blasts of passion,
think it their duty to weigh consequences, and to deliberate fully upon the probable means of obtaining
public ends. Both these kinds of men should bear with
each other; for both are friends to their country.

One thing further let me add, that without order
and just subordination there can be no union in public

bodies; however much you may be equals on other occasions, yet all this must cease in an united and associated capacity; and every individual is bound to keep the place and duty assigned him by ties far more powerful over a man of virtue and honor, than all the other ties which human policy can contrive. It had been better never to have lifted a voice in your country's cause, than to betray it by want of union; or to leave worthy men, who have embarked their all for the common good, to suffer or to stand unassisted.

Lastly, by every method in your power, and in every possible case, support the laws of your country. In a contest for liberty, think what a crime it would be to suffer a freeman to be insulted or wantonly injured in his liberty, so far as by your means it may be prevented.

Thus animated and thus acting, we may then sing with the prophet: "Fear not, O land! be glad and rejoice, for the Lord will do great things. Be not afraid, ye beasts of the field, for the pastures of the wilderness do spring. The tree beareth her fruit, the fig-tree and the vine yield their fruit."

Thus animated and thus acting, we may likewise pray with the prophet: "O Lord, be gracious unto us, we have waited for thee. Be thou our arm every morning, our salvation also in time of trouble. Some trust in chariots and some in horses, but we will remember the name of the Lord our God. O thou hope of Israel, the Saviour thereof in time of need; thou art in the midst of us, and we are called by thy name. Leave us not. Give us one heart and one way, that we may fear thee forever, for the good of ourselves and our children after us. We looked for peace, but

no good came; and for a time of health, but behold
we are in trouble. Yet will we trust in the Lord forever; for in the Lord Jehovah is everlasting strength.
He will yet bind up the broken-hearted, and comfort
those that mourn;" even so, O our God, do thou comfort and relieve them, that so the bones which thou
hast broken may yet rejoice. Inspire us with a high
and commanding sense of the value of our constitutional rights; may a spirit of wisdom and virtue be
poured down upon us all; and may our representatives, those who are delegated to devise and appointed
to execute public measures, be directed to such as
thou in thy sovereign goodness shall be pleased to render effectual for the salvation of a great empire, and
reuniting all its members in one sacred bond of harmony and public happiness! Grant this, O Father,
for thy son Jesus Christ's sake; to whom, with thee
and the Holy Spirit, one God, be glory, honor and
power, now and forever! Amen.

JOHN JOACHIM ZUBLY.

This distinguished man was born at Saltzburg, in Switzerland. He arrived in America in 1760, and became the first minister of the Presbyterian church in Savannah, where he preached to an English and German congregation, in their respective languages, and sometimes to another congregation in French. He possessed a vigorous mind, and was a man of erudition and piety. At the commencement of the revolution he took an active part with the sons of liberty, and in 1775 became a member of the first Provincial Congress of Georgia. In this position he exercised a marked influence. He strongly advocated colonial liberty, and as strongly discountenanced the independence of the colonies. He was appointed a member of the Continental Congress, but differing with most of that body upon the subject of a separation from the crown, he suddenly left Philadelphia, and became an earnest advocate of the English ministry. He was accused of treasonable correspondence with Sir James Wright, and, on his return to Savannah, to avoid the indignation of the people, he was for some time concealed in the cellar of a whig lady friend.

In the ministry, Doctor Zubly labored with the

greatest zeal.   His publications are not numerous,
but are distinguished for learning and power.   He
died in July, 1781.

THE LAW OF LIBERTY.*

So speak ye, and so do, as they that shall be judged by the law of liberty.
.   JAMES, ii. 12.

THERE was a time when there was no king in
Israel, and every man did what was good in his own
eyes.   The consequence was a civil war in the nation,
issuing in the ruin of one of the tribes, and a considerable loss to all the rest.

And there was a time when there was a king in
Israel, and he also did what was right in his. own
eyes—a foolish son of a wise father; his own imprudence, the rashness of his young counsellors, his
unwillingness to redress the grievances of the nation,
and the harsh treatment he gave to those who applied
for relief, also brought on a civil war, and issued in
the separation of the ten tribes from the house of
David.   He sent his treasurer to gather an odious
duty or tribute, but the children of Israel stoned him
that he died; and when he gathered one hundred and
fourscore thousand men, that he might bring again
the kingdom into Roboam, God sent him a message,
" Ye shall not go up, nor fight against your brethren;

* This sermon was preached at the opening of the Provincial Congress of Georgia, in 1775, and was published with a dedication to the
Earl of Dartmouth.

return every man to his house, for this thing is done of me." God disapproved of the oppressive measures and ministry of Roboam, and that king's army appears more ready to obey the command of their God, than slay their brethren by orders of a tyrant. "They obeyed the voice of the Lord, and returned from going against Jeroboam."

The things that happened before are written for our learning. By comparing past times and proceedings with these that are present, prudence will point out many salutary and religious lessons. The conduct of Roboam verifies the lamentation of his father, " Woe to thee, O land, when thy king is a child." A very small degree of justice and moderation might have preserved his kingdom, but he thought weapons of war better than wisdom; he hearkened not, neither to the people, nor to some of his more faithful counsellors; and the consequence was, that, instead of enslaving the ten tribes who stood up for their liberty, God gave Judah to be servants to the king of Egypt, that they might learn the difference between his service and the service of the kingdoms of the nations. A people that claim no more than their natural rights, in so doing, do nothing displeasing unto God; and the most powerful monarch that would deprive his subject of the liberties of man, whatever may be his success, he must not expect the approbation of God, and in due time will be the abhorrence of all men.

In a time of public and general uneasiness, it behooves both superiors and inferiors to consider. It is easy to extinguish a spark; it is folly to blow up discontent into a blaze; the beginning of strife is like the letting out of waters, and no man may know where it will end. There is a rule given to magistrates and subjects, which, if carefully attended to, would secure the dignity and safety of both ; but which, if not duly regarded, is usually attended with the worst conse- quences. The present, my hearers, will easily be allowed is a day of trouble, and surely in this day of adversity we ought to consider. When a people think themselves oppressed, and in danger, nothing can be more natural than that they should inquire into the real state of things, trace their grievances to their source, and endeavor to apply the remedies which are most likely to procure relief. This I take to be the design of the present meeting of persons deputed from every part of the country; and as they have thought proper to open and begin their deliberations with a solemn address unto God, and the consideration of his holy word, I most cheerfully comply with their request to officiate on this occasion; and shall endeavor, as I may be enabled, to point out such directions from the holy Scriptures as may make us wise in the knowledge of time, and direct us how to carry ourselves worthy of the character of good subjects and Christians : what- ever may be necessary for this purpose, I take to be comprehended in the apostolic rule, which I have laid down as the subject of this discourse : " So speak, and so do, as they that shall be judged by the law of liberty." There are two things which properly come before us, viz. :

I. That we are to be judged by the law of liberty ; and

II. The exhortation to act worthily, and under the influence of this important truth on every occasion.

A law is a rule of behavior made under proper

authority, and with penalties annexed suitable to deter the transgressions. As all laws suppose man to be in a social state, so all laws ought to be made for the good of man—a law that is not made by such as have authority for so doing, is of no force; and if authority makes laws destructive in themselves, no authority can prevent things from finally taking their natural course.

Wherever there is society, there must also be law; it is impossible that society should subsist without it. The will, minds, tempers, dispositions, views, and interests of men, are so very different, and sometimes so opposite, that without law, which cements and binds all, every thing would be in endless disorder and confusion. All laws usually wear the complexion of those by whom they were made; but it cannot be denied that some bad men, from a sense of necessity, have made good laws; and that some good men, from mistake, or other weaknesses, have enacted laws bad in themselves, and pernicious in their consequences.

All human laws partake of human imperfection; it is not so with the laws of God: he is perfect, and so are all his works and ways. "The law of the Lord is perfect, converting the soul. The testimony of the Lord is sure, making wise the simple. The statutes of the Lord are right, rejoicing the heart. The commandment of the Lord is pure, enlightening the eyes. All his judgments are truth, and righteousness altogether."

Among men every society and country has its own laws and form of government, which may be very different, and cannot operate beyond their limits; but those laws and that form of government are undoubtedly best which have the greatest tendency to make all those that live under them secure and happy. As soon as we consider man as formed into society, it is evident that the safety* of the whole must be the grand law which must influence and direct every other; men did not pass from a state of nature into a state of society, to render their situation more miserable, and their rights more precarious. That government and tyranny are the hereditary right of some, and that slavery and oppression are the original doom of others, is a doctrine that would reflect dishonor upon God; it is treason against all mankind; it is indeed an enormous faith that millions were made for one; transubstantiation is but a harmless absurdity, compared with the notion of a divine right to govern wrong, or of making laws which are contrary to every idea of liberty, property, and justice.

The law which the apostle speaks of in our text, is not a law of man, but of Him who is the only lawgiver, that can save and. condemn, to whom all owe obedience, and whose laws none can transgress with impunity.

Though all the laws that God ever gave unto man are worthy of God, and tend to promote the happiness of those to whom they were given, yet we may observe a very striking variety in the different laws which he gave at different times and to different people. "He showed his word unto Jacob, his statutes and his judgments unto Israel: he has not dealt so with any other nation."

To the generality of mankind he gave no written

---

* *Salus populi suprema lex.*

law, but yet left not himself without a witness among them; the words of the law were written in their hearts, their conscience also bearing witness, and their thoughts the meanwhile excusing or else accusing one another; it cannot be said they were without law, whilst what they were to do, and what they were to forbear, was written in their hearts.

To Israel God came with a fiery law in his hands; it was given with the most awful solemnity upon Mount Sinai; and as the sum and substance of all their ceremonial, political, and moral law centred in the ten commandments, so the sum and substance of these are comprehended in love to God and love to man, which, as our Lord himself informs us, contain all the law and all the prophets.

All manifestations of the will of God have been gradual; and it is probable the means of knowing God will be progressive through different ages, till eternity gives the good man a full sight of God in his immediate presence. During the dispensation of the Old Testament and the ceremonial law, a spirit of bondage obtained unto fear, the law was a schoolmaster to bring us unto Christ; neither did the law make any thing perfect, but the bringing in of a better hope; grace and truth were brought to light by Jesus Christ; and hence the dispensation of the gospel under which we live, is called the law of liberty.

Though there is a manifest distinction between law and gospel, and sometimes these two things are even opposed to one another, yet the doctrine of the gospel, is also called "the law of faith;" partly because it was usual with the Jewish writers to call every doctrine a law, and partly also because the doctrine of the gospel presents us with a rule of life, which all its professors are bound to obey; hence they are said to be "not without law, but under the law of Christ," and hence our apostle speaks of a royal law, which, though we cannot obey in perfection, nor derive any merit from our imperfect obedience, we cannot neglect without danger, nor disobey without showing our disregard to the doctrine of the gospel in general.

It deserves very particular attention, that the doctrine of the gospel is called a law of liberty. Liberty and law are perfectly consistent; liberty does not consist in living without all restraint; for were all men to live without restraint, as they please, there would be no liberty at all; the strongest would be master, the weakest go to the wall; right, justice, and property must give way to power, and, instead of its being a blessing, a more unhappy situation could not easily be devised unto mankind, than that every man should have it in his power to do what is right in his own eyes; well regulated liberty of individuals is the natural offspring of laws, which prudentially regulate the rights of whole communities; and as laws which take away the natural rights of men are unjust and oppressive, so all liberty which is not regulated by law is a delusive phantom, and unworthy of the glorious name.

The gospel is called a law of liberty, because it bears a most friendly aspect to the liberty of man; it is a known rule, *Evangelium non tollit politias*, the gospel makes no alteration in the civil state; it by no means renders man's natural and social condition worse than it would be without the knowledge of the gospel. When the Jews boasted of their freedom, and that they never were in bondage, our Lord does not reprove them for it, but only observes, that national freedom still admits of improvement: "If the Son shall make you free, then are you free indeed." This leads me to observe, that the gospel is a law of liberty in a much higher sense; by whomsoever a man is overcome, of the same he is brought into bondage; but no external enemy can so completely tyrannize over a conquered enemy, as sin does over all those who yield themselves its servants; vicious habits, when once they have gained the ascendant in the soul, bring man to that unhappy pass, that he knows better things and does worse; sin, like a torrent, carries him away against knowledge and conviction, while conscience fully convinceth him that he travels the road of death, and must expect, if he so continues, to take up his abode in hell, though his decaying body clearly tells him sin breaks his constitution, as well as wastes his substance; though he feels the loss of credit and wealth, still sin has too strong a hold of him to be forsaken; though he faintly resolves to break off; yet, till the grace of God brings salvation, when he would do good, evil is present with him; in short, instead of being under a law of liberty, he is under the law of sin and death; but whenever he feels the happy influence of the grace of the gospel, then this "law of liberty makes him free from the law of sin and death:" it furnisheth him with not only motives to resist, but with power also to subdue sin; sin reigns no longer in his mortal body, because he is not under the law, but under grace. By this law of liberty he is made free from sin, and has his fruit unto holiness, and the end of it eternal life. There is another reason why the gospel is called a law

6

of liberty, which is, to distinguish it from the ceremonial law under the Mosaic dispensation; a yoke, of which an apostle saith, neither they nor their forefathers were able to bear; it was superadded on account of their transgressions, and suited to the character of a gross and stubborn nation, to whom it was originally given. They were so prone to idolatry, and so apt to forget their God, their notions were so gross and carnal, that a number of external rites and ceremonies became necessary, to put them in mind of him and to attach them to some degree of his worship and service. This, however necessary, was a heavy burden; it bid them touch not, taste not, handle not; it required of them expensive sacrifices, and a costly and painful service; it was attended with the most fearful threatenings; if any man brake Moses' law, he died under two or three witnesses; and the very spirit they then received, was a spirit of bondage unto fear: whereas the gospel dispensation breatheth a spirit of confidence, and under the law of liberty we call upon God, as Abba, Father. By this law of liberty the professors of the gospel will be judged.

Every man is a rational, and therefore accountable creature. As a creature he must needs depend on his Creator; and as a rational creature he must certainly be accountable for all his actions. Nothing is more evident than that man is not of himself; and if once we admit that he holds his existence, his faculties and favors from God that made him, it becomes a very obvious conclusion that his Maker must have had some view in giving him existence, and more understanding than to the beasts of the field, neither can it be a matter of indifference to him whether man acts agreeably or contrary to his designs. The creator of the natural world is also its moral ruler; and if he is now the proprietor and ruler of intelligent beings, at some time or other he must also be their judge.

If God had not made his will known unto man, there could have been neither transgression nor judgment. If it should be said that God has not manifested himself alike unto all men, and that some have much smaller opportunities to know his will and their duty than others, it is enough to observe, that no man will be judged by a rule of which it was impossible he should have any knowledge. Every work and every man will be brought into judgment, and the judgment of God will never be otherwise than according to truth; but those that never had the law of liberty will not be judged by that law; and those that have been favored with the revelation of the gospel, will be more inexcusable than any others if they neglect the day of their visitation. " As many as have sinned without law, shall also perish without law; and as many as have sinned in the law, shall be judged by the law." All men are under some law; they feel, they are conscious, that they are so; the thoughts which already excuse or condemn one another, are in anticipation of a final and decisive judgment, when every man's reward will be according to his works.

That all those who heard and professed to believe the gospel will be finally judged by that, we have the fullest assurance. God will judge the secrets of men by Jesus Christ according to his gospel: "The word that I have spoken," saith Christ, "the same will judge them that heard it on the last day." It greatly interests us already to know what is the import and consequence of being judged by the gospel as a law of liberty, and it contains the following things :—

The general character, all the thoughts, words and actions, together with the general conduct of all those who professed the gospel, will be brought to the test and tried by this rule. Man's own opinion of himself, the good opinion of others, will here stand him in no stead ; his character will not be determined by his external appearance, but by his inward reality. "Man looketh on the outward appearance, but the Lord looketh on the heart." The self-righteous Pharisee will be rejected, notwithstanding his fair appearance and boasting; the penitent publican will be received, though he has nothing to plead but "Lord, have mercy on me, a sinner." The law is spiritual, and no law more so than the law of the gospel ; it requires, not merely an external obedience, but an internal conformity to the will of God ; it demands truth in the inward part ; it looks not only to the actions that are done, but to the principle from which they flow ; we must judge of man's inward disposition by his visible action, but God judges of the actions of men according to their invisible spring; thoughts are out of the reach of human cognizance, but they are the first object of divine notice. There is not a word that drops from our tongue but what our judge hears ; whatever we do, or whatever we neglect, is all under his immediate eye; and he not only attends to our general character, but also to every thought, word, or action, and the prevailing complexion of all these taken together forms our true and real character.

In the judgment, according to this law, our character, words, thoughts and actions will be brought to

the test of this rule, our conduct will be compared
with these precepts; this is the balance of the sanctuary in which the professors of the gospel shall be
weighed, and as they shall be found approved or de-
ficient, their case must be determined. Those whose
temper and actions shall be found conformable to the
law of liberty, will be acquitted, graciously accepted,
and made ever happy; and those who turned the
grace of God into wantonness, and made the liberty
of the gospel a cloak for their sins, will be finally rejected. The gospel informs us that a day is already
appointed for that purpose; it acquaints us with the
person of our judge, and every circumstance as well
as rule according to which he will proceed in judgment. Perhaps on that day, when all nations shall
appear before the Judge, and he will divide them as
a shepherd divideth the sheep from the goats, distinct
places will also be allotted to those who are to be
judged by natural conscience and the law of nature,
and those who have been favored with a divine revelation, and especially with the light of the gospel:
the people of Nineveh will arise against empty professors of the gospel and will condemn them. Those
who have been exalted above others in means and
privileges, will sit proportionably lower than those
who have made a better improvement of lesser means;
and notwithstanding the fondest hope and finest profession, it is a determined rule of the law of liberty,
that "except our righteousness shall exceed that of
the Scribes and Pharisees, we shall in no case enter
into the kingdom of heaven."

It deserves our peculiar attention, that the apostle
considers the gospel as a law of liberty, at the same

time when he sets it before us as the rule by which we are to be judged. We are not to imagine, because the gospel is a law of liberty, therefore men will not be judged ; on the contrary, judgment will be the more severe against all who have heard and professed the gospel, and yet walked contrary to its precepts and doctrine. As the transgression of a law of liberty must be more inexcusable than the transgression of a law unjust or oppressive in itself, or even the ceremonial law, which was given only for a certain period, and to answer temporary purposes, so their judgment and doom must be proportionably heavier who have sinned against love and liberty, as well as against power and justice.

According to this law, the fate of men will not only be determined, but sentence will also be put into execution. God sitteth on the throne of judgment every day, and judgeth righteously ; but he hath moreover appointed a particular day when he will manifest his power and justice before the whole creation ; when the dead, both small and great, will stand before God ; when those that acted agreeably to the law of liberty will attain the fulness of glory of the freedom of the sons of God, and when he will also take vengeance on all that have not known God, and have not obeyed his holy gospel. This naturally leads to the second thing proposed, to take a nearer view of the importance of the exhortation : "So speak and so do as they that shall be judged by the law of liberty."

It seems as though the apostle had an eye to some particular branch of the law of liberty, i. e., the love which we owe unto our neighbor, and that his design is to obviate the mistake, as though men might be considered as fulfilling the law of Christ, in paying respect to some of its commands and prohibitions, at the same time that they were entirely regardless of the rest. He assures them, that "whosoever shall keep the whole law, but shall transgress in one point (e. g., having respect of persons), is guilty of all." On this principle the apostle builds the general exhortation: "So speak, and so do, as they that shall be judged by the law of liberty." This implies,

I. Be thoroughly convinced of the certainty of a judgment to come, and that it extends to you, to all your thoughts, words, and actions. There is not any truth of greater moment, nor perhaps more easily forgotten. The belief or unbelief of this important doctrine must have the most sensible effects. All the apostles frequently put their hearers in mind of a judgment to come; and there is not any truth more necessary to be frequently inculcated and daily thought on; and wherever this truth is really believed and felt, it will have a constant and natural influence on the behavior of those who truly believe it.

II. See to it that in judgment you may stand. All men will be brought into judgment, but few will be able to stand; none will be excused, or be able to withdraw, and only those who have acted worthily will meet with the divine acceptance. The difference will be amazing, and beyond all conception—an eternity of happiness, which eye has not seen, ear has not heard, and which never entered into the heart of any man, lies on the one side; and despair, misery, and torment on the other. Those that are able to stand, will meet with the smiles and approbation of their Judge; and to all the rest the King will say: "These mine enemies that would not have me to bear rule over them, bring them here, and slay them before mine eyes." Those that believe and are convinced of this awful alternative, should certainly make it their care that they may be able to stand in judgment; neither should the persuasion of this only influence their conduct in general, but these words ought to be considered as a rule, which we ought to have constantly before our eyes in all our discourses and every undertaking; we should ever "so speak, and so act, as they that shall be judged by the law of liberty."

I shall draw a few inferences, before I conclude, with a more particular address to the worthy gentlemen at whose request I preach on this occasion.

I. *The gospel is a law of liberty.* A late writer* asserts, "Every religion countenances despotism, but none so much as the Christian." This is a very heavy charge against religion in general, but bears hardest on the Christian. Whether it proceeds from malice, ignorance, or misapprehension, it is needless to determine; but if Christianity be a law of liberty, it must be obvious how ill-grounded is such a charge against it. It cannot be denied but some Christian writers have wrote against the rights of mankind. All those who stand up for unlimited passive obedience and non-resistance, may have given but too much cause for such surmises and suspicions; but the truth is, that both those who make this charge, and those who gave occasion for it, were alike ignorant of the spirit and temper of Christianity; and it may well be doubted whether the venders of such odious doctrines,

---

* See a tract entitled "Chains of Slavery." Printed, London, 1775.

who foisted tenets so abominable and injurious to mankind, into the system of Christian religion, have not done that holy religion greater hurt, under the pretence of friendship and defence, than its most bare-faced enemies by all their most violent attacks. Some Christian divines have taught the enormous faith, that millions were made for one; they have ascribed a divine right to kings to govern wrong; but what then? Are such abominable doctrines any part of Christianity, because these men say so? Does the gospel cease to be a law of liberty, because some of its professors pervert it into an engine of tyranny, oppression, and injustice?

The assertion, that all religion countenances despotism, and Christianity more than any other, is diametrically opposite to fact. Survey the globe, and you will find that liberty has taken its seat only in Christendom, and that the highest degree of freedom is pleaded for and enjoyed by such as make profession of the gospel.

There are but two religions which are concerned in this charge; the Jewish and the Christian. Natural religion writers of this kind I suppose would not include in their charge; if they do, they set all religion at variance with the rights of mankind, contrary to the sense of all nations, who are generally agreed, that, abstractly of a world to come, religion is of real service and necessity to mankind, for their better government and order.

As to the Jewish religion, it seems really strange that any should charge it with favoring despotism, when by one of its express rites at certain times it proclaimed " Liberty throughout the land, to the in-

6*

habitants thereof." It required their kings "not to be lifted up in their hearts above their brethren." And the whole system of that religion is so replete with laws against injustice and oppression, it pays such an extraordinary regard to property, and gives such a strict charge to rule in justice and the fear of God, and to consider those over whom they judge as their brethren, even when dispensing punishments, and forbids all excess in them, that it is really surprising any one acquainted with its precepts should declare it favorable to despotism or oppression.

The Christian religion, while it commands due respect and obedience to superiors, nowhere requires a blind and unlimited obedience on the part of the subjects; nor does it vest any absolute and arbitrary power in the rulers. It is an institution for the benefit, and not for the distress, of mankind. It preacheth not only "glory to God on high," but also "peace on earth, and good-will among men." The gospel gives no higher authority to magistrates than to be "the ministers of God for the good of the subject." From whence it must surely follow, that their power is to edify, and not to destroy. When they abuse their authority, to distress and destroy their subjects, they deserve not to be thought ministers of God for good; nor is it to be supposed, when they act so contrary to the nature of their office, that they act agreeably to the will of God, or in conformity to the doctrine of the gospel.

The gospel recommends unto masters to forbear threatenings, and to remember that they also have a Master in heaven. It assures them that the eye of God is equally upon the servant and the master, and

that with God there is no respect of persons. It commands masters, from the most solemn considerations,
to give unto servants that which is just and equal.
It saith to the meanest slave: " Art thou called, being
a servant? care not for it; but, if thou mayest be
made free, use it rather."

The doctrine of the gospel has that regard to property, that it commands even soldiers: " Do violence
to no man, and be content with your wages." That a
Paul sent back a runaway slave, though now converted, and belonging to his intimate friend; and at a
time when he seems to have stood in real need of his
service, from a delicacy that he would do nothing
without the owner's mind, lest his benefit should appear as if it were of necessity, and not willingly.
From the same spirit of justice, a Zaccheus, after his
conversion, restored fourfold what before he had taken
from any by false accusation. Surely, then, the spirit
of the gospel is very friendly to the rights and property of men.

The gospel sets conscience above all human authority in matters of faith, and bids us to stand fast in
that liberty wherewith the Son of God has made us
free." Freedom is the very spirit and temper of the
gospel: " He that is called in the Lord, being a servant, is the Lord's freeman. Ye are bought with a
price: be ye not the servants of men." At the same
time that it commands us to submit to every ordinance of men, it also directs us to act "as free, and
not using liberty as a cloak of maliciousness, but as
the servants of God." Those, therefore, that would
support arbitrary power, and require an unlimited
obedience, in vain look for precedents or precepts for

such things in the gospel—an institution equally tending to make men just, free, and happy here, and perfectly holy and happy hereafter.

II. *The main design of the gospel is not to direct us in our external and civil affairs, but how we may at last stand with comfort before God, the judge of all.*

Human prudence is to be our guide in the concerns of time; the gospel makes us wise unto salvation, and points out the means to be pursued, that it may be well with us in the world to come. As rational creatures, we are to make use of our reason; as Christians, we are to repent and believe the gospel. Motives of a worldly nature may very properly influence us in our worldly concerns; we are created not only for eternity, but also for time; it is not at all improper for us to have a due regard for both. The gospel will regulate our desires and restrain our passions as to earthly things, and will raise us at the same time above time and sense, to objects of a nature more worthy of ourselves. A due regard for, and frequent meditation on, a judgment to come, will greatly assist us in all our concerns; and this very consideration the gospel holds out to us in the clearest manner. It not only affirms as a truth what reason and conscience might consider only as probable, but it takes away as it were the veil from between us and things to come; it gives us a present view of the future bliss of saints, and the terrors and despair of sinners—rather an historical account than a prophetic description of all the proceedings of the dreadful day; it clearly points out the road to destruction, and the way to escape; it affords us a plain and general rule to obtain safety and comfort, when it bids us "So speak, and so do, as they that shall be judged by the law of liberty."

This general rule may also be of considerable service in extraordinary and particular cases. It is impossible to provide express directions for every particular case; and in the course of things, circumstances may happen when a good man may be at a loss to know his duty, and find it difficult so to act as to obtain his own approbation. There may be danger of going beyond, and danger in not coming up to the mark. To act worthy of God, who has called us, is the general rule of the Christian at all times, and upon every occasion; and did we but always follow this rule, what manner of persons should we then be! But in cases of intricacy, we may still be in doubt what may be most for the glory of God, and most consistent with our duty. Sometimes, also, our relative duties may seem to come in competition with one another, and we may hesitate in our own mind which for the present has the strongest call. We should fain obey our superiors, and yet we cannot think of giving up our natural, our civil and religious rights, nor acquiesce in or contribute to render our fellow-creatures or fellow-citizens slaves and miserable. We would willingly follow peace with all men, and yet would be very unwilling that others should take the advantage of a pacific disposition to injure us in hopes of doing it with impunity. We would express duty, respect, and obedience to the king, as supreme, and yet we would not wish to strengthen the hands of tyranny, nor call oppression lawful: in such a delicate situation, it is a golden rule, "So to speak, and so to do, as they that shall be judged by the law of liberty." Nothing has a greater tendency to make men act wrong than the disbelief of a future judgment; and nothing will more effectually restrain and direct them than the full persuasion that such an event will certainly take place; nothing would have a happier tendency to make us act with prudence, justice and moderation, than the firm persuasion that God will bring every work into judgment, and every secret thing, whether it be good or bad.

Neither could I think on any direction more applicable to the design of our present meeting, or which I might more properly recommend to the respectable gentlemen now met together to consult on the recovery and preservation of the liberties of America, and who choose to begin their deliberations with a solemn act of worship to Almighty God, who has established government as his ordinance, and equally abhors licentiousness and oppression, whose singular blessing it is if subjects enjoy a righteous government, and under such a government lead a quiet and peaceable life in all godliness and honesty.

You are met, gentlemen, in a most critical time, and on a most alarming occasion, not in a legislative capacity, but (while the sitting of the usual representatives is not thought for the king's service, or necessary for the good of this province) you are chosen by the general voice of this province to meet on their behalf, to consult on such measures as in our local circumstances may be most to the real advantage, and tend to the honor of our sovereign, as well as the good and safety of this province, and of all this great continent. For the sake of the auditory, I shall briefly state the immediate causes that have given rise to this provincial and a general American Congress, and then offer such humble advice as appears to me most suitable to our circumstances.

. To enforce some acts for laying on a duty to raise a perpetual revenue in America, which the Americans think unjust and unconstitutional, which all America complains of, and some provinces have in some measure opposed,* a fleet and army have been sent to New England, and, after a long series of hardships by that province patiently endured, it is now out of all question that hostilities have been commenced against them; blood has been shed, and many lives have been taken away; thousands, never so much as suspected of having any hand in the action which is made the pretence of all the severity now used against that province, have been and still are reduced to the greatest distress. From this, other provinces have taken the alarm; an apprehension of nearer foes, not unlikely to appear as auxiliaries in an unjust cause, has thrown our neighbors into arms; how far and wide the flame so wantonly kindled may be permitted to spread, none can tell; but in these alarming circumstances the liberty of this continent, of which we are a part, the safety and domestic peace of this province, will naturally become a subject of your deliberations; and here I may well adopt the language of old: "There was no such deed done nor seen, from the day that America was first settled unto this day; con-

---

* This opposition in some provinces consisted in sending the tea on which this duty was to be paid back, to England; not suffering it to be sold or landed, in others; and in Boston, when they were prevented from sending it back, it was entirely destroyed, but no person hurt, nor any blood shed.

sider of it, take advice, and speak your minds." I
mean not to anticipate and direct your counsels; but,
from your desire I should speak on this occasion, I
take it for granted, you will permit me to offer such
hints as may appear suitable to the place and design
of our present meeting.

In the first place, as there is no evil in a city in
which the hand of God may not be seen, so in vain is
salvation looked for from the hills and from the mountains, but can come from him only who has made
heaven and earth. This, undoubtedly, is a day of
trouble, but God saith to his people, " Call upon me
in a day of trouble, and I will deliver thee." " What
nation has God so nigh unto them, as the Lord our
God is in all things that we call upon him for." If
this be our first step, if, first of all, we look unto him
from whom our help cometh, we may hope all will be
well at last. Let us be thoroughly convinced of this,
we must stand well with God, else it can never be
well with us at all ; without him and his help we can
never prosper. The Lord is with you if you are with
him : " if you seek him, you will find him ; but if you
forsake him, you will be forsaken by him." If God
be for us, who can be against us ? If he be against us,
who can be for us ? Before we think on, or look any-
where else, may our eyes be unto God, that he may
be gracious unto us. Let us humbly confess and
speedily turn from our sins, deprecate his judgment,
and secure his favor. "Rend your hearts, and not
your garments, and turn unto the Lord your God, for
he is gracious and merciful, slow to anger and of great
kindness, and repenteth him of the evil; who knoweth
if he will return and repent, and leave a blessing behind

him, even a meat-offering and a drink-offering unto the Lord your God."

Let it be a standing rule with every one that is to sit in council upon this occasion, "so to speak, and so to do, as one that is to be judged by the law of liberty." Let us most carefully avoid every thing that might make us incur the displeasure of God, and wound our own consciences. The effects of your deliberation may become very serious and extensive, and the consequences extremely important : think, therefore, before you speak, deliberate before you execute, and let the law of liberty, by which you are hereafter to be judged, be the constant rule of all your words and actions. Far be it from us to be reduced under laws inconsistent with liberty, and as far to wish for liberty without law; let the one be so tempered with the other, that when we come to give our account to the Supreme Lawgiver, who is the great judge of all, it may appear we had a due regard to both, and may meet with his approbation.

Such always hath been, and such is still the attachment of America to the illustrious house of Hanover, that I need not put you in mind of our duty to the king as supreme. By our law, the king can do no wrong. But of his present majesty, who is universally known to be adorned with many social virtues, may we not justly conclude, that he would not do any wrong, even though he could ? May we not hope, that when the truth of things, the tears of his suffering subjects, the distress caused by acts extremely ill-advised, once reach his notice, a generous pity will force his heart, and that pity, when he feels it, will command redress ? "The heart of the king is in the hand of the Lord, as the rivers of water, and he turneth it as he pleaseth." (Prov. xxi. 1.) Most earnestly, therefore, let us pray, that in this great and most important matter also, God may give unto the king an understanding heart, that power may be governed by wisdom, and the wheels of government roll on with justice and moderation.

Should you think that all our present distress is owing to evil counsellors, nothing need to hinder you from praying that God would turn their counsels into foolishness; you may make it your earnest request, both in public and in private, that the wicked being removed from before the king, his throne may be established in righteousness; that the rod of the oppressor may be broke, and justice and equity take place of tyranny and oppression.

It may be owing to nothing but the firm attachment to the reigning family, that so many Americans look upon the present measures as a deep-laid plan to bring in the Pretender. Perhaps this jealousy may be very groundless; but so much is certain, that none but Great Britain's enemies can be gainers in this unnatural contest.*

Never let us lose out of sight that our interest lies in a perpetual connection with our mother country. Notwithstanding the present unwise and harsh measures, there are thousands in Great Britain that think with us, and wish well to the American cause, and

---

* Were it designed to give the Pretender an opportunity; to raise divisions in Great Britain, starve the manufacturers, scud away troops from Ireland and Scotland, and breed civil war in America, must all be circumstances too favorable, and, I may say, very tempting, to promote such a project.

make it their own; let us convince our enemies that the struggles of America have not their rise in a desire of independency, but from a warm regard to our common constitution, that we esteem the name of Britons, as being the same with freemen; let every step we take afford proof how greatly we esteem our mother country, and that, to the wish of a perpetual connection, we prefer this only consideration, that we may be virtuous and free.*

Let me entreat you, gentlemen, think coolly, and act deliberately; rash counsels are seldom good ones. Ministerial rashness and American rashness can only be productive of untoward compounds. Inconsiderate measures framed on the other side of the Atlantic, are the cause of all our mischiefs; and it is not in the least probable that inconsiderate measures in America can be productive of any good. Let nothing be done through strife and vainglory; let no private resentment nor party zeal disgrace your honest warmth for your country's welfare; measures determined on by integrity and prudence, are most likely to be carried

---

* The idea of a separation between America and Great Britain is big with so many and such horrid evils, that every friend to both must shudder at the thought. Every man that gives the most distant hint of such a wish, ought instantly to be suspected as a common enemy; nothing would more effectually serve the cause of our enemies, than any proposal of this kind; all wise men, and all good men, would immediately speak, write, and act against it; such a proposal, whenever it should be made, would be an inlet to greater evils than any we have yet suffered. But what America detests as the greatest evil, a British ministry has taken the greatest pains to effect; has wasted British blood and treasure to alienate America and Great Britain; the breach is growing wider and wider, it is become like a great sea; every moment is a loss that is not improved toward bringing about a reconciliation.

into execution by steadiness and moderation. Let neither the frowns of tyranny, nor the pleasure of popularity, sway you from what you clearly apprehend just and right, and to be your duty. Consider how much lies at stake; how greatly your religion, your liberty, your property, your posterity, are interested. Endeavor to act like freemen, like loyal subjects, like real Christians, and you will "so speak and so act, as they that shall be judged by the law of liberty." Act conscientiously, and with a view to God, then commit your ways to him; leave the event with God, and you will have great reason to hope that the event will be just, honorable, and happy.

And now, gentlemen, you have the wishes and prayers of every thoughtful person, that your deliberations may be carried on with candor, unanimity, and prudence; may be blessed to preserve the quietness of this province, and co-operate in restoring the rights and tranquillity of all America, as well as promote the prosperity of the whole British empire. This will afford you a heart-felt satisfaction, and transmit your name to posterity with honor, when all those who had opposite views, and sought their greatness in the ruin of others, will be held in abhorrence and detestation.

I have but a few hints to give to my hearers in general.

The times are evil; this is a day of adversity, and in a time of adversity we ought to consider. It may, perhaps, soon become impossible, even to the most indolent, to continue unconcerned; and those that wish no more than to hide themselves in quiet obscurity, may not always have it in their power to remain neuter. To know the signs of the times is a considerable part of human prudence; and it is a still greater to walk circumspectly, and redeem the time, because the days are evil. Whatever part you may think yourselves obliged to take, "so speak, and so do, as they that shall be judged hereafter, and judged by the law of liberty."

In these times of confusion I would press on my hearers a most conscientious regard to the common laws of the land. Let our conduct show that we are not lawless; by well-doing let us put to silence the reproaches of our adversaries. Let us convince them that we do not complain of law, but of oppression; that we do not abhor these acts because we are impatient to be under government, but being destructive of liberty and property, we think them destructive also of all law. Let us act " as free, and yet not make liberty a cloak of maliciousness, but as the servants of God."

While it is yet peace and quietness with us, let us not think ourselves inaccessible to the evils which are already come upon others; there are some evils which we would rather deprecate in private than speak of in public, against which being forewarned, we should be forearmed; every trifling report should not alarm us, but it would be folly still greater not to be on our guard against sudden dangers.

Remember them that suffer adversity, as being yourselves also in the body. Think on those who are driven from their habitations and all their conveniences of life, or confined in their own houses by an enraged soldiery, to starve in their own country in the midst of property and plenty, not permitted to enjoy their own, and distressed in every connection, and this without any cause alleged against numbers of them, without complaint, suspicion, or a legal trial; the like was never heard since the cruel siege of Londonderry, and is a species of cruelty at which even that hard-hearted bigot James II. relented.

Above all, let every one earnestly pray, that He that is higher than the highest would soon make a righteous end of all their confusion; that he would incline the king to hear the cries of his subjects, and that no more innocent blood may be shed in America.

One thing more. Consider the extreme absurdity of struggling for civil liberty, and yet to continue slaves to sin and lust. "Know ye not to whom ye yield yourselves servants to obey? his servants ye are to whom ye obey, whether of sin unto death, or of obedience unto righteousness." Cease from evil, and do good; seek peace and pursue it: who will hurt you while you follow that which is good? Become the willing servants of the Lord Jesus Christ; hearken to and obey the voice of His gospel, for "where the spirit of the Lord is, there is liberty;" and "if the Son makes you free," then, and not till then, "shall you be free indeed."

JOHN HURT.

SCARCELY any thing is known of the personal history of John Hurt. In the journals of the Continental Congress he is mentioned chiefly in the official capacity of chaplain to General Weedon's brigade; but from the tone of his language, such as is used in his printed productions, it is evident that his whole soul was with his country in the revolution, and that he considered success in it as intimately connected with the cause of religion, liberty, and human happiness.

In publishing the sermon which will be found in this collection, he says to his fellow-soldiers: "To your patronage this effort is humbly inscribed; not out of complaisance to your request of publishing it, but from the more certain testimony of being an eye-witness, that you approve its sentiments by your *actions.* For, after all the definitions of patriotism that ever were or ever will be given, this is the quintessence of it: 'The opposing ourselves foremost in the field of battle against the enemies of our country.'" The sermon was preached before the troops in New Jersey, and was printed in 1777, with a dedication to Major-General Stephen, and the officers and soldiers of the Virginia battalions.

THE LOVE OF OUR COUNTRY.

If I forget thee, O Jerusalem, let my right hand forget her cunning. If I do not remember thee, let my tongue cleave to the roof of my mouth; if I prefer not Jerusalem above my chief joy.—PSALM cxxxvii. 5, 6.

REFLECTION upon past enjoyments tends only to the aggravation of present sufferings; and yet—I know not how—the mind of man is ever fondly disposed to draw the painful parallel betwixt the happiness which he once possessed and the misery which he now feels. This was the case of the captive Israelites, as is pathetically described in the Psalm before us: "By the rivers of Babylon," says the divine poet, "there we sat down; yea, we wept when we remembered Zion; we hanged our harps upon the willows which grew in the midst thereof." As the soul in affliction is ever apt to dwell upon every circumstance which heightens the sorrow, he here represents his harp, that sacred instrument devoted to his GOD, now laid aside, silent and neglected; for how, indeed, could he "sing the LORD'S song in a strange land?" Oppression and servitude throw a damp upon every noble faculty: no wonder, then, the sacred musician could ill exert the heavenly harmony under the dispiriting pressure of a foreign tyranny. How shall we sing the LORD'S song in a strange land? Here the faithful patriot turns, by a very natural transition, from lamenting over his country's fate, to the strongest professions of preserving his affection forever inviolable toward her. "If I forget thee, O Jerusalem, let my right hand forget her cunning. If I do not remember thee, let my

tongue cleave to the roof of my mouth; if I prefer
not Jerusalem above my chief joy."

Under the incitement of so animating an example,
I shall offer a few sentiments concerning that virtue
which produced this glorious resolution; and, after
endeavoring to explain the nature and obligation of
love to our country, shall attempt to point out that
conduct which seems requisite to testify the sincerity
of this affection.

The love of our country is a principle which hath
been more celebrated in all ages, hath been the subject of more praise and panegyric, than any other
affection in the whole train of virtue. It hath been
the constant theme of poets, orators and historians;
statues and medals have been erected and struck, and
all the treasures of art and wit perpetually exhausted,
in doing honor to those who have excelled in this
character; and, indeed, the name of patriot implies,
in its true sense, every thing that is most great and
godlike among men; it carries in it the idea of a public blessing; it implies a power of doing good, exerted and extended to whole communities, and resembles
within its sphere, that universal Providence which
protects and supports the world. This is that elevated
passion, of all others the most necessary, as well as
most becoming, to mankind, and yet, if we believe
the common complaints, of all others the least visible
in the world. It lives, we are told, rather in description than reality, and is represented by the first writer
of this age as an antiquated and forgotten virtue.
Wretched picture of the human race! If this be a
just representation, we are degenerate indeed! insensible to the best of all social duties, counteracting the

7

common bond of alliance with our species, and checking the source of our most refined pleasures. The
public is, as it were, one great family; we are all
children of one common mother, *America*, our country; she gives us all our birth; nurses our tender
years, and supports our manhood. In this light,
therefore, our regards for her seem as natural as the
implanted affection betwixt parents and children.

I might here enlarge on the mutual delights given
and received in the social entertainments and conversation of a people connected together with the same
language, customs, and institutions, and from thence
show the reasonableness of an affectionate attachment to the community; but I choose to point out the
obligations to this associating virtue as they arise from
higher and more interesting principles.

The miseries of the state of nature are so evident,
that there is no occasion to display them; every man
is sensible that violence, rapine, and slaughter must
be continually practised where no restraints are provided to curb the inordinancy of self-affection. To
society, then, we must owe our security from these
miseries, and to a wisely-constructed and well-regulated
government we must stand indebted for our protection
against those who would encroach upon the equal
share of liberty which belongs to all, or would molest
individuals in the possession of what is fairly appro-
priated, or justly claimed. And what an unspeakable
satisfaction it is to be free, and to be able to call any
thing one's own! Freedom and security diffuse a
cheerfulness over the most uncomfortable regions, and
give a value to the most inconsiderable possessions;
even a morsel of bread in the most frozen climate

would be more worth contending for, if liberty crowned the meal, than the noblest possessions and greatest affluence under the mildest skies, if held at the merciless will of a civil or religious tyrant. And as such a happiness is only to be established by the love of society—as all the blessings we enjoy spring from this source, gratitude calls upon us to cultivate a principle to which we owe such transcendent obligations. But the obligation rises upon us, when we consider, that from society is also derived a set of amiable duties, unknown to men in a detached and unconnected state. It is from this foundation that hospitality, gratitude and generosity flow, with all the pleasing charities which adorn human nature; for, where have those virtues their theatre? where is their scene of action? or how can they exert themselves, but in society? It is there alone we have opportunities of displaying the moral charms, and of exhibiting the glorious manifestation of good-will to mankind. On this account, therefore, society has a high demand for our affectionate regard.

But to be unmindful of the public, is not only an argument of an ungrateful, it is a proof also of a dishonest temper of mind. God has assigned each of us our station, and a part which we are obliged to discharge in carrying on the great work of social happiness. If, then, I neglect the part appointed me, I am highly unjust; because I take a share of the benefits of society, and yet leave the burden to be borne by others. A greater injustice than this can scarcely be conceived. He who injures particulars is indeed an offender, but he who withholds from the public the service and affection to which it is entitled, is a criminal of a far higher degree, as he thereby robs a whole body of people, and deprives the community of her just demand. If God has given to one man a good understanding, and he does not exert it for the general advantage by advice and counsel; if to another riches, and he will not assist with his liberality; if to a poor man strength, and he will not aid with his labor; if, in short, any be wanting in pursuing the benevolent principle, by directing his talents to their proper ends, he deserves to be treated as a common spoiler, inasmuch as he takes what properly belongs not to him, the title of each man's share of the benefits of society arising only from that proportion which he himself has contributed.

Public good is, as it were, a common bank, in which every individual has his respective share; and, consequently, whatever damage that sustains, the individuals unavoidably partake of the calamity. If liberty be destroyed, no particular member can escape the chains; if the credit of the associated body sink, his fortune sinks with it; if the sons of violence prevail, and plunder the public stock, his part cannot be rescued from the spoil; and some real share (be it more, or less), all, even the meanest, have in this common fund, and a valuable one too, though it were nothing but the lowest earnings of industrious labor. If, then, we have a true affection for ourselves; if we would reap the fruits of industry, and enjoy our property in security, we must stand firm to the cause of liberty and public virtue, otherwise we had better return to the raw herbage for our food, to the inclemencies of the open sky for our covering, go back beyond the mountains to uncultivated nature, where our wants would be fewer, and our appetites less. Such a situation, notwithstanding all its inconveniences, is far preferable to a tyrannical government, and far more desirable than the lot of slaves.

We see, then, how closely the kind Creator has connected our interest with our duty, and made it each man's happiness to contribute to the welfare of his country.

But still, the more noble motive to a generous soul, is that which springs from a benevolent desire of diffusing the joys of life to all around him. There is nothing, he thinks, so desirable as to be the instrument of doing good; and the further it is extended, the greater is the delight, and the more glorious his character. Benignity to friends and relations is but a narrow-spirited quality compared with this, and perhaps as frequently the effect of caprice, or pride, as of a benevolent temper. But when our flow of good-will spreads itself to all the society, and, in them, to distant posterity—when charity rises into public spirit, and partial affection is extended into general benevolence—then it is that man shines in the highest lustre, and is the truest image of his Divine Maker.

But notwithstanding all that has been said in favor of this affection, laudable as it is, we are not, however, to forget, that it may be so conducted as to become a very criminal passion. If any associated body, apprehending themselves superior to other states, should, for that reason only, invade their rights, this would be to undermine the very foundation of society, and, consequently, an unjustifiable enterprise. Does true patriotism inspire such a conduct? Does the love of our country teach us to aggrandize it at the ruin of another? Undoubtedly not. And if we think at all, we must allow such attempts utterly repugnant to the fundamental laws of justice and universal charity. Hard would be his fate who should be commanded to perform such a service, and glorious the triumph of his soul if he resolved to decline it! In vain would he call in the example of ancient Rome for his encouragement; for, after all the extravagant encomiums bestowed upon her patriotism, we shall scarce be able to clear it from the imputation of flagrant tyranny. Rome, early possessed with the high fanaticism of distinction and empire, declared war against mankind; and, out of a feverish fondness for dominion and renown, laid desolate all the known world. Their possessions, their habitations, their paintings, their sculptures, all their riches, were the spoils of injured nations. Thus they erected to themselves an empire as unwieldy as it was unjust, on the ruin of their fellow-creatures. What, then, are all their beautiful lectures, and pompous declamations, on the love of their country? —what their labored orations in praise of liberty! Indisputable proofs, indeed, of their eloquence, but not so of their humanity. If the language of benevolence were to constitute the patriotic character, you must allow it due to these Romans; but if actions are to ascertain the right, we shall find it a difficult task to make good their claim, though we were masters even of their own eloquence.

Look into their city, and behold the inhabitants; there you will find this celebrated freedom spreading itself only amongst particular branches, and giving a few the license to tyrannize over an infinite number of miserable slaves, rendered more wretched by having always before their eyes a disagreeable subject of comparison. Look into their provinces (which they ought to have protected), and you behold scenes of the utmost injustice, barbarity and horror. Their tyrants not content with what might with some degree of propriety be called lawful taxation, but murdering them in cold blood without mercy. Now and then, it is true, you see the conquered enjoying a little ease under a humane, honest governor; but in general their oppressions were intolerable, and their whole administration no better than a course of hostility and plunder.

Let us change the scene, and take a cursory view of our own case. Thanks and praise be given to the Lord God of armies, it is our felicity not to be members of such a society! not to be in so abject and humiliating a state as those Roman colonies were! We have never yet been conquered; we never yet tamely received laws from a tyrant nor never will, while the cause of religion, the cause of nature and of nature's God cry aloud, or even whisper *resistance* to an oppressor's execrated power. The gloomy cloud that has long been gathering over our Jerusalem, is indeed still formidable, and demands our utmost efforts to effectuate its dispersion; and this great and wished for good is in all human probability the most likely to be accomplished by firmness, unanimity, perseverance and a fixed determination strenuously to execute and defend what our Continental Congress, provincial assemblies, commanding officers, and so forth, shall wisely and prudently resolve.

> Let fools for modes of government contest,
> That which is best administer'd is best.

And here I will observe, that it was not through licentious opposition, or for conquest, we drew the sword, but for justice; not to introduce, but to prevent slavery ; not upon a vain principle of ambition to gratify the resentment or pride of any individuals, (as many of our internal enemies have stupidly and falsely asserted) but in defence of the plainest rights, such as all mankind have ever claimed, at the call of a provoked and long injured people, and that after every other method of redress had been tried in vain.

The liberty we contend for is not the license of a few to tyrannize over multitudes, but an equal freedom to all, so far as is consistent with the present circumstances of our country, good order, the constitution, and peace of government. These are circumstances which give a sanction to patriotism, and not only justify, but demand our most active resolutions to promote the welfare of our country by all those methods which become a civilized and numerous people, born with an instinctive love of liberty.

If we bear a true and cordial affection for our country, we shall be warm and active in her cause; a calm concern is inconsistent with true patriotism, which gives ardor to the coldest breast and makes even cowards brave.

There never was a country had stronger motives to unite in active zeal than this, nor was there ever a time required it more than the present. By how much the more the enjoyment of liberty hath been asserted, improved and established amongst us, so much the greater ought to be our resolution to maintain it, and the more scandalous is our folly if we lose it. Liberty with danger is better than slavery with security.

Of all the known parts of the world, and for many ages, Britain hath been the most extolled for the love and protection of liberty; there the heavenly goddess seemed to have fixed her temple; and whilst her sacred fires have been extinguished in so many other countries, there they have till lately been religiously kept alive; there she hath had her saints and her confessors, and a whole army of martyrs. But, alas! how are the mighty fallen! The gates of hell have prevailed against her.

If, then, liberty be that delicious and wholesome fruit on which the British nation hath fed for ages, and to which they owe their riches, their strength, and all the advantages they boast of, surely it is highly incumbent upon us to cherish and cultivate the tree which bears that delicious fruit, and will continue to bear it as long as we are careful to fence it in and trench it round against the beasts of the field and insects of the earth. It is, then, our duty to be ever vigorous and ardent in the support of such a cause; to reverence the majesty of liberty, and conform our conduct to it; to cause all other inclinations to bow to this; to make it, in short, the constant object of our warmest wishes, closest attention, and highest admiration—" to prefer Jerusalem above our chief joy."

We shall give a further proof of our patriotism, if, out of a sense of the obligations we lie under to those on whom the execution or management of our glorious cause is delegated, we endeavor to strengthen their hands, oil the wheels of patriotic power, and smooth the rugged paths of their administration. Whilst they discharge their important duties with ability and honor, they have a just demand to the returns of grateful

7*

acknowledgments, and are entitled to the warmest applause of that people whom they have faithfully served. And as it is incumbent upon us to pay this tribute, so it is natural for them to expect it. Glory is the reward of honorable toils, and public fame is the just retribution for public service; the love of which is so connected with virtue that it seems scarcely possible to be possessed of the latter without some degree of the former. Nor is this any sort of derogation to the benevolence of the character. A good man feels a pleasure from the reputation he acquires by serving his country, because he loves it; but he does not love it merely for the sake of that pleasure; the passion did not spring from the expectation of the delight, but the delight was the consequence of the passion.

But, after all these duties are discharged, we must not stop here: something more is still required at our hands to give the finishing testimony. If the love of your country is indeed the governing principle of your soul, you will give up every inclination which is incompatible with it; nor will you cherish in your hearts any rivals of the favorite passion. All the train of darling vices must therefore be brought forth, and offered up as victims on the altars of liberty. You cannot be said to "prefer Jerusalem above your chief joy" whilst you foster any appetites which have a manifest tendency to her detriment. But what is so pernicious to the common weal as vice? and what vice so much as luxury? It is this which enfeebles the body, corrupts the mind, impoverishes the fortune, and introduces every baneful cause of ruin. This it was which destroyed imperial Rome, and assisted Cæsar to enslave her citizens. She had strength enough left to withstand the attacks of her enemies; but those who seemed to wish her prosperity had not virtue enough to give up their luxury to her interest. Rome, therefore, fell a sacrifice to the vices of her friends. Effects always correspond to their causes. If we pursue the same course, we must expect the same fate.

This consideration is surely sufficient to rouse our virtue, and make us abandon all intemperate pursuits. But if, out of a luxurious vanity, we consume the manufactures of other countries, to the detriment of our own; if our profusion in extravagant expenses render us less able or less willing to assist the public, we violate the most sacred of all social duties, and become flagrant transgressors of the will of our Creator.

It was such a conduct as this which provoked the anger of God against the Israelites, when he sent his prophet (Amos) to them with this denunciation: "Woe unto them that are at ease in Zion! ye that put far away the evil day, and cause the seat of violence to come near! That lie upon beds of ivory, and stretch themselves upon their couches, eat the lambs out of the flock, and calves out of the midst of the stall; that chant to the sound of the viol, and invent to themselves instruments of music; that drink wine out of bowls, and anoint themselves with their chief ointments; but are not grieved for the affliction of Joseph!" A beautiful and pathetic description this of the levity of the Hebrews; who, at a time of public distress, regarded only the indulgence of voluptuous appetites, but never felt one tender sentiment for their bleeding country, "were not grieved for the affliction of Joseph." Thus the children of Israel were brought down (says the Scripture) in that day, and the children of Judah prevailed, because they relied on the Lord their God. These things were written for our admonition, as well as the Jews; and the woe denounced is equally applicable to any other nation in the like circumstances.

Let us, then, not build too much upon human prospects, or shut God out of our councils and designs; but let us flee humbly to him for succor in a pious acknowledgment that without him nothing is strong, that without him no king can be saved by the multitude of an host, nor the mightiest man be delivered by his strength.

Our unnatural enemies have their earthly king, their lords spiritual and temporal to apply to on this occasion; let us leave them to their protection, and let us choose on our part the Lord of lords for our God and for our king. In his name have we set up our banners, who alone "giveth victory unto kings, and saveth from the perils of the sword." Let us every one contribute his endeavor to reduce and lessen the weight of public guilt, by at least reforming and amending himself, and unite in our prayers and in every good work, that "God may be entreated for the land." So we may piously hope, that he will go forth with our armies, and "command deliverance for Jacob;" that through him we shall "cast down our enemies, and keep them under that rise up against us." So shall we not only consult the peace and prosperity of this our Jerusalem, but shall provide in the best manner for our future peace and happiness in a better country, and shall be received as true sons and citizens of that Jerusalem which is above.

To conclude:—Temperance and patriotism go hand

in hand, and adhere together by an inseparable connection. And as there can be no real virtue in that
breast which is not susceptible of the love of the
public, so there can be no genuine love of the public
where virtue is wanting; since that is not only the
truest ornament but the best support of the community. National affection, therefore, if it be derived
from a true principle, must necessarily inspire a moral
conduct, must incline us to quit every baneful vice, to
contract the circle even of what we call innocent
amusements, and, instead of looking out for daily
parties of pleasure, it will prompt us rather to make
• a constant festival of human kindness, the most delicious of all entertainments to a generous mind. If
we behave thus, then we are patriots indeed. It is
thus we are to arm ourselves against our unprincipled
enemies; who, though they should not dread our
strength, will certainly stand in awe of our virtue.
Whilst we act in this manner, our professions will not
only meet with full applause from men, but also with
the approbation of God, when, with the pious ardor
of the text, we cry out: "If I forget thee, O Jerusalem! let my right hand forget her cunning; if I do
not remember thee, let my tongue cleave to the roof
of my mouth—if I prefer not Jerusalem above my
chief joy."

WILLIAM GORDON, D. D.

THIS divine and historian was a native of Hitchin, Hertfordshire, England. In the early portion of his ministerial life he was settled as pastor of a large independent congregation at Ipswich, and after the death of Doctor David Jennings, he was chosen as his successor in the church at Wapping. In both these positions he was an earnest laborer for the cause of Christ, and only relinquished them to emigrate to America, where he thought greater rewards for his work awaited him. He arrived in New-England about the year 1770, and having preached about three years to a congregation in the vicinity of Boston, was ordained as minister of the Third Church at Roxbury. This was in 1772.

During the struggles of the colonists with the crown and ministry of England, he took a bold and active part with the former, and at an early period was chosen chaplain to the Provincial Congress of Massachusetts. Struck with the importance of the scenes that were opening upon the world at that time, he formed a design of compiling their history, which he made known to Washington, and meeting with the desired encouragement from that great man, he devoted himself to the procuring of the best materials, whether oral, written, or printed. In these researches he enjoyed the co-operation of the most distinguished men of the time, and was enabled by them to procure access to their private as well as public papers and documents. At the conclusion of the war he returned to his native country, and in 1788 published the result of his historical researches, in four handsome volumes. In 1793 he again took up the standard of Christianity, and was settled as pastor at St. Neots in Huntingdonshire, but failing intellect caused his early retirement from this position, and he preached but occasionally thereafter. His last days were a blank, his memory left him, and sinking into imbecility, he remained in that state without suffering until the 19th of October, 1803, when he died.

The sermon which follows this imperfect sketch was preached before the general court of Massachusetts on the first anniversary of American Independence. It was published under the title of " The Separation of the Jewish Tribes after the death of Solomon accounted for and applied to the present day."

SEPARATION OF THE JEWISH TRIBES.

THE fulness and variety of Scripture is such, that no occurrence, whether public, domestic, or private, presents itself, but you may find a text suitable to the same. How far I have been directed to choose the right, I submit to the better judgment of this venera-

ble audience: but I mean to improve the present
opportunity by treating on the separation that happened amongst the Jewish tribes in the time of Rehoboam, and to ground the discourse upon these words:

*Wherefore the king hearkened not unto the people: for the cause was
from the Lord.*—1 KINGS, xii. 15.

The sacred oracles enable us to solve many a difficulty in the ancient and modern history of the world.
According to their doctrine, the Lord Jehovah, the
Creator of the universe, governs all his works, whether
material or immaterial, animate or inanimate, rational
or irrational, men or angels, agreeably to an infinitely
wise plan formed from the beginning; and brings to
pass his own purpose, doing all his pleasure and causing his counsel to stand, amidst the various jarring
devices of created intelligent beings. He hath wisdom
and strength. He hath counsel and understanding.
He doeth great things and unsearchable; marvellous
things without number. He setteth up on high those
that be low; that those which mourn may be exalted
to safety. He disappointeth the devices of the crafty,
so that their hands cannot perform their enterprise.
He taketh the wise in their own craftiness: and the
counsel of the froward is carried headlong. The de-
ceived and the deceiver are his. He leadeth counsellors away spoiled, and maketh the judges fools. He
looseth the bond of kings, and breaketh the rod of the
oppressor. He poureth contempt upon princes, and
weakeneth the strength of the mighty. He taketh
away the heart of the chiefs of the people of the earth,
and causeth them to wander in a wilderness where

there is no way. He plucketh up, pulleth down, and destroyeth kingdoms. He buildeth, and planteth, and prospereth nations. In fine, his influence extends to all events, whether more or less important, that so each may work together, in its respective place, toward the accomplishment of that perfect scheme of universal government which He hath projected. Thus we are taught to account for those grand revolutions that take place at times in these lower regions; and that are brought forward by circumstances in themselves apparently trifling; and that might easily have been prevented by a prudent and speedy compliance with the reasonable requests of the aggrieved.

The Jewish state flourished amazingly under the reign of Solomon, whose court was the resort of the wise and noble; for there came of all people to hear the wisdom of Solomon, from all kings of the earth, which had heard of his wisdom. (1 Kings, iv. 34.) The friendship of this wise king was courted by neighboring states, who paid him their annual tributes. He enlarged his dominions, so as to rule over all the region on this side the river, the great river Euphrates, from Tiphsah even unto Azzah, over all the kings on this side the river, and he had peace on all sides around about him. (1 Kings, iv. 24.) Trade and commerce were prosecuted with that spirit, and attended with such success, as that he made silver and gold at Jerusalem as plenteous as stones, and cedar-trees made he as the sycamore-trees that are in the vale for abundance. (2 Chron. i. 15.) His subjects enjoyed not only plenty, but security : Judah and Israel dwelt safely, every man under his vine and under his fig-tree, from Dan even to Beersheba, from one end of

the country to the other, all the days of Solomon.
(1 Kings, iv. 25.)

One would have concluded, from the height the
Jewish empire had reached, when at its meridian in
the reign of Solomon, that, like the summer's sun, it
would have been long in declining.   But, alas! how
soon did the glory and fashion of it pass away, through
the bad policy that prevailed under the reign of his
successor.   Solomon's funeral is scarce closed, before
fatal dissensions arise: the Jewish tribes separate,
through the imprudence and tyranny of Rehoboam,
and the empire is suddenly divided into two independent states.

Thus the most destructive events may be in the rear
of the most successful.   It is not for a community,
any more than a private person, to say, glorying in
present appearances: " My mountain standeth strong,
I shall not be moved, I shall never be in adversity."
When great mercies, bestowed upon a sinful nation,
are productive of great vices, instead of leading to
repentance and the practice of virtue, Divine justice
may hurl it, without further warning, into the depths
of misery.

When George II., of blessed memory, was upon
the verge of eternity, the British nation had nearly
attained the summit of its glory.   That worthy sovereign had the happiness of his reign interrupted by
an unprovoked rebellion, and by wars with foreign
powers ; but its close was like that of the setting sun,
with not a cloud about it, when the storm that lowered in the sky hath been broken and dispersed.   His
loyal subjects enjoyed the glorious circumstances,
while they sincerely mourned its being a setting and

not a rising sun. However, they consoled themselves with the hopes, that his successor would possess the royal virtues of his aged grandsire, and prove the happy instrument of confirming and lengthening out the British glory, and therefore hailed his ascension to the throne with loud and hearty acclamations. These had scarce ceased, ere it was perceived that the baneful influence which George II. foresaw, dreaded as big with misery to his subjects, and spoke of with concern to his trusty servants, was giving a wrong bias to public measures. Old and experienced persons, conversant with business, and who had the confidence of the people, were removed, that so an ambitious favorite of high-flying principles, with his clan of pliant dependents, might be admitted into places of honor, power and profit. The throne was soon surrounded by men of despotic sentiments, and the complexion of the court was such as that not only violent tories, but known Jacobites repaired to it with confidence, while the stanch friends of the House of Hanover were so coolly received as to be really slighted. This occasioned many converts from among those who were attached to the Pretender's family; but, as a political writer wisely and severely observed, though they changed their idol they retained their idolatry. They were, with the party they had joined, for having the king absolute; but as Britons were strenuous for the forms of liberty, though negligent as to liberty itself, they were for making him so by law, which, as the nation was lost to public virtue, might easily be done by corrupting and securing a majority in Parliament. No wonder that, while the leading men had such principles and views, and the sovereign a temper well adapted to second and support them, should he not be thought the first promoter; unwarrantable methods were adopted for procuring moneys for the purpose of ministry, without regarding the rights of those that were to pay them, and that a firm and determined opposition to such proceedings was deemed and treated as disobedience to legal authority. From hence hath originated a separation between those that were as nearly related and as strongly united as the Jewish tribes. Such was the warm affection that the colonists had for Great Britain, that they considered her as their home, and honored her as their mother country. In all her afflictions, they were afflicted; and when she rejoiced, they were glad. With what anxiety did they expect news when her ruin was threatened by rebellions or invasions! how did they wish that they could cross the Atlantic in her defence! how did they exult in her salvations! and how were their hearts enlarged in thanksgivings to God for her successes! But how has the cruelty of the British legislature, and the tameness of the British nation in suffering it, produced such an alienation of heart in the colonists, that many, very many, can scarce wish to be connected with her more, in any way whatsoever. As a friend to the rights of mankind in general, and of this continent in particular, I can but pray that the King of kings would give his sanction to what the Congress declared this day twelvemonth, and by succeeding, make the United States of America perpetually *free and independent;* being assured that there is no alternative but that of the most horrid slavery; and yet as a native of Great Britain, and considering that that is the land of the sepulchres

of your forefathers, I can but wish that, though we
have been drove into an independency, we may
not be forced into a total separation. However, it is
likely that we shall see the words of Rehoboam's
father verified: " A brother offended is harder to be
won than a strong city, and their contentions are like
the bars of a castle, of an unusual size, beyond what
are to be met with in common among strangers."
Prov. xviii. 19.

Return we to the sacred history.

Rehoboam repaired to Shechem, where all Israel
met to make him king. The house of David could
plead a divine right to the throne; and yet God—designing to intimate that its princes were to rule for
the good of the subjects, were not to lord it over his
heritage, and would forfeit their right should they commence tyrants—did leave the investiture in the hands
of the people Thus, upon every new instalment, the
people had an opportunity of relating the grievances
they labored under during the preceding reign, and
of insisting on a redress ere they acknowledged the
successor. Accordingly all the congregation came
and spake unto Rehoboam, saying, Thy father made
our yoke grievous: now, therefore, make thou the
grievous service of thy father, and his heavy yoke,
which he put upon us, lighter, and we will serve thee.
(v. 3, 4.) We are not told what were the particulars on
which this general complaint was grounded. We may
conclude, from the acknowledgment contained in Rehoboam's answer, that it was not without foundation.
The advantages enjoyed under the reign of Solomon
were uncommon; notwithstanding which, there were
some things peculiarly disgustful that the people were

not willing to submit to under his successor; and that
Rehoboam might not construe their silence into an
acquiescence, they determine upon speaking their
minds freely, and stipulating with him upon what
terms they would serve him. Whether they thought
the expenses of government multiplied unnecessarily,
or designedly misapplied; whether they objected to
the taxes as too great, or to the mode of laying and
raising them; or to the imperious, insolent, and oppressive behavior of crown officers; whether any,
some, or each of these, were particular matters of
complaint, must remain in uncertainty; but they considered themselves as having been under a heavy
yoke and grievous servitude. They therefore intimate
to Rehoboam that they will not serve him unless
he would lighten their burdens. This circumstance
plainly proves that they did not apprehend themselves
bound to non-resistance and passive obedience, though
Rehoboam should plead that he was king *jure divino*.
The language of their procedure was: We submit to
no unconditional sovereignty. You must solemnly
promise, before we install you and acknowledge ourselves your subjects. Then we shall know what we
have to trust to, and when our obligation to obedience
ceases. Do we approve of your proposals, we will
serve you; if not, we are at liberty to serve whom we
please. Do we agree to your proposals, we are bound
to serve you while you keep to them; but do you
vary from them without our consent, the contract is
ended—our allegiance is absolved; we have a right
to choose another sovereign, or to alter the mode of
government, as we may judge most expedient. Let
it be observed, that these were the sentiments not of

a disaffected party, but of all the congregation of Israel, at a period not when the nation was overrun with ignorance, and priestcraft influenced, but immediately after the Jews had been tutored in the school of wisdom by the greatest and acutest genius that ever lived.   Here I may introduce with propriety, the following words of the Rev. Dr. Thomas Newton, wrote upon another occasion : "Not only in this particular, but in the general, the Scriptures, though often perverted to the purposes of tyranny, are yet, in their own nature, calculated to promote the civil as well as the religious liberties of mankind.   True religion and virtue, and liberty, are more nearly related and more intimately connected with each other than people commonly consider.   It is very true, as St. Paul saith, that where the spirit of the Lord is there is liberty; or as our Saviour himself expresseth it, 'If ye continue in my word, then are ye my disciples indeed; and the truth shall make ye free.' "   Whether these, which were the sentiments of a private clergyman, continue those of the Bishop of Bristol, since advancement, is immaterial to the public; but they will be perpetuated in his incomparable Dissertations on the Prophecies, volume I., page 313.

Rehoboam having heard what the people had to say, with seeming prudence defers giving them an answer, till he had time to consider the affair, and consult his counsellors, and so sends them away for the present, saying, depart yet for three days, then come again to me.   Had Rehoboam a good design in thus delaying the matter he ought to be commended for it; but the policy of princes is so exceeding intricate and crooked, that he might only mean to gain time by it. He might resent their conduct in presenting such a petition; artfully conceal his displeasure; give it to all appearance a gracious reception; propose by that means to make them secure, to deceive and to divide them; and think that within the three days, what with corrupting some, wheedling others and frightening the timid, he should so weaken the opposition as to have nothing to fear from it. Such policy would only have resembled that of modern times. Rehoboam, however, to keep up the farce, consulted with the old men that stood before Solomon his father, while he yet lived, and said, How do you advise, that I may answer this people? The people when they had heard he had consulted the old statesmen of the former reign, might promise themselves a redress of grievances from their wisdom, and be ready to congratulate each other upon the pleasing prospect. In this George III. did not resemble Rehoboam. The reason for it may easily be conjectured. He was well assured, that had he consulted the old men that stood before his grandfather while he yet lived, they, like Solomon's counsellors, would have advised him to have complied with the petition of the complainants; which, as he had no inclination to do, he might fear would embarrass his affairs and disconcert his favorite projects.

The old men gave counsel to Rehoboam saying, If thou wilt be a servant to this people this day, and wilt serve them, and answer them, and speak good words to them, then they will be thy servants forever. The old men had studied, been long acquainted with, and knew the temper of the people; that they were not given to change; that they did not seek occasion to separate from Solomon's successor; that they sought nothing more than to have their petition complied with; that their proposals were honest, whatever designing and interested men might insinuate; and that they would keep their word with Rehoboam were they gratified; therefore, they do not hesitate to declare positively what would be the happy consequence would he answer them graciously, and speak good words to them.

Whether it was owing entirely to Rehoboam's not relishing this good advice; or partly to that, and partly to the cunning practices of some selfish servants, who were sensible, that, if he followed it, their schemes of aggrandizing themselves and families would be totally ruined; so it was, that he forsook the counsel of the old men, which they had given him, and consulted with the young men that were grown up with him, and which stood before him.

The persons here styled young men, were not so very young in point of years; for, from its being said that they were grown up with Rehoboam, we must conclude that they were of the same age with him; and he was forty and one years old when he began to reign; but they were young men compared with the old men that stood before Solomon; they were young also in point of political knowledge, and the art of governing properly. They had lived long enough to have been good politicians and wise counsellors, if they had applied themselves to the study of human nature, the tempers of mankind, and the history of states and kingdoms; but they had neglected these particulars and had applied themselves to the pleasing and getting the favor of the prince, to whom they

8

had been appointed companions when young, and with whom they were grown up. They were raw and inexperienced, as to state affairs; and no ways fit to be advised with in matters of the first importance, which required the greatest sagacity, and a judgment matured by repeated practice.

Men may have old heads, and yet be incapable of giving proper counsel, for want of understanding what they are consulted about. But as Rehoboam did not approve of the counsel of the old men, he discovered his policy, in applying to the young men that were grown up with him: for there was no danger of their giving advice that would be disagreeable to him. They had been so long about his person, that they knew his temper (perhaps better than what he himself did), what counsel would be acceptable to him; and they would not run the hazard of being turned out of place, and removed from before him, by advising to measures that he might dislike. Not only so, but they might have been so long habituated to adapt their own inclinations to that of the prince, with whom they had grown up, as that harsh proceedings might please them, no less than him. We cannot be surprised, therefore, that they spake unto him, saying: "Thus shalt thou speak unto this people, that spake unto thee, saying, Thy father made our yoke heavy, but make thou it lighter unto us: thus thou shalt say unto them, My little finger shall be thicker than my father's loins. And now, whereas my father did lade you with an heavy yoke, I will add to your yoke: my father hath chastised you with whips, but I will chastise you with scorpions."

Rehoboam, though descended from Solomon, had

very little of Solomon's wisdom, or he must have
known that such an answer as this would only inflame
the people, and make matters worse; but it so suited
his arbitrary disposition, that when they came to him
on the third day, according to appointment, he answered them roughly, forsook the old men's counsel,
and spoke to them after the counsel of the young men.
It must appear strange that any one who was not
quite a natural should commit such a horrid blunder,
and dream of bullying, with great sounding words
of vanity, a high-spirited people struggling for their
liberties, and determined not to submit to past hardships. But our text tells us how it came about, and
wherefore it was that the king hearkened not unto
the people : he did it not, for the cause was from the
Lord, that he might perform his saying, which the
Lord spake by Ahijah the Shilonite unto Jeroboam
the son of Nebat. What the Lord spake by Ahijah
unto Jeroboam was, that He would rend the kingdom
and give ten tribes to him. It was the will and design of Heaven that the ten tribes should be separated from Rehoboam; wherefore it was that the king
hearkened not unto the people. He was left to himself, to act a foolish, obstinate part, and to follow the
worst advice, that so the purpose of the Most High
might be accomplished.

This is the only rational way of accounting for what
happened ; and thus was it according to the Latin
adage—those whom God means to destroy, he first of
all bereaves of sense. Rehoboam being so lost to
common sense as to give the answer above related,
the people resented it with a becoming spirit; and
having nothing good to hope for, from one who could

treat them thus cavalierly, as though they were his beasts of burden, should they enter into further treaty with him; and being confident that it was not the will of Heaven that the Lord's free people should submit to be enslaved by a tyrant, because he was descended from David, whom the Lord had anointed to be king over the tribes of Israel, they had a recourse to the unalienable rights of human nature, declared themselves free and independent, saying: "What portion have we in David? neither have we inheritance in the son of Jesse: to your tents, O Israel; now see to thine house, David."

In the warmth of their resentment, they seem to speak disrespectfully of David; but when persons are enraged with cruel treatment, and that after having meant well and honestly, it is not unusual for them to utter those harsh expressions that they would not adopt in cooler moments. So Israel departed unto their tents. Rehoboam was soon sensible of his error; but in endeavoring to correct it, fell into another that made his affairs still worse. He sent Adoram, who was over the tribute, to treat with them. The tribute, we may suppose, was one ground of complaint; and Adoram might, by his bad management in that department, have made himself peculiarly obnoxious; unless it was so, we can scarce think that he would have fallen a sacrifice to their rage in such a way, for all Israel stoned him with stones that he died. Had Rehoboam sent one or more who had the love and confidence of the people, and were possessed of prudence, some good might possibly have come of it, and a reconciliation have taken place; but that was not to be, and therefore the aggrieved were insulted in the commissioner employed by him. When Adoram was stoned, Rehoboam perceived that it would not be safe for him to remain longer at Shechem, and therefore made speed to mount his chariot, and fled to Jerusalem. When he got there, he thought the ten tribes were of too much consequence to be lost, though before, being far from the seat of government, they might have been slighted, and been spoken of in diminutive terms by the courtiers; and he determined upon reducing them to obedience by arms.

Accordingly he assembled all the house of Judah, with the tribe of Benjamin, an hundred and fourscore thousand chosen men, who were warriors, to fight against the house of Israel, to bring the kingdom to Rehoboam the son of Solomon. What horrid scenes were now likely to commence! Countrymen, brethren in blood, brethren in religion, falling upon and slaughtering each other with the weapons of destruction! Houses on fire! Towns in flames! Women and children shrieking, crying, and flying, without conveniences, without necessaries, into woods and dens and caves for safety! Sons, brethren, lovers, husbands, parents and grand-parents wallowing in blood, and expiring in agonies! Scenes not to be imagined without shuddering! But an infinitely merciful God interdicts the whole by a most timely message. The word of God came unto Shemajah, the man of God, saying, speak unto Rehoboam the son of Solomon the king of Judah, and unto all the house of Judah and Benjamin, and to the remnant of the people, saying, thus saith the Lord, ye shall not go up, nor fight against your brethren, the children of Israel; return every man to his house, for this thing is from me. Did Rehoboam's regard to the divine prohibition influence him to desist, it was more to his credit than had he marched against and subdued the ten tribes; but it is to be apprehended, from the temper he had before showed, that the authority of the man of God to deliver such a message would have been disputed by him, had not the Jews that cleaved to him been fully convinced of the message being from the Lord, which at once disarmed them of all hostile intentions against their brethren, though themselves accustomed to war. They hearkened, therefore, to the word of the Lord, and returned to depart according to the word of the Lord. Thus I have considered the revolution that commenced at the death of Solomon, and the progress of that separation from the house of David, that the ten tribes were drove into, by the insulting and tyrannical conduct of Rehoboam—an event of that nature and so circumstanced, that can be accounted for only upon the principle assigned by the sacred historian—the king hearkened not unto the people, for the cause was from the Lord. And it is upon that principle alone that we can rationally account for the separation that hath taken place between the United States of America and Great Britain. That real friend to America and the rights of human nature, Dr. Price, was he acquainted with all the anecdotes to be gained on this side the Atlantic, relative to our affairs, instead of wording himself so cautiously: " I fancy I see," would not hesitate in saying: "I see in these measures something that cannot be accounted for merely by human ignorance." He would strike out, " I am inclined to think that" and boldly pronounce, "The hand of Providence is in them, working to bring about some great ends."

You must have applied already much of the discourse; for we have not been alluding to things done in secret; and you cannot be dwellers in Massachusetts, and be strangers to them. This continent complained of real grievances, and humbly petitioned. Whatever individuals of uncommon penetration might wish, from foreseeing what would necessarily exist sooner or later; the bulk of the people in every state, not this excepted, the body of the delegates would have been satisfied, would have rejoiced, would have been happy, had their requests been complied with. No set of delegates could have insisted upon more without breaking the union of the colonies. Instead of being heard and relieved, the yoke was increased by fresh acts of cruelty, and new burdens laid upon the continent. Our first grievances were spoken of as if not real; and as though we complained without cause, it was determined that we should have cause for complaining. We had not been accustomed to a state of slavery; therefore could not brook such treatment without resenting it. In the British Parliament we were posted up to the world for poltroons, and the ministry promised themselves a victory over all our resolutions to be free, without any slaughter. "The cabinet was in no disposition to give America any redress. The king was our inveterate enemy, and ordered the ministers to persevere in the old plan; and it was determined by the secret ruling power to distress us as much as possible. This ruler, being the veriest coward that human nature can know," no wonder that he was afraid lest we were falsely aspersed, and wished to have the trifling military stores we had collected for service, in case matters were brought to an extremity, destroyed.* Instructions for doing it were transmitted; blood being wantonly spilt in attempting to execute them, we were at once plunged into a defensive war, with the greatest power in the world, what with her riches, her resources, her alliances, her armies and navies.

When we look back to that important period, and recollect that we were without an army, without money and without ammunition, we are amazed, that instead of being galled to the bone with the yoke of slavery, we are keeping the anniversary of our independency. The sword being drawn and the ground stained with the blood of its inhabitants, the people offered themselves willingly in the cause of liberty, and the colonies united more closely. Still we were desirous, if possible, of an accommodation. We there-

---

* Taken out of a letter from a gentleman at London to his friend in Virginia, copied and sent over by the late Jeremiah Quincy, jun., Esq., whose death was occasioned by his zeal to serve the American cause, no less than if he had been slain in the field, as appears from the following minutes in his journal—" It is a good deal against my own private opinion and inclination that I now sail to America. I have had no letters from thence since they knew of my arrival. I know not what my next letters may contain. Besides, the fine season is now coming on here, and Dr. Fothergill thinks Bristol air and water would give me perfect health. On the other hand, my most intimate friends (except Mr. Bloomfield) insist upon my going directly to Boston. They say no letters can go with safety, and that I can deliver more information and advice *viva voce*, than could or ought to be wrote. They say my going now (if I arrive safe) must be of great advantage to the American cause." He attempted to serve the cause in the way advised to, notwithstanding the personal dangers attending it, and lost his life in the attempt. Let him be numbered therefore with the heroes that have fallen in the dispute.

fore petitioned again, without rising in our requests, only enlarging them to take in new grievances. Instead of having them redressed, we were deemed and were to be treated as rebels. The power of Great Britain was to be employed in reducing us, by fire and sword, by armies and navies. This inclined several of the colonies to wish for independency; but others would not hear of it, though it was known that the British ministry meant to employ Indians, Canadians and negroes against us. Union was essential to our safety: some colonies therefore could not be gratified in their desires after independency, till it was the wish of most or all. The delusive image of an inclination on the part of the ministry to settle the dispute by treaty, with which many in Britain were amused, fascinated numbers on this side the Atlantic; but when it was found that the commission given to the Howes was to be supported by an army of foreign mercenaries, a change of sentiments among the beguiled Americans commenced, and the advocates for independency multiplied greatly, the measure being made absolutely necessary in order to self-preservation.

The deep-laid scheme for destroying the army being discovered in a seasonable moment, removed the difficulties still remaining in the breasts of several well-affected to the cause and liberties of the continent, and brought every colony without exception to unite in declaring for a state of independency; and that they were absolved from all allegiance to the British crown, and that all political connection between them and the state of Great Britain, was and ought to be totally dissolved.

A variety of particulars conspire to evidence, that

8*

it becomes us to say of this great event that it was from the Lord. The union of the colonies was marvellous, considering the methods taken to hinder it; that they had their distinct interests, their mutual jealousies, and their different forms of government. The continuance of that union, notwithstanding the attempts made to prevent it—the general unanimity prevailing successively through the Congress—the ready compliance yielded to their recommendations and resolutions through the continent—the successes attending our military operations—the new modelling of most of our governments, that the people might thereby attain to the enjoyment of their civil rights, to a degree beyond what was before known—the derangement of the plans concerted by the adherents of the British ministry in different colonies—the revolution in people's sentiments, making them fond of a measure that a few months before they abhorred the thought of—the oversight of king and Parliament in neglecting conciliatory measures, while there was an opening for them, though urged strongly to it by the wisest statesmen in the kingdom—the unanimity of the Congress on a point which some weeks before would have occasioned a great division—and Lord Howe's not arriving till independency had been declared, which prevented his having the opportunity of dividing the public, and of obstructing the measure by the subtle arts of negotiation—these are matters so remarkable as not to admit of our excluding the special influence of Heaven. Let others, attached to a false philosophy, ascribe the separation of the United States of America from Great Britain to moral and natural causes, without taking into the account the providential concern of the Most

High in order to the accomplishment of his own divine purpose; but let every religious assembly say, the king hearkened not unto the people, for the cause was from the Lord; this thing is from God. And I heartily congratulate you upon his having brought it to pass, as the only secure way for your continuing free. I see not how it is possible for you to be ever more dependent upon Great Britain, without being in a state of bondage, and feeling all the horrors of slavery. I have not a doubt but that we are fully authorized, by reason and religion, for thus separating; and am persuaded that we are justified by the disinterested and impartial world. May the spirit of wisdom return speedily to the British councils, that so Britain may soon recover our friendship and secure our connection by commercial treaties, ere it is too late, and her ruin is sealed! But of this I have little hope, unless some important event should take place in Europe, and oblige Britons to bethink themselves. I rather expect that they will strain every nerve to subdue us. And such is the impiety of the courtiers (I mean in justice to except the king), such the irreligion of lords and commons, that, was a messenger sent with the word of God to forbid the bloody purpose, he would be rejected without examining his credentials, and would probably be ordered into confinement as a madman. An angel from heaven would have less attention paid him than a threatening express from a neighboring power. Has not the God of nature declared again and again his disapprobation of their bloody proceedings, by scattering their fleets, staying their voyages, disconcerting their plans, delivering many of their stores into our hands, and plunging them continually into greater difficulties. I might enumerate the several interpositions of Providence whereby we have been carried safely through the first year of our independency; but your time will not permit it, and you can scarce have forgot or be ignorant of them. Notwithstanding all, the British ministry will still persist. O! when—when—will the vengeance of Heaven overtake them, by awakening an injured, betrayed nation to avenge itself on such treasonable rulers?

Bear with me somewhat longer, my honorable hearers; for methinks I perceive in a private corner a sly, crafty, and concealed enemy, whispering in the ear of his well disposed but timid neighbor: Why does he not proceed in the history, and observe to us that the separation of the ten tribes weakened and hastened the ruin of all? and may not the like be feared with regard to Great Britain and the United States of America? I answer: The ruin of Great Britain will probably follow, unless prevented in the manner above mentioned. And though, in the heat of the present contest, and while engrossed in attending to our own safety, we can scarce find time to pity her, yet when we have got through our difficulties we shall bitterly lament her fall, and curse the memories of those who made it absolutely necessary for us to give her the mortal wound, that so we might escape with life and liberty. As to the United States of America, there is no reason to fear that it will be with them as it was with the ten tribes, do we improve by their errors. What led on to their ruin was their choosing another king when they had rejected Rehoboam, and not erecting a form of government that should keep out tyranny, after they had cast off the tyrant. They must needs call Jeroboam into the congregation, and make him king over all Israel; and he, through jealousy lest the people, by frequenting the worship of the Lord God at Jerusalem, should be induced at length to return to Rehoboam, adopted a policy that caused Israel to sin, and forfeit the blessing and protection of heaven.

But we are not bound to repair to the metropolis of Great Britain that we may do homage to the Sovereign of the universe. Our separation from her can be no injury to the continent. Should she think of denying episcopal ordination to persons of that persuasion, she only endangers her own establishment, and conscientious persons of that communion will soon be able to procure episcopal ordination elsewhere. No damage can ensue to the continent, on the score of religion, from its separation. Nay, we may derive a benefit from it, even beyond what is enjoyed in Britain, by embracing the present happy moment for establishing to all the peaceable enjoyment of the rights of conscience, while they approve themselves good members of civil society, be their religious principles what they may.

In civil concerns, let us divest ourselves of that selfish partiality, and oppressive temper, which have so disgraced us of late, and benumbed those patriotic principles which animated us in the commencement of the present noble contest, turning numbers into sons of rapine and extortion that once passed for and called themselves high sons of liberty. The nature of the times must unavoidably make the necessaries, no less than the superfluities of life, much dearer than formerly, so that it would be folly to say, that all that advance which has taken place has been owing to oppression and extortion. But, if men in this day will not be content with a livelihood, and will make themselves fortunes, immense fortunes, out of the distresses of the people, I say, let the curse of Heaven fall upon their substance, their unhallowed gains, till the same are providentially dispersed among the sufferers. 'Tis not a curse that is causeless. Says the wisest of men, He that withholdeth corn, the people shall curse him; but blessing shall be upon the head of him that selleth it. (Prov. xi. 26.) To corn, we may add meat, wool, flax, sugar, salt; in a word, all the necessary articles of life, whether raised in the country by the farmer, or brought in by the merchant, or persons engaged in privateering. And I can heartily deliver over to Satan, in the name of the people, such oppressive withholders, for the destruction of their flesh and of their substance, that so their spirits may be saved in the day of the Lord Jesus. I aim not this stroke at any particular order of men, and have been vexed at the weakness and wickedness that have appeared, in that animosity which hath existed between the merchant and the countryman. Fix their proportion, and I will venture to bring as many honest, upright, patriotic individuals from the one as from the other, and as many from each of the opposite character. But to hear some talk against trade and merchandise, as though they were of course a nuisance to society and the country—could do without them—is an exercise for patience. Those very persons forget, that, had it not been for trade and merchandise, the country had never been settled by their forefathers, had never been peopled and cultivated, as now ; had remained a wilderness, and the residence of Indians. They forget, that, without trade and merchandise, we must have been enslaved, for we could have had neither arms, nor ammunition, tents, medicines, and so on.   The countryman says, And remember, sir, that if it had not been for the country, you would not have had your men, your provision, and the like. True, my friend ; and this shows that the country and commercial interest ought not to be contrasted to each other; that, for the public good and the well-being of community, Providence hath designedly joined them together, and, what God hath joined together let no man put asunder.

I am greatly mistaken, or before the sword was drawn, they were both joined in one in whom we are all united, and to whom we are all more indebted than to any one man upon the continent—a—. I recollect myself, and name him not; 'twould be like showing the sun after having described it. Was not the worthy and honorable president of the Congress our own—a merchant also ? Some of the first characters in the civil and military departments were merchants or traders ; and now I have said so much upon this head, I hope little more will be said upon it henceforward, but what will be healing.

I go on to mention : let us mould the governments of the respective states, and the representative body of the united, viz., the Congress, so as not only to exclude kings, but tyranny, and, as ever, to retain the supreme authority in the people, together with the power, no less than the right of calling their delegated agents to an account, whether they sit in the assembly, the council, the chair, or the Congress. We are not fighting against the name of a king, but the tyranny; and if we suffer that tyranny under another name, we only change our master without getting rid of our slavery. Take heed, therefore, my brethren, and stand fast in that liberty wherewith you have been made free. Let no single individual, let no collective body exalt itself above measure, and assume to itself powers that do not belong to it, and with which it has never been entrusted, neither implicitly nor expressly. Now is the golden opportunity for banishing tyranny as well as royalty out of the American states, and sending them back to Europe, from whence they were imported.

I might enlarge, but must forbear. 'Tis expedient and opportune, however, to mention that, would we have our independency perpetuated, let us repent of our sins, attend to religion, and live the doctrines of Christianity; then may we reasonably expect that future generations will joyfully commemorate this anniversary, and that the names of those who boldly stood forth in the cause of liberty, and acted a consistent and uniform part, will be blessed.

My honorable audience, I am as much tired with speaking, as you can be with hearing me; but I must take a little notice of what strikes the ear of my imagination, from one oppressed with the difficulties of the day—if these are the fruits of independence, better be dependent as before. My honest friend, they are not the fruits of independence, but of Britain's trying to enslave us. They originate truly and properly from those we were before dependent upon. Blame them, therefore, for all your difficulties, and hate more than ever being brought into bondage to them. Your difficulties are great, but don't mistake the cause; charge them to the real authors. I pity you under them, and recommend it to every man to ease you of them as far as he is able. But, my friend, have you ever read the history of your own country, wrote by Mather? If not, you have heard of it; let me recommend it to your perusal, you will then find that your difficulties are vastly short of what your forefathers endured. And let me further tell you that I do not recollect reading of any people since the creation, that ever secured their liberties without undergoing far, far more than what we have experienced. I see, or fancy I see, a distant dawning that indicates we are not far from the end of our troubles. But if not, be of good courage, the horrors of slavery, after having exasperated our enemies by so animated and brave an opposition, are more to be dreaded than greater difficulties. Look upon your little ones, the darlings of your souls, and consider what will be their lot should the arms of Britain prevail. They will be forced to cry out: "O that we had been born Africans instead of Americans!" I now leave it with your good sense, and have done, my friend. I cannot but hope that the Lord will save us for his own name's sake.

NATHANIEL WHITAKER, D. D.

AMONG the preachers of the revolutionary period no one manifested a stronger dislike to the usurpations of the British crown than Doctor Whitaker. Possessed of great biblical learning and commanding powers of elocution, which he used upon every opportunity for the service of his suffering country, he exercised a wide influence among the people, and was looked upon as a "great political counsellor." He was a native of Long Island, New York, and was born on the twenty-second day of February, 1732. At the age of twenty, having passed his college life with marked attention to his studies and the cultivation of letters, he graduated at Princeton, and soon after was engaged in the ministry at Norwich, Connecticut. On the twenty-eighth of July, 1769, having agreed with the Third Church in Salem, Massachusetts, "that he would become their minister without public instalment, and that they should be under Presbyterian order, until they saw cause to alter," he preached a sermon and entered upon the duties of that church. Here he continued to labor with increased reputation. In the early part of 1775, his church was destroyed by fire, and his people were obliged to worship in a school-house. A letter of Doctor Whitaker, written at this time mentions the separation of many of his congregation from his church. This circumstance arose from a preference on the part of the seceders for the congregational form of government, under which Doctor Whitaker refused to preach. This spirit of dissension continued to increase until 1783, when the Third Church expressed a desire to return to congregationalism, and Doctor Whitaker retired from the pulpit. Soon after he visited Virginia, where he died. The records of his life are scanty, but enough remains in his printed sermons to entitle him to the name he has received, "an uncompromising man, pious, learned and charitable." His sermon "An Antidote against Toryism," was delivered at Salem, Massachusetts, and printed in 1777, with an extended dedication to General Washington.

ANTIDOTE AGAINST TORYISM.

Curse ye Meroz, said the angel of the Lord, curse ye bitterly the inhabitants thereof, because they came not to the help of the Lord against the mighty.—JUDGES, v. 23.

THE sum of the law of nature, as well as of the written law, is love. Love to God and man, properly exercised in tender feelings of the heart, and beneficent actions of life, constitutes perfect holiness. The gospel breathes the same spirit, and acknowledges none as the disciples of Christ but those who love not their friends only, but even their enemies. Bless and curse not, is one of the laws of his kingdom. Yet the aversion of men to this good and benevolent law prompts them to frequent violations of it, which is the source of all the evils we feel or fear. And so lost are many to all the tender feelings required in this law, as to discover their enmity to their Creator, by opposing the happiness of his creatures, and spreading misery and ruin among them.

When such characters as these present themselves to our view, if we are possessed with the spirit of love required in the law and gospel, we must feel a holy abhorrence of them. Love itself implies hatred to malevolence, and the man who feels no abhorrence of it, may be assured he is destitute of a benevolent temper, and ranks with the enemies of God and man. For, as God himself hates sin with a perfect hatred from the essential holiness of his nature, and sinners cannot stand in his sight, so the greater our conformity to him is, the greater will be our abhorrence of those persons and actions which are opposite to the divine law. David mentions this as an evidence of his love to God: "*Do not I hate them, O Lord, that hate thee?· and am I not grieved with them that rise up against thee? I hate them with a perfect hatred. I count them mine enemies.*"* True benevolence is, therefore, exercised in opposing those who seek the hurt of society, and none are to be condemned as acting against the law of love, because they hate and oppose such as are injurious to happiness.† But the weakness and

---

* Psalms cxxxix. 21, 22.

† Even God's hatred of sin, and the punishment he inflicts on the wicked, arise from his love of happiness, from the benevolence of his nature.

corruption of nature, in the best, is such, that God hath not intrusted to men at large the exercise of the resentment due to such characters, nor allowed them to inflict those punishments which their crimes call for, even in this world, except in some special cases. On the contrary, he hath strictly prohibited all his subjects taking vengeance for private or personal injuries in a private and personal manner, and required, that if "one smite us on the one cheek, we turn to him the other also;"* and, in the language of love, exhorts us: "Dearly beloved, avenge not yourselves." Yet there are cases in which he requires us, as his servants, to take vengeance on his enemies. And it deserves our particular notice, that all these cases respect crimes which tend to destroy human happiness.

Even his commands to punish blasphemy and other sins which strike more directly against himself, are not given because his own happiness is thereby diminished, but because they tend to erase from our minds that sense of his glorious majesty, authority, and government, without the belief of which, all order and peace among men would come to an end. So God requires us to execute vengeance on the murderer, the thief, the adulterer, reviler, and the like; all which sins strike at the peace and happiness of human society. God's heart is so much set upon diffusing happiness among his creatures, by which he most displays his glory, that he perfectly abhors whatever tends to frustrate this end; and has threatened the least opposition to it with everlasting death in

---

* Matthew, v. 39.

the world to come. But some (through the corruption of nature by sin) have not faith in a future state of rewards and punishments sufficient to influence them to their duty, or deter them from opposing God's gracious purpose, therefore, to strike our senses with full conviction of his anger against such as counteract his benevolent designs, he has commanded every society of men, to inflict punishment on them in this world, and has specified the crimes, the punishments, and the officers who are to inflict them.

Every punishment involves in it a curse, and presupposes some crime ; and the curse or punishment is by God exactly proportioned to the nature, heinousness, and circumstances of the crime. Therefore, when a grievous punishment is inflicted, we justly infer the aggravation of the offence. To inflict punishment, is actively to curse, and when we pronounce a curse, we do, as far as we can, consign over the object to some punishment. But when God commands us to curse any person or people, we are bound by his authority actually to punish them.

These observations may lead us to some apprehension of the aggravated nature of the sin of Meroz, whom Israel are commanded to curse bitterly for their conduct in an affair of a public nature.

The text I have chosen as the theme of my discourse, is part of a song uttered by Deborah and Barak, in holy triumph and praise for a signal victory obtained over Jabin, king of Canaan, and Sisera, the captain of his host. This powerful prince, who had nine hundred chariots of iron, and a mighty army, had brought Israel into subjection, and grievously oppressed them for twenty years. This cruel and galling yoke awakened

them to a sense of their sin against God, and to cry to
him for deliverance. No sooner are they made sensible of their sin against, and dependence on him, and
to repent and seek his favor and protection, than he appears for their help, and raises up and inspires Deborah
and Barak with courage, and faith in his power and
grace, to oppose the tyrant, and shake off his yoke.
A few men of Zebulon and Naphtali, viz., ten thousand, were designed by God to have the honor of
conquering this potent king; for ten other tribes mus-
tered and were ready for the war, yet it seems Zebulon and Naphtali only, were the people that jeoparded
their lives to the death, in the high places of the field.*
And the little army—raised from two tribes only
out of twelve—of Deborah and Barak march out and
wage war against their oppressor, for the recovery of
their freedom.†

---

* Context, ver. 18.

† Some people, not the inhabitants of Meroz, fear the event of our
present struggle, (1), on account of our inability, however we may
exert ourselves, to oppose the power of the tyrant; and hence, though
desirous of freedom, through want of faith in the power and grace of
God, dare not act, and so weaken the cause they wish might succeed.
Or, (2), they despair of success, because of so many in these states
who are lukewarm in the cause, and secretly or openly friends to the
tyrant. And, (3), some serious people despair of success because of the
abounding sins of our land. For the relief and establishment of such,
I entreat them to consider that none of the twelve tribes are mentioned
as entering the field but Zebulon and Naphtali; and not another as re-
motely favoring the cause, but Ephraim, Benjamin, Issachar, and Ma-
chir, of the family of Caleb. Their divisions then were much greater
than ours. For the divisions of Reuben there were great searchings of
heart . . . . As to their power, their army was but ten thousand, and
these without arms; for Deborah informs us, that neither shield nor spear
was seen among forty thousand in Israel. As to their sins, they had

Jabin, it seems, had no knowledge or thought that Israel was arming against him. The first intelligence brought him was, that Barak was gone up to Mount Tabor, that he had already marched, and was on his way to invade his country. Some traitors, who pretended friendship to Israel, carried him the news, hoping, doubtless, to ingratiate themselves with Jabin, by giving him the earliest notice possible of this revolt.

No doubt, both Jabin and Sisera despised this small body of undisciplined, unarmed troops, and were confident they should carry all before them, and quickly reduce those rebels (as he, doubtless, termed them) to their former obedience. But God, who disposes all events, not only gave the victory to Israel, but utterly destroyed the whole host of Jabin, that not one escaped, except Sisera the captain-general, and him God delivered to be slain by the hand of a woman. Women have sometimes been the deliverers of their country, and can, when God inspires them with courage, face the proudest foe. Oh, how easy is it with God to save from the greatest danger, and, by the weakest instruments, conquer the most powerful enemies!

Deborah and Barak, deeply impressed with a sense of God's mercy in this deliverance, sang this song as an expression of their joy and gratitude, from which, would time allow, many instructive lessons might be

---

greatly revolted, and chosen them new gods, which was high treason against their king. But, notwithstanding all the discouragements, we find victory declaring for them on their repentance, and proper exertion of the little power they had. This must surely remove all our fears in our present struggle, unless impenitence and unbelief still rule in our hearts, by which we shall incur the curse of Meroz.

deduced. But the words of my text lead us more directly to consider some things most worthy our attention this day, and therefore I have chosen them as the theme of the following discourse, and in them we may observe:

I. The crime for which this bitter curse is denounced on the inhabitants of Meroz. Probably this was some town or state in Israel, who, being called to furnish their quota of men and money for the war, through fear of bad success and, in that case, of a heavier burden; or from a secret lurch to the enemy, arising from hope of court preferment, or favors already bestowed on some of their leading men; or from some other sinister motive, thought best to lie still, and not meddle in the quarrel. So much is certain, they did not go with Barak to the war. The crime they are charged with, is not their aiding, assisting, or furnishing the enemy, or holding a secret correspondence with, or taking up arms to help them; they are not charged as laying plots to circumvent the rest, or striving to discourage their neighbors from going to the war, or as terrifying others with descriptions of the irresistible power of Jabin's nine hundred chariots of iron and the like. No, the inhabitants of Meroz were innocent people compared to these; they were only negatively wicked; they only failed in their duty; they did not arm to recover their liberties when wrested from them by the hand of tyranny. This is all the fault charged on them, yet for this they incurred the fearful curse in my text. Now, if for mere negligence they deserved this curse, what must they have deserved who aided and assisted the enemy? Surely a sevenfold bitterer curse.

9

II. Observe the curse pronounced: "Curse ye Meroz, curse ye bitterly the inhabitants thereof." Their conduct, on that occasion, was such as deserved a severe punishment from the other states, who are commanded to separate them unto evil, as a just reward of their neglect.

III. We observe by whom this curse was to be pronounced and inflicted. Not by Deborah and Barak alone, in a fit of anger, as profane persons in a rage curse their neighbors, and undertake to punish them; such often pronounce curses without cause, but the curse causeless shall not come. This curse was to be pronounced and inflicted by all the people, who are here required to be of one heart, and engage seriously, religiously, and determinately in cursing them, and as God's ministers to execute his wrath upon them. We may not suppose that this work was left to the people at large, or to a mob; but the rulers are first to proceed against them,* and all the people to support and assist them in this work; and so all were to join, as one man, to curse them, and that bitterly, i. e., they were fully and without hesitation to condemn them to severe punishment, and inflict it on them. They were not to deal gingerly with them, nor palliate their offence. They are allowed to make no excuses for them, nor to plead "that they were of a different opinion; that they thought it their duty not to take up arms against their king that ruled over them, but to submit to the higher powers; that liberty of conscience ought to be allowed to every one, and that it

---

* This is evident from the order of government God established in Israel.

would be hard to punish them for acting their own judgments."* No such pleas might be made for them, nor one word spoken in their favor, their sin being against the great law of love and light of nature; but all, with full purpose of heart, were to curse those cowardly, selfish, cringing, lukewarm, half-way, two-faced people, and to treat them as outcasts, and unworthy the common protection or society of others.

IV. Observe by whose command they were required to curse Meroz. It was not by the command of Deborah and Barak, but of God himself; yea by the command of Jesus Christ, the meek and compassionate Saviour of men. Curse ye Meroz, said the angel of the Lord. This was the angel of God's presence, who then fought for Israel, and who was so offended with the people of Meroz for their selfishness and indifference in this important cause, that he not only cursed them himself, but commands all the people to curse them, and inflict his wrath on them in this world.

V. Observe the circumstances which aggravated their crime, viz.: the enemy that enslaved them was mighty. Had the foe been weak and contemptible, there had been less need of their help. But when a powerful tyrant oppressed them, and they were called upon to unite with their suffering brethren in shaking

---

* Liberty of conscience is often pleaded in excuse for the worst of crimes. In matters of mere conscience the plea is valid, but nothing else. Those are matters of mere conscience in which none are concerned but God and the person acting; as in matters of faith and worship. But when actions respect society, and become injurious to the civil rights of men, they are proper subjects of civil laws, and may be punished, notwithstanding the plea for liberty of conscience.

off his yoke, and all their strength little enough to
oppose him, then to excuse themselves, was highly
criminal, and in effect to join with the tyrant to rivet
slavery and misery on the whole nation. This was
highly provoking to God, whose great end is, to diffuse
happiness, and not misery, among his creatures, and
who never punishes but when his subjects oppose
this design.

This was the crisis when their all lay at stake. They
well knew that their brethren (however they themselves might be distinguished with court favors by the
tyrant) were groaning under cruel bondage. But as
selfishness renders people callous and unfeeling to the
distresses of others, so they were easy and satisfied to
see their brethren tortured by the unrelenting hand
of oppression, if so be they might sleep in a whole
skin. They were contented that others should go
forth and endure the hardships of war, but refused to
engage in the work, or bear any part of the burden
with them, though all was hazarded through their
neglect. How base was this conduct, while they
knew the strength of the enemy? This consideration
was enough to have engaged every one, not lost to all
the feelings of humanity, to the firmest union, and the
most vigorous exertions. But these servile wretches
would rather bear the yoke, and see the whole land
involved in slavery, than enter the field, and share the
glory of regaining their freedom from a powerful foe.
They preferred their present ease, or some court favor,
with chains and slavery, to the glorious freedom they
were born to enjoy.

From this view of the text and context, we may
deduce the following doctrinal observations:

I. That the cause of liberty is the cause of God and truth.

II. That to take arms and repel force by force, when our liberties are invaded, is well-pleasing to God.

III. That it is lawful to levy war against those who oppress us, even when they are not in arms against us.

IV. That indolence and backwardness in taking arms, and exerting ourselves in the service of our country, when called thereto by the public voice, in order to recover and secure our freedom, is an heinous sin in the sight of God.

V. That God requires a people, struggling for their liberties, to treat such of the community who will not join them, as open enemies, and to reject them as unworthy the privileges which others enjoy.

I. The cause of freedom is the cause of God. To open this, I will inquire:

1st. What we are to understand by liberty, or freedom? and then,

2d. Prove that this is the cause of God

1. What is meant by liberty, or freedom?

It is sufficient to my present purpose to distinguish liberty into moral, natural and civil.*

---

* I purposely omit what Dr. Price, in his excellent Observations on Civil Liberty, p. 2, calls physical liberty; which, I venture to say, with deference to this great man, is not to be found, as he defines it, in any intelligent agent in the universe. For, that actions may be "properly ours," he makes them the effects of self-determination only, "without the operation of any foreign cause." This, at one blow, demolishes all the power and value of motives. which are always foreign to the actions they produce, as the cause is to the effect. And thus the issue is, that we must act without any reason, motive, aim, or end of our actions, in order that they may be properly our own. But this reduces us to mere machines.

Moral liberty lies in an ability, or opportunity, to act or conduct as the agent pleases.

He that is not hindered by any external force from acting as he chooses or wills to act, is perfectly free in a moral sense ; and so far as he possesses this freedom, so far, and no farther, is he a moral, accountable creature, and his actions worthy of praise or blame.

` By natural liberty, I mean that freedom of action and conduct which all men have a right to, antecedent to their being members of society. This Mr. Locke defines to be " that state or condition in which all men naturally are to order all their actions, and dispose of themselves and possessions as they think fit, within the bounds of the law of nature, without asking leave, or depending on the will of any man." In this state all men are equal, and no one hath a right to govern or control another. And the law of nature or the eternal reason and fitness of things, is to be the only rule of his conduct; of the meaning of which every one is to be his own judge.

But since the corruption of nature by sin, the lusts and passions of men so blind their minds, and harden their hearts, that this perfect law of love is little considered, and less practised; so that a state of nature, which would have been a state of perfect freedom and happiness had man continued in his first rectitude, in a state of war, rapine and murder. Hence arises an absolute necessity that societies should form themselves into politic bodies, in order to enact laws for the public safety, and appoint some to put them in execution, that the good may be encouraged, and the vicious deterred from evil practices;   and these laws should always be founded on the law of nature.*

Hence it appears, that perfect civil liberty differs from natural only in this, that in a natural state our actions, persons and possessions, are under the direction, judgment and control of none but ourselves; but in a civil state, under the direction of others, according to the laws of that state in which we live; which, by the supposition, are perfectly agreeable to the law of nature. In the first case, private judgment; in the second, the public judgment of the sense of the law of nature, is to be the rule of conduct. When this is the case, civil liberty is perfect, and every one enjoys all that freedom which God designed for his rational creatures in a social state. All liberty beyond this is mere licentiousness—a liberty to sin, which is the worst of slavery. But when any laws are enacted which cross the law of nature, there civil liberty is invaded, and God and man justly offended. Therefore, when those appointed to enact and execute laws, invade this liberty, they violate their trust, and oppress their subjects, and their constituents may lawfully depose them by force of.arms, if they refuse to reform.

Now, if it be unlawful for magistrates in a state, to bind their subjects by laws contrary to the law of nature, and if in this case it is lawful for their subjects to depose them, it follows, *a fortiori*, that should the rulers of one state assume a power to bind the

---

* Civil liberty is the freedom of bodies politic, or states. This is well defined by Dr. Price, p. 2, to be "the power of a civil society or state to govern itself by its own discretion, or by laws of its own making, without being subject to any foreign direction or the impositions of any extraneous power."

people of another state who never intrusted them with a legislative power, by such unrighteous laws, those oppressed people would be under no kind of obligation to submit to them, but ought, if in their power, to oppose them and recover their liberty. Therefore the freedom of a society or state consists in acting according to their own choice, within the bounds of the law of nature, in governing themselves independent of all other states. This is the liberty wherewith God hath made every state free, and which no power on earth may lawfully abridge, but by their own consent; nor can they lawfully consent to have it abridged, but where it appears for the greater good of society in general: and when this end cannot be attained, they have a right to resume their former freedom, if in their power.

2. I proceed to prove that the cause of civil liberty is the cause of God. This follows from what hath now been said. For if the law of nature is the law of God, and if God hath given every society or state liberty independent of all other states, to act according to their own choice in governing themselves within the bounds of the law of nature, then it follows that this freedom is of God, and he that is an advocate for it espouses the cause of God, and he that opposes it opposes God himself. This liberty hath God not only given, but entailed on all men, so that they cannot resign it to any creature without sin. Therefore, should any state, through fear, resign this freedom to any other power, it would be offensive to God. Thus, had America submitted to, and acquiesced in the declaration of the British Parliament, "That they have a right to bind us in all cases whatsoever," we should

have greatly provoked God by granting that prerogative to men, which belongs to God only; nor could
we have reason to hope for pardon and the divine favor on our land, without unfeigned repentance; but,
as repentance implies a change of conduct as well as
of mind, so we must have exerted ourselves to undo
what we had done, and by every method in our power
to cast off the chains and resume our liberty.   But, to
leave the dim light of reason, let us hear what divine
revelation says in my text and context.

Israel were a free, independent commonwealth,
planted by God in Canaan, in much the same manner
that he planted us in America.   The nations around
always viewed them with an envious and jealous eye,
as well they might, since they drove out seven nations
more powerful than themselves, and possessed their
land.   But when, by their grievous sins they provoked God, he often permitted those neighboring nations to invade their rights, that they might be brought
to a sense of their sin and duty.

Jabin, the king of Canaan, one of those states, was
God's rod to humble them.   He invaded Israel, robbed them of their rights, and held them in slavery
twenty years; in all which he acted the part of a
cruel tyrant, and provoked God, to his own destruction.   Jabin had long ruled over Israel; but this gave
him no right.   His dominion was still mere usurpation, as he robbed them of the liberty God had given
them; and with a single view to recover this and punish the invader, God commanded them to wage war
on the tyrant, and shake off his yoke.   They obey the
divine mandate, assemble their forces, call on the
various states to join them in the glorious conflict;

9*

and God himself curses those who would not assist to punish this oppressor.

No doubt, Jabin called this rebellion, and made proclamation that all who were found in arms, or any way aiding the revolt, should be deemed and treated as rebels, and their estates confiscated; but that all who would make their submissions, should enjoy all their privileges, as before, at his sovereign disposal. A glorious offer! How worthy the joyful and thoughtful acceptance of men born to freedom! Rather where's the wretch so sordid as not to feel this as an insult to human nature? or where's the Christian that does not view it as a reproach of his God? and who will not, with good Hezekiah, spread before the Lord, in humble prayer, the words of this Rabshekah, published to reproach our God, as unable to defend us, though engaged in his cause? Or where is the man, so lost to all noble and generous feelings, that would not choose to die in the field of martial glory, rather than accept such insulting terms of peace, or rather of misery; to live and see himself, his friends, his wife, children and country, subjugated to the arbitrary will and disposal of a merciless tyrant?

But doubtless these inviting, gracious terms of peace, had great influence on some. The inhabitants of Meroz seem to have been such dastardly, low-spirited, court sycophants; and also many in the tribe of Reuben, for whose divisions there were great searchings of heart. These probably trembled at the power of Jabin, and thought him invincible, though opposing God himself, whose cause they were called to espouse. Some might call the war rebellion, and others, by open or secret practices, discourage and weaken the cause.

This is very applicable to our present case. We are declared rebels by the king of England. His servants offer pardon to all those who will lay themselves at his feet to dispose of as he shall see fit, and "to bind them, their children and estates, at his pleasure, in all cases whatsoever." What gracious terms of peace! Must not this yoke sit with peculiar ease and pleasure on the necks of freeborn Americans! Yet, with horror be it spoken, there are freeborn sons of America so lost to all sense of honor, liberty, and every noble feeling, as to join the cry, and press for submission. O tell it not in Gath, publish it not in the streets of Ashkelon. We have some, but blessed be God, that we have no more of the inhabitants of Meroz scattered among us; some whose endeavors to divide us, cause great searchings of heart. But be it known to them, and to all men, that they, as Meroz, are fighting against God. This assertion is confirmed by the curse denounced on Meroz by God's command; for had they not opposed him, he would not have cursed them. They, then, were the rebels, in the judgment of God, and not those who took up arms to recover their liberties: rebels against the God of Heaven; and therefore fell under his and his people's curse; as well as those shall, who oppose or neglect to promote the like glorious cause.

From what hath been said, the truth of the second observation appears, viz.:

II. That to take arms, and repel force by force, when our liberties are invaded, is well pleasing to God.

This is a natural consequence from what is said above, and from the text itself. Deborah and Barak, in taking arms against Jabin, acted agreeably to the law of nature, which is the law of love; were also particularly excited, directed, and commanded thereto by God himself.* They did not, by this war, aim at dominion over others, nor seek to deprive any of their natural rights; but only to recover and secure the liberties and rights which had been wrested from them, that they might thereby spread peace and happiness through all the tribes of Israel; while the real happiness of others would not thereby be diminished. This, by the law of nature, was sufficient to justify them. If, then, they conformed to the law of love in taking up arms, and if God required them to make war on Jabin, then it was undeniably pleasing to him. But, if God approved their conduct in this case, he certainly will approve the like conduct in all similar cases. Therefore, when one country or state invades the liberties of another, it is lawful, and well pleasing to God, for the oppressed to defend their rights by force of arms. Yea, to neglect this, when there is a rational prospect of success, is a sin—a sin against God, and discovers a want of that benevolence, and desire of the happiness of our fellow-creatures, which is the highest glory of the saints.

I need not spend time to prove that our struggle with Great Britain is very similar to that of Israel and Jabin. As they had, so have we been long oppressed by a power that never had any equitable right to our land, or to rule over us, but by our own consent, and agreeably to a solemn compact. When they violated this, all their right ceased, and they could have no

---

* Judges, iv. 6, 7.

better claim to dominion than Jabin had over Israel. A power, indeed, has been usurped by Great Britain, "to bind us in all cases whatsoever;" which claim hath already produced many most unrighteous and oppressive laws, which they have attempted to enforce by their fleets and armies; in all which they can be no more justified than Jabin in his tyranny over Israel. Therefore, if it was their duty to fight for the recovery of their freedom, it must likewise be ours. And to neglect this, when called to it by the public voice, will expose us to the curse of Meroz. Yea,

III. It is lawful, yea duty, to levy war against those who oppress us, even when they are not in arms against us, if there be a rational probability of success.

I say, if there be a rational probability of success. For the law of love or nature will not justify opposition to the greatest oppression, when such opposition must be attended with greater evils than submission. Therefore, the primitive Christians, and many of later ages, did not oppose their cruel persecutors; as it would, without a miracle, have brought on them inevitable destruction. But where there is a rational probability of success, any people may lawfully, and it is their duty to, levy war on those who rob them of their rights, whether they be rulers in the state they live in, or any more distant powers, even before war is waged against them.

The truth of this appears from the instance before us. Jabin at this time was not at war with Israel; no, they had been conquered and under his government twenty years; and nothing was heard, but the groans and cries of the oppressed. How then, it may be asked, can they be justified in commencing a war? Doubtless they had often petitioned for redress of grievances, as we have done, and to as little purpose. What more could they do in a peaceable way? They were reduced to the dreadful alternative, either tamely to submit themselves and children after them, to the galling yoke of merciless tyranny, or wage war on the tyrant. The last was the measure God approved, and therefore, by a special command, enjoined it on them. This we are sure he would not have done, had it been offensive to him. He did not require Israel to wait till Jabin had invaded their country and struck the first blow (as we did in respect to our British oppressors), but while all was peace in his kingdom, for aught we find, God commands Israel to raise an army, and invade the tyrant's dominions.

The moral reason of this is obvious. For usurpation or oppression, is offensive war, already levied. Any state which usurps a power over another state, or rulers who, by a wanton use of their power, oppress their subjects, do thereby break the peace, and commence an offensive war. In such a case opposition is mere self-defence, and is no more criminal, yea, as really our duty as to defend ourselves against a murderer, or highway robber. Self-preservation is an instinct by God implanted in our nature. Therefore we sin against God and nature, when we tamely resign our rights to tyrants, or quietly submit to public oppressors, if it be in our power to defend ourselves.

A rebel, indeed, is a monster in nature, an enemy not only to his country, but to all mankind; he is destitute of that benevolence which is the highest honor and glory of the rational nature. But what is a rebel?—what those actions, for which a man or people deserve this opprobrious charge? Those only are rebels who are enemies to good government, and oppose such as duly execute it. A state of nature is a state of war. Civil government, which is founded in the consent of society to be governed by certain laws framed for the general good, and duly executed by some appointed thereto, puts an end to this state, and secures peace and safety. He, therefore, who transgresses this compact, even he opposes good government, and is a rebel, *rebellat*—he raises war again.

In this, it matters not whether the person be a king or a subject; he is the rebel that breaks the compact, he renews the war, and is the aggressor; and every member of the body politic is bound, by the eternal law of benevolence, to set himself against him, and, if he persists, the whole must unite to root him from the earth, whether he be high or low, rich or poor, a king or a subject. The latter, indeed, less deserves it, by how much less mischief he is capable of doing. But when a king or ruler turns rebel (which is vastly more frequent, in proportion to their numbers), being armed with power, he ever spreads desolation and misery around his dominions before he can be regularly and properly punished, and therefore is proportionably higher in guilt. Witness Pharaoh, Saul, Manasseh, Antiochus, Julian, Charles I., of blessed memory, and George III., who vies with the chief in this black catalogue, in spreading misery and ruin round the world.

The ruler who invades the civil or religious rights of his subjects, levies war on them, puts them out of his protection, and dissolves all their allegiance to him; for allegiance and protection are reciprocal, and where one is denied the other must cease.

If these observations are true (and they cannot be denied with modesty), then it is as lawful, and as strongly our duty, to prosecute a war against the king of England for invading our rights and liberties as to bring an obstinate rebel to justice, or take arms against some foreign power that might invade us.   Oppression alone, if persisted in, justifies the oppressed in making war on the oppressors; whether they be rulers or private persons, in our own or a foreign state.   The reason is, because oppressors are enemies to the great law of nature, and to the happiness of mankind.   For this, God commanded Israel to commence a war against Jabin, that, being free from his power, happiness and peace might be restored.

In our contest with the tyrant of Great Britain, we did not, indeed, commence the war.   No.   But though under a load of almost insupportable insult, abuse and reproach, we raised our humble and earnest petitions, and prayed only for peace, liberty and safety, the natural rights of all men.   But, be astonished, O heavens! and tremble, O England! while our dutiful supplications ascended before the throne, the monster was meditating the blow; and ere we rose from our knees, he fixed his dagger in our heart!   If this is to be a father, where can be the monster?   If this be the exercise of lenity and mercy, as he vainly boasts,* what must be his acts of justice?   O, merciful God, look down and behold our distress, and avenge us of our cruel foe.

---

* See Gen. Howe's proclamation of November 30th, 1776.

Can we reflect on those scenes of slaughter and desolation which he hath spread before our eyes, and doubt
of our duty ? Is it any longer a scruple whether God
calls us to war ? If such insults and abuse will not
justify us, no abuses ever can. Yea, had George withheld his hand from shedding our blood, the grievous
oppressions we groaned under before, and the contempt
and insult with which he treated our petitions, were
fully sufficient to justify us in the sight of God, and all
wise men, had we begun the war, and expelled his
troops from our country by fire and sword. Is it possible that Jabin could treat Israel with greater insult
or more unjustly invade their rights ? But for this,
God commanded Israel to make war on him, and pronounces a heavy curse on those who refused to join in
carrying it on.

This leads me to show,

IV. That those who are indolent, and backward to
take up arms and exert themselves in the service of
their country, in order to recover and secure their
freedom, when called thereto by the public voice, are
highly criminal in the sight of God and man.

This doctrine is wrapt up in the very bowels of my
text. "Curse ye Meroz, said the angel of the Lord,
curse ye bitterly the inhabitants thereof, because they
came not to the help of the Lord, to the help of the
Lord against the mighty." The curse of God falls on
none but for sin; for he delights in blessing, not in
cursing. And he never permits any of his subjects
to execute his curses on their fellow-subjects, but
where the crime is highly aggravated ; much less does
he allow them to curse them bitterly, unless their guilt
is exceeding great. Now, since God commands Is-

rael to curse Meroz bitterly, we fairly infer, that their
sin was of a crimson dye, and most provoking to him
and his people. And whoever is guilty of the like
conduct in our contest with Great Britain, incurs the
like guilt.

This needs no further proof; for if it be allowed
that the state of the case between Great Britain and
America, is, in its main parts, parallel with that between
Jabin and Israel, as hath been shown, then the crime
of negligence is as heinous in this struggle as in that.
And as Israel were required to curse bitterly those
cowardly, selfish, half-way people, so are we to curse
the like characters at this day. And as those people,
for their neglect, exposed themselves to the loss of all
the privileges and blessings of a free state in this
world, and to the eternal vengeance of God in the
next; so it highly concerns all to take heed that they
do not fall under the same condemnation. That we
may avoid the rock on which they were lost, I will,

1. Give their character.

2. Mention some aggravations of their sin.

3. I will hint at some things which discover people to be like the inhabitants of Meroz.

Few, I fear, are perfectly clear in this matter. Alas,
there is too great negligence among people in general.
Private interests and selfish considerations, engross
the thoughts and cares of many, who wish well the
cause of liberty, and divert their attention and exertions from the main thing which calls for our first and
chief regard, viz., the defence of our country from
tyranny, and securing our civil and religious freedom.
It is mournful to see most men eagerly pursuing
worldly gain, and heaping up unrighteous mammon

by cruel oppression and grinding the faces of the poor, while our country lies bleeding of her wounds, and so few engaged to bind them up. Let such consider that they are guilty of the sin of Meroz, and, though they may not feel the curse of men in this world, they shall not, without sincere repentance, escape the wrath and curse of God in the world to come. Every one is called, at this day, to come to the help of the Lord against the mighty; either to go out to war, or in some way vigorously exert himself for the public good. There are various things necessary for the defence of our country besides bearing arms, though this is the chief; and all may, one way or other, put to a helping hand. There are various arts and manufactures essential to the support of the inhabitants and army, without which we must soon be overcome. In one or other of these, men and women, youth, and even children, may be employed, and as essentially help in the deliverance of their country as those who go out to war. All are now called to have more than ordinary frugality and diligence in their respective callings;* and those of ability should be liberal and forward to encourage manufactures for the public good.† But alas, that so few make the interest and

---

* Suppose every fifth man to be employed in the army, and the number of dependents to be as great as before, then every man must labor one-fifth more than formerly, in order to support those in the army and their dependents, allowing them to live as cheap in the army as at home, which is not the case.

† There hath been a laudable spirit, especially in some towns, to encourage manufactures. I have been informed that Newbury, by a town vote, encouraged erecting works, and carrying on the making saltpetre. And in Salem, where the first was made in this state, several gentlemen

welfare of the public the main object of their pursuit. Yet there are some, and I hope many, who with truth can say, they have done their best, according to their circumstances, for the defence and safety of their country. Such, however the contest may arise, will enjoy the approbation of God, their own consciences, and of all the friends of mankind.

But not to make our case appear better than it really is, I fear there are many among us, in one disguise or other, who, when stript of their vizards, will appear to be of the inhabitants of Meroz; and who, if their characters were justly drawn, would secretly, if not openly, say, as the Pharisees in another case, In saying this, thou reproachest us also. But as birds which are hit, show it by their fluttering, and it may serve to bring such contemptible characters to view, and expose them to the curse they deserve, and on the other hand, may convince some real friends to freedom of their sinful negligence in the common cause; I will venture to point out a few.

Among these characters I do not include such as aid, or in words or actions defend, or openly declare for the enemy, and plead the right of Great Britain "to bind us in all things whatsoever." Of such there are not many among us, owing, probably, to their fear of a vast majority, which is on the side of freedom; and therefore they put on the guise of friendship, while they endeavor secretly to work destruction to

---

generously subscribed to assist me in making experiments, and erecting the works. And this winter they have subscribed above £500 to enable me to erect large salt-works—a manufacture most necessary for the good of the state.

the cause. These may be known by the following marks:

1. Observe the man who will neither go himself, nor contribute of his substance (if able) to encourage others to go into the war. Such do what in them lies to break up the army. These incur the curse of Meroz.

2. Others will express wishes for our success, but will be sure to back them with doubts of the event, and fears of a heavier yoke. •You may hear them frequently magnifying the power of the enemy, and telling of the nine hundred chariots of iron, the dreadful train of artillery, and the good discipline of the British troops, of the intolerable hardships the soldiers undergo, and of the starving condition of their families at home; and by a thousand such arts endeavoring to discourage the people from the war.

3. There are other pretended friends whose countenance betrays them. When things go ill with our army, they appear with a cheerful countenance, and assume airs of importance, and you'll see them holding conferences in one corner or another. The joy of their hearts, on such occasions, will break through all disguises, and discover their real sentiments; while their grief and long faces in a reverse of fortune, are a plain index pointing to the end at which they really aim.

4. Others, who talk much for liberty, you will find ever opposing the measures of defence proposed; making objections to them, and showing their inconsistency, while they offer none in their stead, or only such as tend to embarrass the main design. They are so prudent that they will waste away days, yea

months, to consider; and are ever full of their wise cautions, but never zealous to execute any important project. When such men get into public stations—especially if they fill a seat in our public councils—they greatly endanger the state. They protract business, and often defeat the best councils. Prudence and moderation are amiable virtues; and the modest mind feels pain in being suspected as sanguine, rash, and imprudent. This gives the overprudent great advantage to obstruct every vigorous measure, which they brand with the name of rashness; and every friend to vigorous action feels the reflection—who, without great fortitude, sits down abashed, and with grief sees his counsels defeated. But, if the measure be adopted, the next motion of the prudent man is to delay the execution, that the happy moment, on which all depends, may be lost.* These over and over pru-

---

* We have a remarkable instance of this nature in 2 Samuel, xvii. 1–14. David had just retreated from Jerusalem, with only six hundred men, when Absalom entered the city, and night came on. Ahithophel counselled for an immediate pursuit. This was wise and good counsel in the case. But Hushai, a friend in heart to David, and firm to Absalom in appearance, disapproved the counsel of Ahithophel as rash and imprudent at that time, and advised to more moderate and cautious measures. And, to carry his point, he magnifies the generalship of David, and the valor of his troops. He hints the great danger there was that his own troops, so near in opposition to their king, would be thrown into confusion, and melt away through fear of the valor of David and his men, and probably desert and join him on a mere report that there was a slaughter among Absalom's army; and that a defeat would be utter ruin. He therefore moves that all Israel be gathered together, as the sand of the sea, that so they might swallow up David in a moment. But mark his design! Was it to gain advantage of David? No; but to give him an opportunity to retreat, collect a larger force, and dispose his army for battle. Happy should we be if all

dent men ought to be suspected, and viewed with a watchful eye. And the discerning mind will soon be able to discover whether such counsels spring from true wisdom, or from a design to ensnare us.

5. Some are discovered by the company they keep. You may find them often with those who have given too much reason to suspect their enmity to our cause, and rarely with the zealous friends of liberty, except by accident; and then they speak and act like creatures out of their element, and soon leave the company, or grow mute, when liberty is the subject of discourse.

6. There are others who in heart wish well to our cause; but, through fear of the power of our enemies, they are backward to join vigorously to support it. They really wish we might succeed; but they dread the hardships of a campaign, and choose so to conduct, that, on whatever side victory may declare, they may be safe.

7. Others wish well to the public cause, but have a much greater value for their own private and personal interest. They are high sons of liberty, till her cause crosses their private views; and, even then, they boast in her name, while, like George III., they stab her to the heart, by refusing submission to those regulations which are essential to her preservation.

All these, and many others of a like kind, might doubtless have been found in Meroz, and yet the best

---

Hushais were banished from our councils, or their stratagems discovered and defeated. Prudence and caution are highly necessary. But to be always deliberating, and opposing vigorous measures, and slow in executing, at such a crisis as this, is strongly characteristic of an inhabitant of Meroz.

of them all fell under this bitter curse. For whatever were their private sentiments, they tended to the issue, viz. : to keep them back from those vigorous efforts that the cause of liberty then required, and for want of which, it was greatly hazarded. And whatever motives influence men at this day, whether a desire of ease, hope of power, honor, or wealth ; if they do any thing against, or neglect to assist all in their power, this glorious cause of freedom, now in our hands, they, in a greater or less degree, incur the curse of Meroz. Now, if ever, is that text to be applied to such, *"Cursed be he that doeth the work of the Lord deceitfully ; and cursed be he that holdeth back his sword from blood."** This leads me

II. To mention some aggravations of this sin.

1. This conduct is a violation of the law of nature, which requires all to exert themselves to promote happiness among mankind. Love is the fulfilling of the law, but this implies a benevolent frame of heart, exercised in beneficent actions toward all men, as we have opportunity. When therefore we see our fellow-creatures, especially our friends and brethren, whose happiness is more immediately our care, reduced to a state of misery, robbed of their most dear and unalienable rights, and borne down with a heavy load of oppression and abuse by the hands of tyrants; this law requires us to stand forth in their defence, even though we are not involved with them in the same evils, and how much more, when our own happiness is equally concerned. Moses, though enjoying all the honors and pleasures of a court, from the pure benev-

---

* Jeremiah xlviii., 10.

olence of his heart, interposed and smote an Egyptian whom he saw cruelly oppressing one of his brethren. This conduct is spoken of with approbation, and was no mark of his want of meekness, in which he excelled all men on the face of the earth. How opposite to this is the character of many great pretenders to meekness in our day, who can tamely see their brethren abused and plundered, and are so meek, or rather selfish, as to pay their courts to the oppressors. One would think, that like some heathens they worship the devil to keep him in a good mood, that he may not hurt them. The man who can stand by, an idle spectator, when a murderer or robber assaults his brother, and not exert himself in his defence, is deservedly accounted as criminal, in law and reason, as the murderer or robber himself, and is exposed to the same punishment. Inactivity, in such a case, is justly esteemed an approbation of the crime. But as freedom is an inheritance entailed on all men, so whosoever invades it, robs mankind of their rights, endeavors to spread misery among God's creatures, and violates the law of nature, and all who refuse to oppose him, when in their power, are to be considered and treated as confederates and abettors of his conduct, and partakers in his crimes.

2. This sin is against posterity; our children after us must reap the fruit of our present conduct. If we nobly resist the oppressor, we shall, under God, deliver them from his galling yoke; at least shall avoid the guilt of riveting it on them. But if we bow tamely to have it fastened on our necks, unborn generations, through unknown centuries may never be able to shake it off; but must waste away a wretched existence in

10

this world, without any other claim to the fruit of their labors, or even to the dear pledges of conjugal love, the fruit of their own bodies, than such as depends on the uncontrolled will of a haughty tyrant.

3. Let us, for a moment, glance an eye on the next and succeeding generations. What a scene opens to view! Behold these delightful and stately mansions for which we labored, possessed by the minions of power; see yonder spacious fields, subdued to fruitfulness by the sweat and toil of our fathers or ourselves, yielding their increase to clothe, pamper, and enrich the tyrant's favorites, who are base enough to assist him in his cursed plots to enslave us. Does this rouse your resentment? Stop a moment, and I will show you a spectacle more shocking than this. What meagre visages do I see in yonder field, toiling and covered with sweat, to cultivate the soil? Who are those in rags, bearing burdens and drawing water for those haughty lords, and cringing to them for a morsel of bread? They are— O gracious God, support my spirits—they are my sons and daughters, the pledges of conjugal love, for whose comfort I thought myself happy to spend my days in labor, my nights in care! Thus are my hopes blasted. Oh that they had never been born, rather than to see them loaded with irons, and dragging after them wherever they go, the heavy, galling, ignominious chains of slavery. But may we not hope for an end of these miseries? Alas, what hope! Slavery debases the human faculties, and spreads a torpor and stupidity over the whole frame! They sink in despair under their load; they see no way, they feel no power to recover themselves from this pit of misery; but pine away and die in it, and

leave to their children the same wretched inheritance.
What then does he deserve? or rather, what curse is
too heavy for the wretch that can tamely see our country enslaved?

4. This is a sin against our forefathers. They left
us a fair inheritance; they forsook their native land,
the land of tyranny and the furnace of iron; and, by
their blood, treasure, and toil, procured this sweet,
this peaceful retreat, subdued the soil when covered
with eternal woods, raised for us the stately domes
which afford us shelter from the storms, and safe re-
pose, and were exceedingly careful to instruct us in
the things which concern our temporal and eternal
liberty and peace. And shall we resign this patri-
mony, so dearly bought by them, and entailed to us by
their will, living and dying? Shall we, I say, resign
it all to that tyrant power which drove them from
their native land to this then howling wilderness?
Shall we bow our necks to the yoke which they,
though few in number, nobly cast off? Should our
fathers rise from their graves they would disown such
children, and repent their care and toil for such degenerate sons.

5. This is a sin against contemporaries. How provoking in the sight of God and man is it to see some,
quite unconcerned for the good of the public, rolling
in ease, amassing wealth to themselves, and slyly
plotting to assist our enemies in their murderous designs, while others endure the fatigues of war, and
hazard all that's dear to secure the peace, liberty, and
safety of the whole! Surely, every benevolent heart
must rise with indignation, and curse these enemies
to God and nature.

6. This is a sin against the express command of God. He commands us to *stand fast in the liberty wherewith he hath made us free,* and not to bow to any tyrant on earth, when it is in our power to oppose him.

V. I proceed to show that God requires a people, struggling for their liberties, to treat such of the community who will not join them as open enemies, and to reject them as unworthy the privileges of society.

The single crime of Meroz is said to be this. When they were called to arm, in order to shake off the yoke of tyranny, they did not join in the glorious cause. For this, and only this, they fell under the curse of God and man. Not only eternal wrath in the world to come was the just reward of this sin, but so highly was God provoked thereby, as to command his people to inflict his vengeance on them in this world, that, being held up as the monuments of his wrath, others might hear and fear, and do no more so wickedly.

A curse is something more than wishing ill to a person. It implies a separating him to some evil, or punishment. The command in my text therefore required Israel to separate the inhabitants of Meroz from some temporal good the rest of Israel enjoyed, and inflict on them some severe punishment; for they were to curse them bitterly.

And why may we not suppose that this curse consisted in these things:

1. That they should be deprived of that delightful freedom and liberty Israel had regained from the tyranny of Jabin. As these wretches discovered their servile temper in refusing to exert themselves for the

recovery of their liberty, why should they not be condemned to the slavery they chose ? Jabin (like George) probably claimed a right to lay any taxes on them he pleased, and " to bind them in all cases whatsoever ;" and they, rather than jeopard their lives in defence of their rights, tamely submitted to his demands. Well, since this was their choice, why should it now be denied them ? Let them be taxed at the sovereign will of the other states, without allowing them any representation. Since they loved, and sought to involve all Israel with themselves in slavery, they should have it from the rest, and receive but the just reward of their conduct. With what face could they complain of such treatment, since they chose to submit to the same from Jabin ? The change of masters made no change in the task ; and if they preferred slavery then, rather than fight for their liberties, let them have it now, since they would do nothing to regain them.

How absurd is their conduct who prefer, to our glorious struggle for liberty, a tame submission to the claims of the British Parliament ! If we submit, we must be slaves ; for to be governed and guided by the will of another, and not our own, is perfect servitude. If we fight and are conquered, we can but be slaves. If we conquer, we gain our freedom. On one hand, the event is certain, the chains are riveted. On the other, there is a possibility, and a probability, too, of a glorious deliverance ; yea, were all united, there would be a moral certainty of success. On those, therefore, who, like Meroz, refuse to come to the help of the Lord in the present war, will be the sin of involving millions, besides themselves, in the most abject misery and cruel slavery. Consider this, ye inhabitants of Meroz; remember, that there is a God that judgeth in the earth, and tremble at your fearful doom. If murdering one man deserves death, what does the murder of thousands deserve? If God made the enslaving one of his people a capital crime, to be punished with death (Exodus, xxiv. 7), what does your crime deserve, who are endeavoring to enslave a whole nation? If you choose slavery for yourselves, don't force it on others who abhor it. You may enjoy it, though others are free. It is your due. And the curse in my text, when inflicted on you aright, will give it you in full tale.

2. Why may we not suppose that they were deprived of their estates, and reduced at least to a state of tenantage at will? They had implicitly joined with the enemy, by which they put to hazard every dear and valuable enjoyment of the whole nation. Through their neglect all might have been lost. And their fault was not the less because victory declared for Israel; and all their possessions could never countervail the damage their conduct had exposed the nation to.

The application of this to our times is easy. The present war, 'tis probable, had never been commenced had none of the inhabitants of Meroz been in our land; or, if begun, could not have been carried on to this day. On them, therefore, as the confederates, abettors and supporters of the tyrant, lies the guilt of this war. And as they are partners with him in the sin, so they ought to be involved in the punishment he deserves. If it is lawful to deprive the inhabitants of Great Britain of their property, when in our power, and convert it to our use; if this be a just retaliation for the injury they have done us, and all too little to countervail the damage; much more the interest of those who live among us, and yet assist the enemy in their cruel designs, ought to be confiscated for the service of the public, by how much more mischief they have done, and are capable of doing these states, and by how much greater their sin.

I cannot but think it would have been happy for these states, had our rulers, long ere now, declared all who should be found any way aiding and assisting the enemy, or holding a correspondence with them, should be deemed enemies to these states and forfeit all their estates at least. Yea,

3. As the curse of Meroz, no doubt, extended to a depriving the inhabitants of a capacity to enjoy any place of honor in the government, and the ordinary privileges of freemen; and also inflicted some corporal punishment at least on their principal leaders; so the like characters among us, ought to share the same punishment. And I am persuaded, these states will still be unsafe, and all our efforts for deliverance from tyranny attended with great hazard and uncertainty, till there shall be some more effectual and vigorous means adopted by our rulers, to distinguish friends from foes, and expose the latter to some exemplary punishment. The law of retaliation is sometimes just and necessary, even when the persons offending are not made the subjects of it; how much more when the transgressors themselves are in our power.* Nor can we do justice to ourselves or the

---

* It was a righteous act in Tamerlane the Great, to carry Bajazet, the grand Turk, in an iron cage, round the world in triumph. The magnanimous, the benevolent Tamerlane marches with a great army to repel

public, or to our brethren now suffering in hard and cruel durance among the enemy; nor to our posterity;

Bajazet, who was made prisoner. "Being brought into his presence, Tamerlane asked him why he endeavored to bring the Greek emperor into his subjection? He answered, 'Even the same cause which moved thee to invade me, namely, the desire of glory and sovereignty.' 'Wherefore, then,' said Tamerlane, 'dost thou use such cruelty toward them thou overcomest, without respect to age or sex?' 'That I did,' said he, 'to strike the greater terror into mine enemies.' Then Tamerlane asked him if he had ever given thanks to God for making him so great an emperor?' 'No,' said he; 'I never so much as thought of any such thing.' 'Then,' said Tamerlane, 'it is no wonder so ungrateful a man should be made a spectacle of misery; for you,' said he, being blind of one eye, and I lame of a leg, was there any worth in us, that God should set us over two such great empires, to command so many men far more worthy than ourselves? But', continued he, 'what wouldest thou have done with me, if it had been my lot to have fallen into thine hands, as thou art now in mine?' 'I would,' said Bajazet, 'have enclosed thee in a cage of iron, and carried thee in triumph up and down my kingdom.' 'Even so,' said Tamerlane, 'shalt thou be served.' And causing him to be taken out of his presence, and turning to his followers, he said: 'Behold a proud and cruel man, who deserves to be chastised accordingly, and to be made an example to all the proud and cruel of the world, of the just wrath of God against them.'" (See Clarke's Life of Tamerlane the Great, pages 37, 38.)

But it too rarely happens, that the perpetrators of these crimes fall in the way of justice; in which case it is sometimes lawful, yea, duty, to retaliate on some of their connections. For instance, the commanders of the British troops and their master are the cruel monsters who treat such as fall into their hands with unexampled barbarity, confining them in prisons and vessels, in the extreme cold, without fire or food sufficient to preserve life; by which hundreds, yea, thousands of our dear friends have suffered the most cruel and painful deaths, and others lost their limbs by the frost. The real criminals are out of our reach. What, then, can be done? Nothing, but to inflict a like punishment on a like number of their prisoners in our hands. Accordingly, the honorable Congress, long ago, assured the public that they would retaliate all abuses offered to prisoners taken from us. Depending on this promise as the means to secure good treatment, should they fall into the

nor lastly, to the manes of our murdered friends who
have fallen in the field, or expired in the loathsome

---

enemy's hand, many who cheerfully offered themselves for the war
have been made prisoners, and froze or starved to death, and no retaliation that I have heard hath yet been made—I hope for wise
reasons. Hence the enemy exercise their more than brutal cruelty
without fear, and many, dreading the like usage, are disinclined to the
war.

If something be not speedily done to convince our foes that we are
not afraid to retaliate, the consequence, I fear, will be fatal to our cause.
Lenity and mercy are due prisoners; and nothing can justify acts of
severity, but where cruel usage makes them necessary, and then acts of
severity become acts of mercy. I cannot persuade myself to put an
end to this note, already too long, without transcribing a passage from
the aforesaid life of Tamerlane, which at once represents the true cause
of making war, and also that noble, benevolent spirit which should inspire every soldier to enter the field; both of which are exemplified in
this heathen warrior, in whose presence most Christian princes have
reason to blush.

After the battle before mentioned, the emperor of Constantinople sent
ambassadors to Tamerlane offering him his empire, and his person as
his most faithful subject, in gratitude and as a reward for the deliverance he had obtained for him from the most cruel tyrant. But Tamerlane, with a mild countenance, beheld them and said, "That he had not
come so far, nor taken such pains to enlarge his dominions, big enough
already (too base a thing to put himself into so great danger and hazard for), but rather to win honor, and make his name famous to future
posterity; and that he would make it appear to the world that he came
to assist their master, as his friend and ally, at his request; and that his
upright intentions therein, he believed, were the cause that God from
above had favored him and made him instrumental to bruise the head of
the greatest and fiercest enemy of mankind under heaven; and therefore, to get him an immortal name, his purpose was, to make free so
great and flourishing a city as Constantinople. That he always joined
faith to his courage, which should never suffer him to make such a
breach in his reputation as to have it reported of him that, in the color
of a friend, he should come to invade the dominions of his ally. That
he desired no more, but that the service he had done for the Greek emperor might remain forever engraven in the memory of his posterity, that

10*

prisons with cold and hunger; till we inflict some just and exemplary punishment on those who have brought these calamities on us.

This discourse shows us, how defensive war is consistent with true benevolence, and a sincere desire of the happiness of mankind; and how it is consistent for the soldier to love and pray for the happiness of those he opposes and endeavors to root from the earth.

Every soldier should enter the field with benevolent, tender, compassionate sentiments, which is the temper of Jesus Christ. A morose, cruel, revengeful, unmerciful temper, is no more consistent with the character of a Christian soldier, than with that of a minister of the gospel of peace; nor can it be justified even in the height of the fiercest battle. He should ever be possessed with a disposition to pray for those he endeavors to destroy, and to wish their best, their eternal good. These are no more inconsistent in a soldier, engaging in battle and doing his best to kill his enemies, than they are in a judge and executioner, who take away a murderer from the earth. For, as the judge and executioner are God's ministers to execute vengeance on the wicked who endeavor to destroy the happiness of society; so the soldier, engaged in a just defensive war, is the minister of God to render ven-

---

they might ever wish well to him and his successors, by remembering the good he had done for them." p. 41.

This was truly noble ambition, to seek an immortal name and honor, not by actions which the ambitious call great, but by those which God pronounces good. The battle being ended, Tamerlane said: "This day hath God delivered into my hand a great enemy, to whom, therefore we must give thanks," which was publicly done. Excellent example!

geance to the invaders of others' right : and as the executioner may and ought to pray for the suffering criminal, so should the soldier for his foe ; as benevolence is the source of vindictive laws in the states, so it should ever be of defensive war ; and they both tend to the same end, the happiness of mankind. How absurd then is the pretence that the gospel of Jesus Christ forbids us to take up arms to defend ourselves ! and that defensive war is inconsistent with the patient, meek long-suffering temper it requires ! It may with as much reason be said, that to punish a murderer or robber is forbidden by the gospel ; which is in effect to say, that the gospel of peace forbids the exercise of love and benevolence in acts absolutely necessary, in this sinful world, for the peace and happiness of society and individuals.

From what has been said, we may clearly infer, that to levy offensive war is murder, and all who engage in it are murderers in God's sight. They are guilty, not only of the murder of those they kill in battle, or who otherwise perish in the war, but they are self-murderers—they put themselves to death— their blood is on their own heads. Well, then, might Solomon say : " *With good advice make war.*"

The characters, therefore, of two states or armies at war, are as opposite as their actions. The aggressor is a murderer and robber, and all who assist him are involved in his guilt. Every soldier who fights for him is a murderer too. But we know that no murderer hath eternal life. How should this make those shudder who engage on the side of the aggressor ! If they fall in battle, what hope can they have of God's approbation, since they die murdering others and themselves too? But such who oppose them in defence of their own and country's peace, liberty and safety, are God's ministers, commissioned and ordered by him to punish his and his people's enemies. They, therefore, may draw their swords with a quiet, approving conscience, and with pity view the wretches slain by their hands as self-murderers; or, if they fall, they can die, in regard to the war, free of the blood of all men, and in peace resign their spirits into the hand of their Redeemer.

This consideration surely must animate every man, inspired with the benevolent temper of the gospel—which disposes to the greatest advancement of human happiness, and to relieve the miserable and oppressed—to vigorous exertions in defence of our bleeding land; bleeding under the hand of oppression, rapine and murder. Would you, my friends, count it an honor to be employed by God to restore peace and happiness to the oppressed and miserable? do you wish to perform acts of love and kindness to mankind, and therein be like your Creator and Redeemer? Do you fear the wrath and curse of God pronounced on all who spread misery among his creatures, and on all that aid or assist them, or so much as connive at, or neglect to oppose them? Do you desire to be workers together with God in restoring peace and felicity to your groaning country, and to be owned of him as his servants when you die? Are these the objects of your desire and pursuit? I know they are if the love of God and your neighbor rules in your hearts. Well, then, here is an opportunity presented to you, to manifest your love, by coming to the help of the Lord against the mighty. The cause we are engaged in is the cause of God ; and you may hope for his blessing and fight under his banner. In supporting and defending this cause, you may, you ought to seek for glory and honor; even that glory and honor which come from God and man for acts of benevolence, goodness and mercy, for the performance of which the fairest opportunity now offers.

But what shall I say of those whose religious principles forbid the performance of any such labors of love, and necessarily involve them in the curse of Meroz? If their religion be right, love itself must be wrong. But arguments are vain. May God in his mercy show them their error, give them repentance, and inspire them with the love which the law and gospel require, before they fall under the wrath and curse of God, for neglecting to come to his help against the mighty.

This discourse also shows us how we ought to treat those who do not join in the cause of freedom we have espoused.

1. As they are accursed of God, and we are commanded to curse them, we ought, at least, to shun their company. What a shame is it, to see those born to freedom and professing zeal for her cause, associating themselves with the willing slaves of an abandoned tyrant and murderer? Oh, how do such debase themselves, and give occasion to suspect them as belonging to the same herd. But it may be asked, how shall they be distinguished from friends? Attend to the characters already given, and you may see enough to justify you in avoiding intimacy with them ; though they may so disguise that no evidence appears to condemn them to open and condign punishment. Happy

would it be should our civil fathers draw some determinate line of distinction between freemen and these slaves of power.* For want of this we have suffered greatly already, and if this be not speedily done, the consequences, I fear, will be fatal.

2. As soon as they are discovered, we ought to disarm them; for, as they will not assist us, we should put it out of their power to hurt us or our families, when we at any time shall be called to action. Yea,

3. As such forfeit all the privileges of freemen, their estates should be forfeited and applied to support the war; and themselves banished from these states. The curse we are commanded to inflict on the inhabitants of Meroz, must imply as much as this; and benevolence to millions demands this of us; not out of hatred to their persons, but their crimes, which strike at the life and happiness of these states. This punishment must be inflicted, not by the people at large, but by our rulers, with whom, under God, we have intrusted our safety; and in whose wisdom we confide, to take proper vengeance on them in due time. But should this be delayed, without proper reasons assigned, we shall have no cause to wonder, though there should be great thoughts of heart among a people, beholding their friends and brethren barbarously murdered, or wandering forlorn, destitute of food or shelter; while the detested authors of these unparalleled distresses smile unnoticed and unpunished, at these dire calamities,

* Since the above was copied for the press, a proclamation by his excellency General Washington has been published, and also two acts to punish treason and other crimes of less enormity against this state; by which this line of distinction is, in a good measure drawn, which is cause of joy to all the friends of liberty.

and triumph in our distress. But should delay happen, we must look on.it as another instance of divine displeasure, which speaks to all, to search after, and, by sincere repentance and thorough reformation, remove, the moral cause of God's controversy with us.

When this shall take place, we shall then see our councils filled with men inspired with wisdom to know what Israel ought to do; our arms victorious and triumphant; the inhabitants of Meroz justly punished; peace, liberty and safety restored; the rod of tyranny broken; pure and undefiled religion prevailing, and the voice of joy and gladness echoing round our land. May God hasten the happy, happy day! And let all the people say, Amen, and Amen. Hallelujah!

HISTORY affords no record of the ancestry of Mr. Hart. He was born in Warminster, Bucks county, Pennsylvania, on the fifth day of July, 1723. Being early impressed with the importance of religion, he entered the ministry, and in 1749, at the age of twenty-six, was ordained. The same year he went to Charleston, South Carolina, where he succeeded Mr. Chanler, and continued pastor of the Baptist church in that city for thirty years.

At the commencement of the Revolution he warmly espoused the cause of the colonists; and in such estimation was his character for patriotism held by the Council of Safety of Carolina, that he was soon after appointed by it to accompany William Tennent to the frontiers, in order to reconcile some of the disaffected inhabitants to the change which had occurred in public affairs. Shortly before the British laid siege to Charleston, in 1780, owing to his active connection with the affairs of the Americans, he was advised to leave the place, lest he should be made a prisoner to the British, and suffer from the excesses that their soldiers were at that time committing throughout the Southern colonies. He left Charleston in February, 1780, and journeyed to Hopewell, in New Jersey, where, in

the December following, in consequence of the warmest solicitations, he took charge of the church in that
place, and remained its pastor until his death, which
occurred on the thirty-first of December, 1795.

Mr. Hart was "blessed with such strong natural
abilities as to lay a foundation for those grateful services which, from his youth to a good old age, he
rendered both to church and state. His imagination
was lively, and his judgment firm. Although he
never enjoyed the advantages resulting from a regular progress through any public school or university,
yet such were the improvements of his mind by self-
application, close reading, and habitual reflection,"
that few men more richly deserved the highest literary honors. As a preacher, Mr. Hart was pleasing in
manner, and animated in his delivery. As a citizen,
he was a firm and decided patriot, always engaged in
the great work of promoting the happiness of his fellow-men.

In the preface to the sermon which succeeds this
notice, Mr. Hart says: "It would have slept in
oblivion had not the practice inveighed against been
revived, and attended to in a frantic manner, at a time
when every thing in Providence is calling us to different exercises. The judgments of God are now opened
over the land, and the inhabitants ought to learn
righteousness. The alarm of war; the clangor of
arms; the garments rolled in blood; the sufferings of
our brethren in the northern states, and of others in a

state of captivity; together with the late dreadful conflagration in this town; are so many loud calls to repentance, reformation of life, and prayer that the
wrath of God may be turned away from us. Instead
of which, we are smothered up in pleasure and dissipation. It will hardly be credited that the fire was
scarcely extinguished in Charleston, before we had
balls, assemblies, and dances in every quarter; and
even in some of those houses which miraculously escaped the flames. . . . Is it thus we requite the
Lord for our deliverance? The monumental ruins of
the town will rise up in judgment against the inhabitants, and condemn them for such impieties. . . .
I am no prophet, nor the son of a prophet; and
yet will venture to predict that other, and perhaps
greater judgments will yet light upon us unless we
repent."

DANCING EXPLODED.*

Their children dance.—Job xxi. 11.

THE bare reading of my text hath, I doubt not,
occasioned a strange emotion of spirits in many of my
hearers; by some I may be pitied for my folly, by
others, despised and ridiculed. Be this as it may, it
gives me little or no concern. If I had not been will-

---

* A sermon, showing the unlawfulness, sinfulness and bad consequences of balls, assemblies, and dances in general; preached in
Charleston, S. C., March 22, 1778.

ing to endure the scoff of the world, I should never have made an open profession of the religion of Jesus; much less should I have become a preacher of his much despised gospel. He, however, who ventures to attack vice in a public manner, ought to be possessed of some degree of fortitude and resolution; for sin is a monster of more than a thousand heads; should he slay some, there will be many yet remaining, and he may expect to be attacked on every side; especially if he should dare to level at some popular darling vice; one that hath been much caressed, and that too by the more polite part of the world; in this case, there will be a mighty uproar among the people. The whole city, or country, will be filled with wrath, as *Demetrius* and his associates were, when they cried out, "Great is *Diana* of the *Ephesians*," or as *Micah*, when stripped of his idols, exclaimed: "Ye have taken away my gods, and what have I more?"

However, in leaving the event to God, I am determined, in faithfulness to my trust, to maintain an open and vigorous war with all the vices and sinful diversions of the age. Were I to act otherwise, my own conscience would condemn me, and the world justly reproach me for my unfaithfulness. This, therefore, may justify me, for entering on such a subject; which I shall introduce by making some remarks on the context; in which *Job* seems to be at a loss to account for the dispensations of divine Providence, with regard to the prosperity of the wicked.

The friends of *Job* were far from comforting him, as they proposed, under his afflictions, and which they might have done by observing to him, that one event often happeneth to the righteous and to the

wicked; so that no man can certainly judge of love
or hatred by all that is done under the sun; and that
chastisements are so far from being positive tokens of
divine wrath, they sometimes rather indicate love—
for whom the Lord loveth he chasteneth, and rebuketh
every son whom he receiveth. Such hints as these
might have afforded *Job* some consolation under his
heavy trials. But his three friends took a contrary
method, which wounded instead of comforting him.
The doctrine which they laid down and endeavored to
maintain was this, that wicked men *only* are severely
afflicted in this world. Hence, instead of comforting
Job as an afflicted saint, they censure him as a vile
sinner and a hypocrite. *Job* labors to refute their
arguments and maintain his own innocence. He
affirms that the wicked often flourish, and become rich
and great in the world; when the righteous, on the
other hand, are greatly afflicted, and stripped of all
their worldly possessions. He instances his own
case, and then proceeds to point out the prosperous
circumstances of the wicked, together with their vain
and impious practices.

Mark me, says Job, consider my present dolorous
condition, *and be astonished* at the dealings of God
with me. Can you justly charge me with any gross
and impious practices, which according to your hy-
pothesis should bring down the judgment of God upon
me? You cannot: therefore *lay your hand upon
your mouth.* Try no more to vindicate your opinion,
when you have a living instance, in opposition to it,
before your eyes. As for my own part, *even when I
remember* my former flourishing circumstances, and
consider how I am stripped naked and bare, and visited

with the most painful and loathsome disorders, *I am afraid* of those judgments of the Almighty, *and trembling taketh hold on my flesh.* Not being able to account for my being thus afflicted, while the wicked go on unpunished. Tell me, if you can, *wherefore do the wicked live, become old, yea, are mighty in power ?* How doth this coincide with your opinion, that God will surely take vengeance on the wicked, in this life ? The reverse of this seems to be the case, for *their houses are safe from fear, neither is the rod of God upon them.* They are not afflicted, or plagued like other men. They swim in affluence and roll in pleasure ; there is no end to their wealth. And with their riches, their families increase, so that they shall not want heirs. *Their seed is established in their sight, and their offspring before their eyes.* They live to see their children's children a numerous progeny around them ; so that *they send forth their little ones like a flock,* for multitude, they going before them like a shepherd ; not to the house of God to engage in solemn devotion, rather to balls, assemblies and the playhouse, where they take the timbrel and harp, and suchlike instruments of music, which they play, *and their children dance.* Thus merrily they go on, regardless of a future state or eternal judgment. *They spend their days in wealth,* which they squander upon their lusts and pleasures in great abundance, although they can spare little or nothing for the poor, or any other pious purposes.

After they have thus run their race, *in a moment they go down to the pit,* without any apprehension of danger. The wicked have no bands in their death. Their principal concern in life is to gratify their corrupt inclinations; *therefore they say unto God, Depart from us; for we desire not the knowledge of thy ways.* The thoughts of God are disagreeable to them; and his ways, which are the ways of holiness, they cannot endure. Like *Pharaoh*, they know not the Lord, neither will they obey him. *What is the Almighty,* say they, *that we should serve him?* And what profit should we have, if we pray unto him? Thus, fulness of riches, honor and pleasure swell men's minds with pride, and beget in them mean, absurd and atheistical notions of the Deity. They look upon him as a mere idol, as nothing in the world; and therefore conclude that they can derive no advantage from praying unto him.

This is the character of the wicked, as drawn by *Job*, a perfect and upright man, who feared God, and eschewed evil. In the midst of which description, and as a part of it, stands that very polite and much-esteemed practice of *dancing*, a diversion which, in all ages, hath had admirers and votaries. To oppose it, will be to incur the censure of all the gay gentry, and with them, however to forfeit all pretension to polite breeding and good manners, I am willing to risk greater consequences than these, that I may maintain a conscience void of offence toward God and toward man. Bear with me, then, while I bear my testimony against a practice which I look upon as sinful, and opposed to the Christian character, and which *Job*, in our text, certainly speaks of as constituting part of the character of the wicked. *And their children dance.* Observe, it is *their* children—*i. e.,* the children of such wicked parents as he was describing. By *children*, we do not always understand children as to *age;* sometimes it intends those who have descended from such or such parents, although they themselves may have arrived at men's or women's estate. And if we take the word *children* in our text in this sense, the meaning of *Job* appears evidently to be this, that the families or posterity of wicked parents give into this practice. Would to God that none of the descendants of pious parents ever imitated their bad example, and that it might never be said of any but wicked parents, *And their children dance.*

On treating this uncommon subject, I design

I. To state the argument, by giving a scriptural definition of the word *dance.*

II. Prove, by various arguments that dancing, according to the common mode, is absolutely sinful.

III. Reply to the most popular arguments used in favor of dancing.

IV. Conclude with a brief improvement.

I. I am to state the argument, by giving a scriptural definition of the word *dance.*

Dancing, according to the Scripture account, is sometimes to be taken in a good sense ; and then it is expressive of the inward spiritual joy of the heart, which was commonly manifested by a comely motion of the body ; attended with songs of praise to God, for some deliverance obtained, or mercy received. Thus was dancing attended to, or practised by the good people of old, in a religious way. When their songs were spiritual, and the music, as also the motion of their bodies, were suited thereto. Agreeable to which are the words in Psalm cxlix. 3, " *Let them praise his name in the dance ; let them sing praises unto him with the timbrel and harp.*"

It was thus *David* danced before the ark (2 Sam., vi. 16.) And in this manner most of the dances, which the children of *Israel* had, were attended to; as you may see by consulting the passage in Scripture where they are recorded. As, for instance, when the Lord had destroyed *Pharaoh* and his army in the Red Sea, the *Israelitish* women sung and danced. (See Exod. xv. 20, 21.) "*And Miriam, the prophetess, the sister of Aaron, took a timbrel in her hand, and all the women* went out after her, with timbrels and dances. *And Miriam answered them, Sing unto the Lord, for he hath triumphed gloriously; the horse and his rider hath he thrown into the sea.*" Such a song as this becomes a rational mind, and is suitable to the taste of the greatest saint in the world. But it would not be so agreeable to our modern dancers; were it to be sung in their assemblies, it would be to them as smoke to the eyes or vinegar to the teeth. Unto such music and dancing our Lord alludes, in the parable of the prodigal son. Such kind of dancing was lawful and holy, and by no means to be condemned.

But there is another sort of dancing spoken of in Scripture, which consists in a motion of the body, seemly or unseemly, stirred up by natural or carnal joy, to please or satisfy ourselves or others, without any view to the glory of God, or the benefits of souls. Thus that fine young lady, the daughter of *Herodias*, danced, on Herod's birthday; it should seem that she opened the ball, and performed so well as to fill the king with raptures of joy; whereupon, in a courtly dialect, he promised the young lady whatsoever she should ask, even to the half of his kingdom. She, being afore instructed by her mother, very modestly

asked no greater reward than the head of *John* the
Baptist in a charger. Thus, as a reward for dancing,
the harbinger of Christ lost his life—enough, one
would think, to cause every serious person to abhor
the practice forever. It is this profane kind of dancing
that is intended in our text; the same with what is
now in vogue, and which, if it were set in a proper
light, would not appear altogether such an innocent
diversion as is generally imagined. I proceed, therefore,

II. To prove that dancing, according to the common, modern mode, is absolutely sinful.

Some may be ready to think this is a strange undertaking, and that I shall certainly fail in the attempt.
It will be but fair, and therefore I have a right to
expect, that you should suspend your judgment until
I have done; hear with candor, then weigh the arguments in the balance of the sanctuary; and if they
prove too light, or insufficient to prove the point, reject
them.

1. Then, I argue that dancing, according to the modern mode, is sinful, because it contributes nothing to
the chief end of man; nay, is contrary to it. You
know that the chief end of man is to glorify God.
And this ought to be our principal aim in every thing
we do. (1. Cor. x. 31.) " *Whether, therefore, ye eat or
drink, or whatsoever ye do, do all to the glory of God.*"
Now I would ask our advocates for dancing, what tendency that practice has to glorify God? Can you say
that you have any view to the glory of God in it? I
am persuaded you will not dare thus to give your conscience the lie. And if it should be proved, as I suppose it will, that dancing contributes rather to pro-

11

mote the interest of Satan than the glory of God, it follows that the practice is directly contrary to the chief end of man. Only give this one argument its proper scope and due weight, and dancing will soon cease.

2. A corroborating argument may be drawn from *Romans*, xiv. 23: " *Whatsoever is not of faith is sin ;*" but dancing is not of faith, therefore it is sin. But perhaps some may query :

" What has this text to do with our diversions, or any of our trivial concerns ?"

I shall answer in the words of a learned expositor : " This is a general rule or axiom, which is not only applicable to the present case, but to any other, whether of a natural, civil, moral, or evangelical kind ; whatever is not agreeable to the word and doctrine of faith, ought not to be done ; whatever is done without faith, or not in the exercise of it, is culpable, for without faith nothing can be pleasing to God."

Therefore, until it can be proved that dancing is of faith, you must excuse me if I insist that it is a sinful practice.

III. Whatever action in life we cannot pray for a blessing upon, must be unlawful and sinful, and such an one is dancing; therefore it ought to be avoided. Will any say " we are not bound to seek the blessing of God upon our ordinary concerns ?" I will confront them with the words of *Solomon : " In all thy ways acknowledge him, and he shall direct thy paths."* (Prov. iii. 6.) Such universal piety may not, indeed, suit the taste of frolickers and dancers, but it well becomes the character of all the professed disciples of Jesus Christ. But should any query : " Why may we not pray for a blessing on our dances?" I answer, you may not, because God has never promised to give a blessing to such practices; therefore, such a prayer would be sin. Nay, you cannot do it because it would be a profanation of the deity, and your consciences will not admit it.

IV. The injunction which is laid upon us to redeem the time, prohibits our misspending it in such practices. Time is a precious jewel, put into our hands to improve for eternity, and those who trifle it away, are (in the Scripture account) very fools. (Eph. v. 15, 16.) "*See then that ye walk circumspectly, not as fools, but as wise, redeeming the time.*" Can it with truth be said, that the time spent at balls, assemblies and dances is redeemed? No such thing. It is squandered away; it is murdered; it is consumed on our lusts; and how our dancers will be able to answer to God for all the time they have thus shamefully misimproved, another day will determine.

V. It occasions an extravagant waste of money; with which great good might be done. After enough hath been thrown away upon a child, at the dancing-school, to have educated two or three poor children, then truly miss must be dressed up, *cap-a-pie*, to make a shining figure at the ball; which expends enough to relieve a virtuous family in distress, or clothe half a dozen orphan children. If this is to be good stewards of our money, I confess I am very much mistaken. And *stewards* we certainly are, and *only* stewards, of all we possess, and must be accountable unto God for the spending of our substance. I am apprehensive our dancers think but too little of this. Sirs, you would do well to consider, that in a little time the

Lord will say: "Come, give an account of thy stewardship, for thou mayest be no longer steward."

VI. The thoughts of having thus squandered our precious time must occasion very uneasy reflections on a dying bed, unless the conscience should then be asleep—which would avail but for a little while; for at death the illusion must vanish, and then it would be still more terrible to awake in hell. However, those diversions, which were so pleasing to the carnal mind while in health and strength, can afford no comfortable reflections in a dying hour. The dancer will then ·be ready to say: "Wretch that I was, thus to squander away my precious time, my health, strength, and estate, upon my idle diversions! How much better might I have improved the blessings which Providence bestowed upon me! How much might I have done for God and my own soul! But, alas! they were objects too much neglected! How ought I to have redeemed my time in preparing for death and eternity! But, fool that I was, I spent my life in vain mirth and sinful pleasures. Oh for those precious moments which I have lost! But they are gone—they are lost forever; and I am afraid my God, my heaven, my soul, are lost too! Pity and pray for me, O my friends; and let my late repentance be a warning to you. Oh guard against those sinful diversions on which my poor soul hath been shipwrecked!" Such a scene might affect one of our dancers, and for a little time make him serious. But how soon do such impressions wear off! And then the libertine returns to his folly.

VII. It behooves us to live each day and hour as we would wish to die, and not to engage in any thing

that would alarm us, in case death should overtake
us in the act. The truth and utility of this assertion
none will deny. Let me then ask, Would you be
willing to meet with death at a ball, or a dance?
You would not. And how do you know, when you
venture on the enchanted ground, that you shall come
away alive? And is this to hold yourselves in readiness? Think, O my friends, how you would look,
how you would feel, should this ever happen. Horror
would fasten on your countenance, trembling seize
every joint and nerve, and the convulsive pangs of
conscience would be more intolerable than the tortures
of the bloody inquisition. You would probably use
the language of a fair lady, in a dialogue with Death:

> " I little thought you would have called so soon.
> And must my morning sun go down at noon?"

Oh, dreadful! to be cut off in the midst of my pleasures—to be hurried from a ball to the bar, without
any time to repent, or prepare for eternity! But,
perhaps you will say: " Would you have us always on
our knees, waiting for death?" I answer, No; you
may boldly meet death when engaged about your
secular concerns, or any of the duties of life.

I remember to have read, I think, in the life of
Lord Chief Justice Hale, that at the time of sessions,
while one of the attorneys was pleading, there came
on a most terrible thunderstorm, which silenced the
attorney; upon which the Judge said to him: " Sir,
why don't you go on?" " Go on, my lord," said the
attorney, " don't you see how black the heavens are,
and the lightning rolling on the ground, while the
thunder roars as though the last day were come?"

"And suppose it is," said his lordship, "are you not in the way of your duty?" I am here about my business, and I am as willing to go hence to judgment as I should be if I were on my knees in my closet. The way of duty is the way of safety, and while thus engaged we have nothing to fear; but who would manifest such fortitude at a dance?

VIII. The conversation at dances is inconsistent with Christianity. I will appeal to the conscience of those who frequent such places, whether or no flattery, lying, ribaldry, and nonsense, do not abound there? Little, I fear, is to be heard that hath any tendency to reform the manners or improve the mind; much less to minister grace to the hearers. There may be enough to corrupt the morals and vitiate the taste of both sexes. Is it not from hence, at least in part, that we have so much obscene, vulgar, and profane conversation amongst us? Our merry gentry, who delight so much in frolicking and dancing, would do well to consider how they will answer for all their filthiness, foolish talking, jesting, and suchlike things, when they come to stand at the bar of God.

IX. Again, many dances are extremely immodest, and incentive to uncleanness. This is acknowledged by Mr. Addison, although an advocate for dancing. "As for country dancing, saith he, it must indeed be confessed, that, the great familiarity between the two sexes on this occasion, may sometimes produce very dangerous consequences." But modesty bids me be sparing here, otherwise more might be said. My soul, come not thou into their secrets, and unto their assemblies, mine honor, be not thou united.

X. Farther, the music which leads the dance, is

often very obscene; the tunes being adapted to the most vulgar and filthy songs; which have a tendency to pollute the imagination, and to raise unchaste thoughts in the mind. Thus the heart becomes a sink of uncleanness—a cage of all manner of abominable and filthy lusts.

XI. Moreover, the practice we are speaking of, cannot be endured in the minister. And why so? If there is no harm in it, and if it may be attended to with advantage, why must ministers be prohibited the practice? The thing speaks for itself; people are conscious that it is an evil, and therefore, although they will indulge themselves in it, they will not allow it in those who have the care of their souls.

As for my own part, I think indeed a dancing parson, is an odd character, and a dancing Christian is not much better. And our advocates for dancing would do well to consider that the Almighty hath no more allowed them dispensation in this case, than their ministers.

XII. Once more. This practice renders persons the most unlike to Christ, our great pattern and example. Did Jesus ever indulge himself in mirth? No. Frequently did he mourn over such impieties, but never did he countenance them, in any way whatever. The doctrines, precepts and examples of Christ, all prohibit vain mirth—idle and sinful diversions. Those who indulge themselves in these, act diametrically opposite to the religion of Jesus; which enjoins temperance, mortification, self-denial and the like virtues.

XIII. In fine, the greatest and best of men have ever bore a testimony against the practice of dancing. I shall quote some passages from several authors, which I shall do in their own words; hoping that their sentiments may make some impression upon your minds. We shall begin with the observations of that truly great and good man, Mr. Caryl, upon our text and context.

"*Their children dance,* that is, saith Mr. Caryl, they are instructed and taught the art of music and dancing ; or there is rejoicing among them ; this is proper to the age and state of children. Christ, himself, speaks as if this were the trade of children. (Matt. xi. 16.) '*Whereunto shall I liken this generation ? They are like children sitting in the market-place.*' What do they there? Are they buying or selling? Are they bargaining or trading ? No, that is the business of men. What do the children there ? They call to their fellows and say : '*We have piped to you, and ye have not danced ; we have mourned to you, and ye have not lamented.*' *They take the timbrel and the harp.* They live in pleasure ; hence observe, worldly men breed their children vainly. Here is a description of their education : they are sent forth as a flock in a dance, playing upon the timbrel, &c. Here is all the knowledge and literature they are brought up to ; here is all their religion, all the catechism that they are taught.

"The Lord giveth this report of *Abraham,* who had a numerous family : '*I know him that he will command his children, and his household after him, and they shall keep the way of the Lord.*' (Gen. xviii. 19.) Abraham did not teach his family to dance. Here was education in the fear of the Lord."

Thus far are the words of *Mr. Caryl.* The pious *Mr. Henry,* upon the place, saith :

"They are merry, and live a jovial life. They have

their balls and music-meetings, at which *their children dance;* and dancing is fittest for children, who know not how better to spend their time, and whose innocency guards them against the mischiefs which commonly attend it. Their children do not pray, or say their catechism, but dance and sing, *and rejoice at the sound of the organ.* Sensual pleasures are all the delights of carnal people; and as men are themselves, so they breed their children."

I shall add the words of the learned and judicious *Dr. Gill,* in his exposition of the text:

"*And their children dance,* either in an artificial way, skip and frisk, and play like calves and lambs, and are very diverting to their parents, as well as showing them to be in good health; which adds to their parents' happiness and pleasure; or in an artificial way, being taught to dance; and it should be observed, it is *their* children—the children of the wicked, and not of the godly—that are thus brought up; so Abraham did not train up his children, nor Job his; no instance can be given of the children of good men being trained up in this manner, or of their children dancing in an irreligious way."

This is the testimony of the great Dr. Gill. Mr. Baxter, speaking of dancings, revellings and idle diversions, interrogates thus:

"Dost thou not know that thou hast higher delights to mind? And are these toys beseeming a noble soul, that hath holy and heavenly matters to delight in? Dost thou not feel what a plague the very pleasure is to thy affections? How it bewitcheth thee, and befooleth thee, and maketh thee out of love with holiness, and unfit for any thing that is good? Again,

11*

is it sport that thou needest? Dost thou not more need Christ, and grace, and pardon, and preparation for death and judgment, and assurance of salvation? Why, then, are not these thy business? Farther—Hast thou not a God to obey and serve? And doth he not always see thee? And will he not judge thee? Alas! thou knowest not how soon. Though thou be merry in thy youth, and thy heart cheer thee, and thou walk in the ways of thy heart and the sight of thine eyes, yet know thou that for all these things God will bring thee into judgment."

I shall conclude this head with a passage from Moreland's history of the evangelical churches of the valleys of Piedmont. Here I would observe, that these were the only pure churches in the world for several centuries. When the world wandered after the beast, these people adhered strictly to the religion of Jesus. They were remarkable for piety, and endured the most cruel persecutions for the cause of Christ. In the tenth article of their discipline, which treats of balls and dances, they say:

"A ball is the devil's procession, and whosoever entereth there, entereth into his procession. The devil is the leader, the middle, and the end of the dance. So many paces as a man maketh in a ball, so many leaps he maketh toward hell. They sin in dancing sundry ways. First, in walking, for all their paces are numbered; they sin in touching, in their ornaments, in their hearing and seeing, in speaking, in singing, in lies and vanities. A ball is nothing but misery, sin and vanity."

They observe that the dancing of a damsel caused John the Baptist's head to be cut off; and the dancing of the children of Israel caused Moses to break the two tables of the law. They also prove that the ten commandments are violated by balls. They cite a passage from St. Augustine, wherein he saith: "The miserable dancer knoweth not that so many paces as he maketh at a ball, by so many leaps he draweth nearer to hell."

Thus have I offered some reasons and arguments which have determined me against dancing; which I have enforced by the testimony of several great and good men; whether or no the whole hath sufficient force to prove the unlawfulness and sinfulness of the practice, must be left to the candor of serious minds.

After all, it may be thought that my work is but half done, unless I can answer whatever may be brought in support of this favorite and falsely called polite diversion. And this brings me,

III. To reply to the most popular arguments used in favor of dancing.

1. One of the most popular arguments (or rather excuses) for this practice is: " I can see no harm in it, therefore it can be no crime in me." Poor creature; you can *see* no harm in it. This is of as much force as if a blind man was to tell us that he could neither distinguish colors nor see the light. We may pity your unhappiness, but cannot give you eyes. But, you conclude, it cannot be a crime in you, because you do not view it in that light. If we are not cognizable for sins of ignorance, Saul was not chargeable with guilt when he persecuted the Church, and yet for this reason he accounted himself the chief of sinners. But it may be you are wilfully blind. You might be better instructed if you would. Let me therefore ad-

vise you to pray to God for instruction in this matter, laying yourself open to conviction; and I am persuaded you will soon see an evil in dancing, for which you must be accountable to God.

2. It may be said, "Dancing is a part of good breeding, without which we are not qualified for company, but shall appear singular, and be laughed at."

Perhaps custom may have induced the world to look upon dancing as a branch of good breeding, rather than any excellency in itself. However, to give this plea all its force, I will grant that some advantages might be derived from the dancing-school, if properly managed ; and possibly may as it is, so far as it teaches a graceful mien and easy carriage, and a genteel behavior. But these advantages will by no means compensate for the disadvantages which attend it. For, first, miss, who is educated at the dancing-school, soon swells with pride and self-importance, looks down, with an air of disdain, on those who are not as well accomplished as herself, and but too much copies the description in Isaiah (iii. 16): "*The daughters of Zion are haughty, and walk with stretched forth necks, and wanton eyes, walking and mincing as they go.*" However, the young lady's fine acquirements are not to be buried in those avocations which industry inspires ; therefore, in the next place, immense sums are expended to equip her for public view. And so, rustling in her silks, powdered *à la mode*, and studded with brilliants, she makes her appearance at the ball; where she is introduced into fine company—gets a taste for pleasure and dissipation, which often ends in the destruction of soul and body. "*The woman who liveth in pleasure, is dead while she liveth.*" (1 Tim. v, 6.)

And now, suppose you are not qualified for such company, what is the loss? "*The friendship of the world is enmity with God.*" (James, iv. 4.) And our greatest danger lies in our becoming too familiar with it. But you say that you shall be singular, and laughed at. This, indeed, may be mortifying. But are you as careful not to be singular in religious society? Perhaps, when there, you have nothing to say; yet this gives you no concern. As to your being laughed at, it need give you no pain; for, if you will shun vice, and pursue piety, you shall endure the laugh of the world, although you should behave ever so well.

3. To vindicate dancing, it is said that "it unbends the mind, and recreates the body." This plea can suit none but such as live a studious, sedentary life; and there are many exercises less exposed to temptation, that will answer those salutary purposes equally as well. Walking, riding, or manual labor, may be as profitable and efficacious. Besides, it doth not appear that dancing hath such a beneficent tendency as alleged. Strange, that being deprived of natural rest, exposed to night-damps and inclement air, in a profuse sweat, should be so salutary. The truth is, the reverse is the case; and many have danced themselves into eternity.

4. But, perhaps, we shall meet with some champion in the cause of dancing, who comes forth, Goliah-like, bidding defiance to the armies of Israel, and hath the effrontery to assert, that "the lawfulness of dancing may be supported by Scripture." Can it, indeed? If so, our business will be done for us, and we will promise to give up the point. "Why," says this hero,

"did not David dance?" Yes; we know, as well as he, that David danced; but then it was religiously, before the ark. I have already shown in what sense we are to understand David's dancing; and it is insolent, as well as perverting of Scripture, to bring this passage to support our irreligious, modern dances. "But," says this champion, "Solomon tells us *there is a time to dance.*" True; and Solomon tells us also *there is a time to die.* If our dancers thought more of this, they would find less time for that. But let it be proved, if it can, that Solomon intends dancing according to the common mode; and, suppose he should, all that can be drawn from hence is, that there is a time in which numbers will be profane enough to dance.

5. Another plea for dancing often made use of is this: "We may spend our time a great deal worse." I reply, it always indicates a bad cause when one vice is subpœnaed to vindicate another. Nothing, therefore, need be said to show the weakness of this excuse, only, that we may spend our time a great deal better, themselves being judges.

6. Some have endeavored to plead for this practice by quoting the example of professors of religion, and whom we believe to be good people, who will go to heaven, and yet they can dance as well as any body. More is the pity that they should lay a stumbling-block in the way of others. Often they are heartily despised by the people of the world, for their sinful compliances. However, all professors are not Christians. Some who have Jacob's voice, have Esau's hands. And even the best are liable to err. Therefore follow none, unless they follow Christ. It will be no excuse

in the day of judgment, that you saw professors go to balls and assemblies, and therefore you thought there could be no harm in such diversions.

Thus, having given a scriptural definition of the word dance; and proved that dancing according to the modern mode is sinful and attended with bad consequences; also replied to the most popular arguments in favor of dancing; I now come, in the last place,

IV. To make some improvement of the subject.

1. From what hath been said we may see the folly of those parents who put their children to the dancing-school, and spend such immense sums of money to bring them up in pride, gayety, and all the vanities of life. Is this to bring up our children in the fear of the Lord, as Abraham did? Is it to train up a child in the way it should go, as Solomon directs? Would it not be much better to devote our money to pious and charitable uses? Do such parents take as much care of their children's souls? Do they instruct them in the principles of the Christian religion, and warn them against sin and vanity? I fear they do not. Look to it, parents! you have the charge of your children's souls, as well as of their bodies; and a much weightier charge it is. Think how dreadful it will be to have the blood of your dear children's souls crying against you, in the day of judgment. How awful would it be to have a child thus to address you, on that day: "O cruel parent! you were the instrument of my being, or I should not have existed, to have been thus miserable. You cared indeed for my body, but why did you not care for my soul, and labor to make that happy? You might, and you ought to

have restrained me, when pursuing vanity and folly? But, instead of that, you placed me in the way of temptation; yea, you went with me yourself to the devil's seminaries, where I was taught to practise sinful pleasures. And now, alas! I am to reap the fruit of our doings to all eternity." Is the thought shocking? Oh, give no occasion for the dolorous complaint.

2. What hath been said, reproves those who are attached to, and engaged in the practice of frolicking, dancing, and suchlike sinful divisions, I say, *suchlike* diversions; for you would do well to consider, that the arguments against dancing will generally hold good against gaming, horseracing and all sinful diversions. My dear friends, you are highly reprovable; but I rather choose to address you in soft language. Let the time past suffice you, to have gone on in sin and folly. Forsake the foolish and live and walk in the way which leads to eternal life. You are surely making work for repentance. God grant that it may be in time.

If after all that hath been said, you still remain unconvinced, and can see no harm in these things—suffer me to advise you to pray earnestly, that you may be enabled to see things in a proper light; and particularly, that you may have a discovery of the wretchedness of your own wicked and deceitful heart. Then seriously ask yourselves these following questions.

For what was I made? Do I answer the end of my being? Is God glorified by all my actions? Is living in pleasure to live like a Christian? Must I not shortly die, and give an account of my actions to God? Have I any time to spare from transacting business for eternity? If this advice were universally regarded, we should hear no more of balls, assemblies and dances; instead of· which, our temple-gates would be crowded, and the general cry would be: Lord, what shall I do to be saved? May God send us the happy day, and to his name shall be all praise.

SAMUEL STILLMAN, D. D.

This eminent divine was a native of Philadelphia, in Pennsylvania, where he was born, February twenty-seventh, 1737. While quite a child, his parents removed to Charleston, South Carolina, at which place he was educated; soon after he attained his twenty-second year, he was ordained and settled at James's Island. Ill health prevented his remaining in this position but for eighteen months, at the termination of which he removed to Bordentown, New Jersey. In 1762, he visited New England, and after being an assistant about a year, in the Second Baptist Church, in Boston, he was installed the minister of the First, as successor of Mr. Bound, in January, 1765.

Dr. Stillman was by nature endowed with a good capacity, and an uncommon quickness of apprehension. His feelings were peculiarly strong and lively, which gave activity to whatever he did, and, under the influence and control of religious principles, served to increase that eminent piety, in which nature no less than grace, seemed to have aided him. To this constitutional ardor, both of sentiment and action, which led him to enter with his whole heart in whatever he engaged, he united a delicacy, that he would not intentionally wound the feelings of any one; and such easy, affable, and gentlemanly manners, as would adapt themselves to almost any society, without diminishing in the smallest degree his personal respect on the one hand, or carrying the least mixture of austerity or precision on the other. The lively interest he appeared to take in whatever affected the happiness or increased the pleasures of his friends, the gentleness of his reproofs and the gratification he seemed to feel in commending others, united to his social qualities, endeared him to all who knew him.

The popularity of a preacher commonly declines with his years. Dr. Stillman, however, was a singular exception to this general remark. He retained it for upward of fifty-two years, and his congregation, which, upon his first connection with it, was the smallest in the town, at the age of seventy, the period of his death, he left among the most numerous.

As a minister of Christ his praise was in all the churches. Nature had furnished him with a most commanding voice, the very tones of which were admirably adapted to awaken the feelings of an audience; and he always managed it with the greatest success. His eloquence was of the powerful and impressive, rather than of the insinuating and persuasive kind, and his manner so strikingly interesting, that he never preached to an unattentive audience: and even those who dissented from him in some minor points of theology, were still pleased with hearing him—for they knew his sincerity—they knew him to be a good man.

There was a fervor in his prayers that seldom failed to awaken the devotion of his hearers; for coming from the heart, it failed not to reach the hearts of others. In his sermons he was animated and pathetic. His subjects were often doctrinal, but he commonly delivered practical inferences from them, and every one acknowledged his great usefulness. He preached much to the feelings and the heart; and numbers on whose minds naked reason and simple truth could produce no serious effects, his powerful eloquence was a means of both touching and reclaiming. Nor was he only a preacher of righteousness; what he taught that others should do, he lived himself.*

The integrity of Dr. Stillman's character was such as produced universal confidence in him. Expressive of this was his election by the town of Boston as a member of the Senate Convention for the formation of the state constitution in 1779; as also for the adoption of the federal constitution in 1788; in the last body he delivered a very eloquent speech in its support, and was considered at the time as having contributed much toward its adoption, and confirmed many members in its favor who were previously wavering upon that question. To that constitution he ever after continued a firm, unshaken friend, and a warm approver of the administration of Washington and Adams.

---

* See the *Palladium* and *New-York Advertiser* of March, 1807.

His domestic character was in perfect unison with the other parts of it. His habit of body through life was weak, and he was not unused to occasional interruptions of his ministerial labors. It was his constant prayer that "his life and his usefulness might run parallel," and in this he was gratified. Without any previous symptoms, on the morning of the 13th of March, 1807, he was suddenly attacked with paralysis, and on the night following, having received another shock, he passed into eternity.

THE DUTY OF MAGISTRATES.*

Then saith he unto them, Render therefore unto Cæsar the things that are Cæsar's, and unto God the things that are God's.—MATT. xxii. 21.

THE Pharisees, who in appearance were the strictest religious sect among the Jews, observing the growing reputation of the Son of God, and finding that he had eclipsed their glory, took counsel how they might entangle him in his talk. A conduct this that is repugnant to every principle of genuine religion. But those men who are determined upon their own aggrandizement are seldom scrupulous about the means of obtaining it. Hence these ambitious religionists sent out to him their disciples, with the Herodians, men fit for their purpose, *saying*, in the language of hypocrisy

---

* This sermon was preached before the Supreme Court of Massachusetts, on the 29th of May, 1779. It was published the same year.

and insult, "*Master, we know that thou art true, and teachest the way of God in truth, neither carest thou for any man : for thou regardest not the person of men. Tell us, therefore, what thinkest thou? Is it lawful to give tribute unto Cæsar, or not?*"

The Jews entertained an extreme aversion to the Gentiles, and could not be brought to submit to a heathen magistrate but with great reluctance, and through absolute necessity.

These Pharisees, therefore, judging of our blessed Lord by their own sentiments and feelings, supposed that by this question they should extort something from him derogatory to Cæsar's honor; or that would subject him to an impeachment as an enemy to the Roman government. But he taketh the wise in their own craftiness: "*Show me,*" said he, "*the tribute money. And they brought him a penny. And he saith unto them, Whose is this image and superscription? They say unto him, Cæsar's. Then saith he unto them, Render therefore unto Cæsar the things that are Cæsar's : and unto God the things that are God's.*" Upon their being thus defeated in their infamous attempt, they marvelled and went their way to report to their masters their humiliating disappointment; for Christ had said nothing in his reply to them which Cæsar himself would not approve.

It is a matter of very little consequence to us, on this occasion, which of the Cæsars was on the throne at the time referred to in the text; because the duties here inculcated are not affected by this circumstance. The people were taught by Christ, to render such obedience to Cæsar, or to the civil magistrate, as would be consistent with the natural and the civil rights of

men, and the obligations they were under to the eternal God. It is unreasonable to suppose that he meant
to inculcate any other subjection than this. Besides,
his address is properly guarded : " Render therefore to
Cæsar, *the things that are Cæsar's.*" That is, those
things which he may lawfully claim. What these
were, our Lord does not ascertain. Nor is it necessary that we should, as they relate to Cæsar and his
subjects. I shall therefore proceed to apply this sacred
passage to ourselves, in our present situation, by considering :

I. What those duties are which the people owe to
the civil magistrate.

II. The duties of the magistrate to the people. And
then,

III. Endeavor to draw the line between the things
that belong to Cæsar, and those things that belong to
God.

I. We are first to inquire, what those duties are
which the people owe to the civil magistrate.

I apprehend that this question implies another,
which is previously necessary to be determined, viz. :
How came the men whom we call magistrates with
any power at all over the people? Were they born
to govern? Have they a higher original than
other men? Or do they claim the sovereignty *jure
divino?*

The time has been when the divine right of kings
sounded from the pulpit and the press ; and when the
sacred name of religion was brought in to sanctify
the most horrid systems of despotism and cruelty.
But, blessed be God, we live in a more happy era,
in which the great principles of liberty are better

understood. With us, it is a first and fundamental principle, that God made all men equal.

"Nothing is more evident," says Locke, "than that creatures of the same species and rank, promiscuously born to all the same advantages of nature, and the use of the same faculties, should also be equal one amongst another, without subordination or subjection, unless the Lord and Master of them all should, by any manifest declaration of his will, set one above another, and confer on him, by evident and clear appointment, an undoubted right to dominion and sovereignty."

Until such a declaration of the divine will shall be produced, we ought firmly to maintain the natural equality of all men.

And as they are equal, so they are likewise in a state of entire freedom. Whatever they possess is their own, to be disposed of solely agreeably to their own will. None have a right to claim any part of their property, to disturb them in their possessions, or to demand subjection in any degree whatever, while they act consistently with the laws of nature. He who attempts to do either is an usurper; puts himself into a state of war, and may be opposed as a common highwayman.

If we admit the truth of these principles, we come, by an easy transition, to the foundation of civil society, viz., the consent of the people. For, if all men are equal by nature, it must depend entirely upon themselves whether they will continue in their natural condition, or exchange it for a state of civil government. Consequently the sovereignty resides originally in the people.

As their leaving a state of nature for a state of civil society is a matter of their own choice, so they are equally free to adopt that form of government which appears to them the most eligible, or the best calculated to promote the happiness of themselves and of their posterity.

Which is the best form of civil government, is a question of the first magnitude to any people; and particularly to us who have lately considered this weighty matter; and who expect, at some future period, finally to determine it. May that God by whom all human events are controlled, inspire my fellow-citizens with that wisdom that shall be profitable to direct!

From the premises, the following is a natural conclusion—*That the authority of the civil magistrate is, under God, derived from the people.*

In order therefore to determine with accuracy, what the powers of the civil magistrate are, and also the duties that the people owe him, we must have recourse to the constitution; by which, in all good governments, the authority of the former, and the rights of the latter are determined with precision.

That it should be so, is a dictate of common sense. For upon a supposition of the contrary, how shall the rulers or subjects determine their respective obligations?

From hence arises, in my view, the indispensable necessity of a BILL OF RIGHTS drawn up in the most explicit language, previously to the ratification of a constitution of government; which should contain its fundamental principles, and which no person in the state, however dignified, should dare to violate but at his peril.

12

As we are at present without a fixed form of government, I shall treat the subject rather according to my wishes, than the present state of things. For the constitution ought at least to have a general existence in idea before the reciprocal duties of magistrates and people can be ascertained.

Some of those principles which, I apprehend, may be called *fundamental*, have been mentioned; to which I beg leave to subjoin:

That the great end for which men enter into a state of civil society is *their own advantage*.

That civil rulers, as they derive their authority from the people, so they are accountable to them for the use they make of it.

That elections ought to be *free* and *frequent*.

That representation should be as equal as possible.

That as all men are equal by nature, so, when they enter into a state of civil government, they are entitled *precisely* to the same rights and privileges, or to an *equal degree* of political happiness.

That some of the natural rights of mankind are unalienable, and subject to no control but that of the Deity. Such are the SACRED RIGHTS of CONSCIENCE; which, in a state of nature and of civil society, are exactly the same. They can neither be parted with nor controlled by any human authority whatever.

Attempts of this kind have been repeatedly made by an ambitious clergy, assisted by rulers of despotic principles; the consequence of which has been, that crowds of the best members of society have been reduced to this dreadful alternative, either to offend God and violate the dictates of their own minds, or to die at a stake.

That the right of trial by jury ought to be perpetual.

That no man's property can, of right, be taken from him without his consent, given either in person or by his representative.

That no laws are obligatory on the people but those that have obtained a like consent. Nor are such laws of any force, if, proceeding from a corrupt majority of the legislature, they are incompatible with the fundamental principles of government, and tend to subvert it.

"All human things have an end," "says Montesquieu, "the state we are speaking of (meaning Great Britain) will lose its liberty, will perish. Have not Rome, Sparta and Carthage perished? It will perish when the legislative power shall be more corrupt than the executive."

Let us cast our eyes to the land of our fathers, to the kingdom from whence we descended, and we shall find that she now totters on the brink of a most dangerous precipice. And that she hath been brought into her present deplorable situation by a *venal majority.*

Some of that people foresaw their catastrophe approaching with hasty strides; they petitioned and remonstrated. And several excellent things were published in vindication of their constitutions and their injured rights; but all was in vain.

The very men who were appointed the guardians and *conservators* of the rights of the people, have dismembered the empire; and by repeated acts of injustice and oppression, have forced from the bosom of their parent country, millions of Americans, who might have been drawn by a *hair*, but were not to be driven by all the thunder of Britain.

A few soft words would have fixed them in her interest, and have turned away that wrath which her cruel conduct had enkindled. The sameness of religion, of language and of manners, together with interest, that powerful motive, and a recollection of that reciprocation of kind offices which had long prevailed, would have held America in closest friendship with Great Britain, had she not "governed too much."

It can afford the inhabitants of that once happy country, no consolation in their present threatening condition, that it hath been brought on with all the *formality of law.* Rather, this circumstance adds to the calamity, seeing the men who should have saved them, have betrayed them.

Where is now the boasted freedom of the British government? Bribery and corruption seem nearly to have accomplished the prediction of the great Montesquieu. Nor is such an event to be wondered at, while we reflect on the inequality* of their representation and the base methods that are used in their elections of members of the House of Commons, together with the length of time they are suffered to continue in their places.

If they are chosen for a long term, by a part only

---

* In Great Britain, consisting of near six millions of inhabitants, five thousand seven hundred and twenty-three persons, most of them of the lowest of the people, elect one-half of the House of Commons; and three hundred and sixty-four votes choose a ninth part. This may be distinctly made out in the *Political Disquisitions,* vol. I., book 2, ch. 4.—Dr. Price.

of the state, and if, during that term, they are subject to no control from their constituents, the very
idea of liberty will be lost, and the power of choosing
in constituents becomes nothing but a power lodged
in a *few* to choose, at certain periods, a body of *masters* for themselves and for the rest of the community.
And if a state is so sunk that the body of its representatives are elected by a handful of the meanest
persons in it, whose votes are always paid for ;* and
if, also, there is a higher will on which even these
mock representatives themselves depend, and that
directs their voices ; in these circumstances, it will
be an abuse of language to say that the state possesses liberty. This appears to be a just description
of the present state of the country from which we
descended.

Such an instance affords us many important lessons,
and calls upon us to guard as much as possible in *our
beginning*, against the corruption of human nature.
We should leave nothing to human virtue, that can
be provided for by law or the constitution. The more
we trust in the hands of any man, the more we try
his virtue, which, at some fatal hour, may yield to a
temptation ; and the people discover their error, when
it is too late to prevent the mischief.

Upon the truth of the principles advanced, I observe, that the authority of the magistrate is derived
from the people by consent—that it is limited and
subordinate—and that so long as he exercises the
power with which he is vested, according to the orig-

---

* They who *buy* their *places* will *sell* the *people*, for they mean to
make something by the bargain.

inal compact, the people owe him *reverence, obedience* and *support*.

Inspiration teaches us to *give honor to whom honor, fear to whom fear*.

When any men are taken from the common rank of citizens, and are intrusted with the powers of government, they are by that act ennobled. Their election implies their personal merit, and is a public declaration of it. For it is taken for granted, that the people have been influenced in their choice by worthiness of character, and not by family connections, or other base motives. They are, therefore, entitled to a certain degree of respect from their constituents—who, while they pay them due reverence, will feel it reflected upon themselves, because they bear their commission. Both interest and duty oblige them to reverence the powers that be. It is their duty in consequence of their own appointment. And their interest, because the good of the community depends much upon it. For as far as any of the citizens unjustly depreciate the merit of rulers, so far they lessen the energy of government, and put it out of their power to promote the public good.

With reverence to the person of the magistrate, we connect *obedience to his authority*—such obedience as is compatible with the principles already laid down. The term *government* implies this *subordination*, which is essential to its very existence.

When, therefore, any persons rise in opposition to such authority, they are guilty of a most daring offence against the state; because, as far as it prevails, it tends to destroy the social compact, and to introduce confusion and every evil work. Consequently,

It is the duty of the people to *support the magis-trate, in the due execution of the laws against such,* and *all other offenders.* To choose men to office, and not to support them in the execution of it, is too great an absurdity, one would think, to find any abettors.

There is also a *pecuniary support* which the magis-trate hath a right to receive from his constituents. It is most reasonable that those persons whose time and abilities are devoted to the service of their country, should be amply provided for while they are thus en-gaged. The compensation should be adequate to the services they render the state. Let it be sufficient, but not redundant.

While speaking of that support which the servants of government are entitled to, I beg leave to mention those brave men of every rank who compose our army. They have stepped forth in the hour of danger, have exchanged domestic ease and happiness for the hard-ships of the camp, have repeatedly fought, and many of them have bled, in the cause of their country. Of their importance no man can be ignorant.

With deference to this venerable assembly, I am constrained to observe, that our first attention is due to them, because, under God, they have been, now are, and, we trust, will be, our defence. For them let us make the most ample provision, and rest assured of their most vigorous exertions to defend and save their country.

But it is time to pass to the —

II. Consideration of the duties of the magistrate to the people.

As a free government is founded in a compact, the

parties concerned in it are consequently laid under mutual obligations. These, it hath been said, are determined by the constitution. If so, it follows, that the rulers of the people ought to make themselves thoroughly acquainted with it, together with the different laws of the state. Therefore they should be men of leisure and abilities, whether they are called to act in a legislative or executive department.

It is taken for granted, that the rulers of the people will not forget the source of their power, nor the design of their appointment to office—that they have no authority but what they derived from the people; who, from a confidence in them that reflects great honor on them, have put it into their hands, with this sole view—that they might thereby promote the good of the community.

Whether this great end is accomplished, by the exercise of the authority of civil rulers, the people are to judge; with whom the powers of government originate, and who must know the end for which they intrusted them in the hands of any of their fellow-citizens. This right of judging of their conduct implies, that it lies with them either to *censure* or *approve it.*

These considerations are happily calculated to prevent the abuse of power, which has already happened in repeated instances. And of which there ever will be danger, while mankind remain in their present state of corruption.

A spirit of ambition, which is natural to man, tends to tyranny; and an undue attachment to personal interest, may issue in fraud; or in an accumulation of offices, which, in their own nature, are incompatible with each other; and which no man, let his abilities be what they may, can discharge with honor to himself, and advantage to his country.

A faithful ruler will consider himself as a trustee of the public, and that he is accountable both to God and to the people for his behavior in his office. He will, therefore, be very careful not to involve himself in more public business than he can perform with fidelity.

It would have a happy tendency to render the duty of the magistrate easy and successful, were he to cultivate an intimate acquaintance with the genius and temper of the people over whom he presides. By such an acquisition if prudent, he would be capable of pursuing a mode of conduct that would not fail of gaining him the affections and confidence of his subjects. The importance of which is self-evident.

"He *who ruleth over men*," says David, "*must be just, ruling in the fear of God.*" In his exalted station, he should go before the people as an example of every moral virtue; and as a hearty friend of that constitution of government which he hath sworn to protect. To the meanest of the people he should act the part of a political father, by securing to them the full enjoyment of life, liberty, and property. To him they are to look that justice is not delayed, nor the laws executed with partiality; but that all those who united in clothing him with the authority of the magistrate may uninterruptedly enjoy that *equal liberty*, for the security of which they entered into a state of civil society. Thus will he be *as the light of the morning when the sun riseth, even a morning without clouds.*

There are many things that belong to this part of

12*

the subject. Such as, that the people have a right to expect that the honorable their rulers, will by all lawful means in their power encourage agriculture and commerce, endeavor to *suppress vice* and immorality,* lend all necessary assistance to our schools and colleges ; it being a matter of high political importance that knowledge should be diffused through the state, amongst all ranks of men. The propagation of literature is connected with the security of freedom. Ignorance in politics, as well as in religion, is fatal in its tendency.

These subjects have been often considered with great ability and address, on these anniversaries. Therefore, I forbear to enlarge on them, and reserve the remainder of my time for the consideration of a point of peculiar delicacy, and of the greatest importance to the happiness of my country—viz. :

III. To attempt to draw the line between the things that belong to Cæsar, and those things that belong to God.

To this inquiry I am naturally led by the text :— *Render, therefore, to Cæsar the things that are Cæsar's,*

---

* Had this sentence been duly attended to at the time the sermon was delivered, the following objection which some of my friends have made viz.: "That upon the principles contained in the sermon, the civil magistrate ought not to exercise his authority to suppress acts of immorality." I say, had what is said above been properly observed, this objection had been superseded. Immoral actions properly come under the cognizance of civil rulers, who are the guardians of the peace of society. But then I beg leave to observe, in the words of Bishop Warhburton, "That the magistrate punishes no bad actions as sins or offences *against God*, but only as crimes injurious to, or having a malignant influence on society." In this view of the matter he keeps within the line of his own department.

and unto God the things that are God's. It is most evident in this passage, that there are some things which Cæsar, or the magistrate, cannot of right demand, nor the people yield. The address has its limits. To determine what these are, was never more necessary to the people of these United States than it is at present. We are engaged in a most important contest; not for power, but freedom. We mean not to change our masters, but to secure to ourselves, and to generations yet unborn, the perpetual enjoyment of civil and religious liberty, in their fullest extent.

It becomes us, therefore, to settle this most weighty matter in our different forms of government, in such a manner, that no occasion may be left in future for the violation of the all-important rights of conscience.

"I esteem it," says the justly-celebrated Mr. Locke, "above all things, necessary to distinguish exactly the business of civil government from that of religion, and to settle the just bounds that lie between the one and the other. If this be not done, there can be no end put to the controversies that will be always arising between those that have, or at least pretend to have, on the one side a concernment for the interest of men's souls, and on the other side a care of the commonwealth.

"The commonwealth seems to be a society of men constituted only for the procuring, preserving, and advancing their own *civil interests.*

"Civil *interests* I call life, liberty and health, and the possession of outward things, such as money, lands, houses, furniture, and the like.

"Now, that the whole jurisdiction of the magistrate

reaches only to these civil concernments, and that all
civil power, right and dominion, are bounded and confined to the only care of promoting these things; and
that it neither can nor ought in any manner to be extended to the salvation of souls, these following considerations seem to me abundantly to demonstrate:

"First, because the care of souls is not committed
to the civil magistrate any more than to other men.
It is not committed to him, I say, by God; because it
appears not that God has ever given any such authority to one man over another, as to compel any one to
his religion. Nor can any such power be invested in
the magistrate by the *consent of the people;* because
no man can so far abandon the care of his own salvation, as blindly to leave it to the choice of any other,
whether prince or subject, to prescribe to him what
faith or worship he shall embrace. For no man can,
if he would, conform his faith to the dictates of another. All the life and power of true religion consist
in the inward and full persuasion of the mind; and
faith is not faith without believing.

"In the second place. The care of souls cannot
belong to the civil magistrate, because his power consists only in outward force; but true and saving religion consists in the inward persuasion of the mind,
without which nothing can be acceptable to God. And
such is the nature of the understanding, that it cannot
be compelled to any thing by outward force.

"In the third place, the care of the salvation of men's
souls cannot belong to the civil magistrate, because,
though the rigor of laws and the force of penalties
were capable to convince and change men's minds,
yet would not that help at all to the salvation of their

souls; for, there being but one truth, one way to
heaven, what hope is there that more men would be
led into it if they had no other rule to follow but the
religion of the court, and were put under the necessity
to quit the light of their own reason, to oppose the
dictates of their own consciences, and blindly resign
up themselves to the will of their governors, and to
the religion which either ignorance, ambition, or superstition had chanced to establish in the countries
where they were born? In the variety and contra-
diction of opinions in religion, wherein the princes of
the world are as much divided as in their secular interests, the narrow way would be much straitened,
one country alone would be in the right, and all the
rest of the world put under an obligation of following
their princes in the ways that lead to destruction.
And what heightens the absurdity, and very ill suits
the notion of a Deity, men would owe their eternal
happiness or misery to the places of their nativity.

"These considerations, to omit many others that might
have been urged to the same purpose, seem to me sufficient to conclude that all the power of civil government relates only to men's civil interests, is confined
to the care of the things of this world, and hath nothing to do with the world to come."

These sentiments, I humbly conceive, do honor to
their author, and discover a true greatness and liberality of mind, and are calculated properly to limit
the power of civil rulers, and to secure to every man
the inestimable right of private judgment.

They are also perfectly agreeable to a fundamental
principle of government, which we universally admit.
We say, *That the power of the civil magistrate is de-*

rived from the people. If so, it follows, that he can neither have *more*, nor *any other kind of power,* than they had to give.

The power which the people commit into the hands of the magistrate is wholly confined to the things of this world. Other power than this they have not. They have not the least authority over the consciences of one another, nor over their own consciences so as to alienate them or subject them to the control of the civil magistrate in matters of religion, in which every man ought to be fully persuaded in his own mind, and to follow its dictates at all hazards, because he is to *account for himself* at the judgment-seat of Christ.

Seeing, then, that the people have no power that they can commit into the hands of the magistrate but that which relates to the good of civil society, it follows that the magistrate can have no other, because he derives his authority from the people. Such as the power of the people is, such must be the power of the magistrate.

To these observations I beg leave to add, that *the kingdom of Christ is not of this world.* By his kingdom we mean his church, which is altogether spiritual. Its origin, government and preservation are entirely of Him who hath upon his vesture and upon his thigh written, KING OF KINGS, AND LORD OF LORDS.

The doctrines that we are to believe, the duties that we are to perform, the officers who are to serve in this kingdom, and the laws by which all its subjects are to be governed, we become acquainted with by the oracles of God, which are the Christian's infallible directory; to which he is bound to yield obedience, at the risk of his reputation and life.

They who enter into this kingdom do it voluntarily, with a design of promoting their spiritual interests. Civil affairs they resign to the care of the magistrate, but the salvation of their souls they seek in the kingdom of Christ.

This kingdom does not in any respect interfere with civil government, but rather tends to promote its peace and happiness, because its subjects are taught to obey the magistracy, and to *lead peaceable and quiet lives in all godliness and honesty.*

The subjects of the kingdom of Christ claim no exemption from the just authority of the magistrate, by virtue of their relation to it. Rather they yield a ready and cheerful obedience, not *only for wrath but also for conscience sake.* And should any of them violate the laws of the state, they are to be punished as other men.

They exercise no *secular* power, they inflict no *temporal* penalties upon the persons of one another. All their punishments are *spiritual.* Their *weapons are not carnal, but mighty through God.* They use no other force than that of reason and argument, to reclaim delinquents; nor are such persons to be punished for continuing incorrigible, in any other way than by rebuke, or exclusion.

They pretend not to exercise their spiritual authority over any persons, who have not joined themselves to them of their own accord. " *What have I to do,*" says Paul, " *to judge them also who are without? do ye not judge them who are within?*"

The subjects of this kingdom are bound by no laws in matters of religion, but such as they receive from Christ, who is the only lawgiver and head of his church. All human laws in this respect are inadmissible, as being unnecessary, and as implying a gross reflection on our Lord Jesus Christ, as though he was either unable, or unwilling to provide for his own interest in the world. Nor will he stand by, an idle spectator, of the many encroachments that have been made on his sacred prerogative by the powers of the world.

Should the most dignified civil ruler become a member of his church, or a subject of his spiritual kingdom, he cannot carry the least degree of his civil power into it. In the church he is, as any other member of it, entitled to the same spiritual privileges, and bound by the same laws. The authority he has derived from the state, can by no means be extended to the kingdom of Christ, because Christ is the only source of that power, that is to be exercised in it.

It may be said, that religion is of importance to the good of civil society; therefore the magistrate ought to encourage it under this idea.

It is readily acknowledged that the intrinsic excellence and beneficial effects of true religion are such that *every man* who is favored with the Christian revelation ought to befriend it. It has the *promise of the life that now is, and of that which is to come.* And there are many ways in which the civil magistrate may encourage religion, in a perfect agreement with the nature of the kingdom of Christ, and the rights of conscience.

As a *man*, he is *personally* interested in it. His everlasting salvation is at stake. Therefore he should search the Scriptures for himself, and follow them wherever they lead him. This right he hath in common with every other citizen.

As the *head of a family*, he should act as a priest in his own house, by endeavoring to bring up his children in the nurture and admonition of the Lord.

As a *magistrate*, he should be as a nursing father to the church of Christ, by protecting all the peaceable members of it from injury on account of religion; and by securing to them the uninterrupted enjoyment of equal religious liberty. The authority by which he acts he derives alike from *all the people;* consequently he should exercise that authority *equally* for the benefit of *all*, without any respect to their different religious principles. They have an undoubted right to demand it.

Union in the state is of absolute necessity to its happiness. This the magistrate will study to promote. And this he may reasonably expect upon the plan proposed, of a *just and equal treatment of all the citizens.*

For though Christians may contend amongst themselves about their religious differences, they will all unite to promote the good of the community, because it is their interest, so long as they enjoy the blessings of a free and equal administration of government.

On the other hand, if the magistrate destroys the equality of the subjects of the state on account of religion, he violates a fundamental principle of a free government, establishes separate interests in it, and lays a foundation for disaffection to rulers and endless quarrels among the people.

Happy are the inhabitants of that commonwealth, in which every man sits under his vine and fig-tree, having none to make him afraid; in which all are *protected* but none *established*. Permit me, on this occasion, to introduce the words of the Rev. Dr. Chauncey,

whose age and experience add weight to his sentiments. "We are," says this gentleman, "in principle
against all civil establishments in religion. We desire not, and suppose we have no right to desire, the
interposition of the state to establish our sentiments
in religion, or the manner in which we would express
them. It does not, indeed, appear to us, that God
has intrusted the state with a right to make religious
establishments." And after observing that if one
state has this right, all states have the same right, he
adds: "And as they must severally be supposed to
exert this authority in establishments conformable to
their own sentiments in religion, what can the consequence be, but infinite damage to the cause of God
and true religion? And such, in fact, has been the
consequence of these establishments in all ages and
in all places. What absurdities in sentiment, and ridiculous follies, not to say gross immoralities in practice, have not been established by the civil power, in
some or other of the nations of the world?"

To which I take the liberty to add the following
passage of a very ingenious author:

"The moment any religion becomes national, or established, its purity must certainly be lost, because it
is impossible to keep it unconnected with men's interests; and if connected, it must inevitably be perverted
by them. Again, that very order of men, who are
maintained to support its interests, will sacrifice them
to their own. By degrees knaves will join them, fools
believe them, and cowards will be afraid of them; and
having gained so considerable a part of the world to
their interests, they will erect an independent dominion among themselves, dangerous to the liberties of

mankind, and representing all those who oppose tyranny, as God's enemies, teach it to be meritorious in His sight to persecute them in this world, and damn them in another. Hence must arise hierarchies, inquisitions and Popery; for Popery is but the consummation of that tyranny which every religious system in the hands of men is in perpetual pursuit of."

It is well known to this respectable assembly, that Christianity flourished remarkably for the space of three hundred years after the ascension of Christ, amidst the hottest and most bloody persecutions, and when the powers of the world were against it, and began to decline immediately upon its being made a *legal establishment* by Constantine, the first Christian emperor, who heaped upon it his ill-judged favors and introduced a train of evils which he had not designed.

The preachers of this divine religion were no sooner taken into the favor of the prince, and their sentiments established by law, than they began to quarrel who should be the greatest; and anathemized one another. Every man who has read the history of the four first general councils, is fully satisfied of the truth of these remarks.

Seeing, then, Christianity made its way in the beginning, when the powers of the world were against it, let us cheerfully leave it to the force of its own evidence, and to the care of its adorable author; while we strictly attend to all those means which he hath instituted for the propagation of it. The ministers of Christ are particularly called upon to *preach the word, to be instant in season, out of season*, to teach the people *publicly and from house to house;* always encouraging themselves with that gracious promise,

Lo, I am with you alway, even unto the end of the world.

Upon the whole, I think it is a plain as well as a very important truth, that the *Church of Christ* and a *commonwealth are essentially different.* The one is a *religious* society, of which Christ is the sole head, and which he gathers out of the world, in common, by the dispensation of his gospel, governs by his laws in all matters of religion, a complete code of which we have in the sacred Scriptures; and preserves it by his power.

The other is a *civil* society—originating with the people, and designed to promote their *temporal interests*—which is governed by men, whose authority is derived from their fellow-citizens, and confined to the affairs of this world.

In this view of the matter, the line appears to me to be fairly drawn between *the things that belong to Cæsar* and *the things* that belong to God. The magistrate is to govern the *state*, and Christ is to govern the *church.* The former will find business enough in the complex affairs of government to employ all his time and abilities. The latter is infinitely sufficient to manage his own kingdom without foreign aid.

Thus have I considered the important principles of civil and religious liberty, according to that ability which God hath given; and with a freedom that becomes a citizen when called upon, at a most critical period, to address the rulers of a free people; whose patriotic minds, it is taken for granted, would at once despise the language of adulation.

In order to complete a system of government, and to be consistent with ourselves, it appears to me that we ought to banish from among us that cruel practice, which has long prevailed, of reducing to a state of slavery for life the freeborn Africans.*

·The Deity hath bestowed upon them and us the same natural rights as men; and hath assigned to them a part of the globe for their residence. But mankind, urged by those passions which debase the human mind, have pursued them to their native country; and by fomenting wars among them, that they might secure the prisoners, or employing villains to decoy the unwary, have filled their ships with the unfortunate captives; dragged them from their tenderest connections, and transported them to different parts of the earth, to be hewers of wood, and drawers of water, till death shall end their painful captivity.

To reconcile this nefarious traffic with reason, humanity, religion, or the principles of a free government, in my view, requires an uncommon address.

Should we make the case our own, and act agreeably to that excellent rule of our blessed Lord, *Whatever ye would that men should do to you, do ye to them likewise*, the abolition of this disgraceful practice would take place.

Nor can I conceive that we shall act a consistent part, till we brand this species of tyranny with perpetual infamy. Shall we hold the sword in one hand

---

* Congress, early in the controversy with Great Britain, protested against the slave-trade in the following resolve:

"Secondly, We will neither import nor purchase any slaves imported after the first day of December next; after which time we will *wholly discontinue the slave-trade;* and will neither be concerned in it ourselves, nor will we hire our vessels, nor sell our commodities or manufactures to those who are concerned in it."

to defend our just rights as men; and grasp chains with the other to enslave the inhabitants of Africa? Forbid it heaven!—Forbid it all the freeborn sons of this western world!

May the year of jubilee soon arrive, when Africa shall cast the look of gratitude to these happy regions, for the *total emancipation of her sons!*

This matter, among others, deserves the serious attention of our honorable rulers, in whom their fellow-citizens have reposed uncommon confidence, which is apparent in calling them forth to public service at such a difficult period as this, which undoubtedly calls for the united exertions of the greatest abilities.

The voice of the people is, as mentioned before, and the importance of the matter justifies the repetition of it; I say, the voice of the people is, that government should pay their first attention to the war. If America is respectable in the field, the greater will be the prospect of success in arms, and of an honorable peace.

Let us not amuse ourselves with a prospect of peace, and in consequence thereof abate in our preparations for the war. If we should, it may prove greatly injurious to *the freedom and glory of this rising empire.*

But it is not for me to attempt to specify the weighty affairs which, during the course of the present year, and particularly of the present session, are likely to come before the honorable gentlemen who have this day called us to the place of public worship. God grant unto them that wisdom that is from above!

While transacting public business, may they remember that Jehovah *standeth in the congregation of the mighty, and judgeth among the gods.* Under the influence of this solemn consideration, may the elections of this day be conducted. This being the case, every elector, before he gives his vote for any person to sit in council, will take pains to satisfy himself whether he possesses the qualifications that are necessary for so exalted a station—such as wisdom, virtue, firmness, and an unfeigned love of his country. Tried friends deserve the preference—an experience of whose capacity and fidelity in times past, recommends them as worthy of our present confidence.

To the direction of Unerring Wisdom we commit both branches of the honorable court, heartily wishing that they may conduct themselves in every respect as those who are to be accountable to God, the judge of all. Thus will they enjoy the testimony of conscience, and may expect to be accepted of the multitude of their brethren.

In fine, seeing the body of Christians, however divided into sects and parties, " are entitled precisely to the same rights," it becomes them to rest contented with that equal condition, nor to wish for pre-eminence. Rather, they should rejoice to see all men as free and as happy as themselves.

They should study to imbibe more of the spirit of their Divine Master, to love as brethren, and to preserve the unity of the spirit in the bond of peace. In the present state of ignorance and prejudice, they cannot expect to see eye to eye. There will be a variety of opinions and modes of worship among the disciples of the same Lord—men equally honest, pious, and sensible—while they remain in this world of imperfection. Let them, therefore, be faithful to their respective principles, and kind and forbearing toward one another. Their chief study should be to advance the cause of morality and religion in the world, and by their good works to glorify their Father who is in heaven.

They are to be subject to the civil magistrate, not only for wrath, but also for conscience sake; and to pray for all who are in authority, that under them they may lead a quiet and peaceable life in all godliness and honesty. For this is good and acceptable in the sight of God. To whom be glory forever.

DAVID TAPPAN, D. D.

THE subject of this sketch was the son of the Reverend Benjamin Tappan, minister, of Manchester, and was born on the twenty-first of April, 1753. Under the guidance of his father he acquired the rudiments of knowledge, and having passed a short period at the Dummer academy, he was, at the youthful age of fourteen, admitted to Harvard college. There, "rising above juvenile follies and vices," he applied himself diligently to his studies; "was considerate and sober-minded," and graduated in 1771. Within three years after, he commenced the work of the ministry, and at once took a place among the foremost in the esteem of the public. In his earliest performances his hearers were surprised at the extent of his learning, and the animation and fervor of his devotions. At the age of twenty-one he was ordained pastor of a church at Newbury, and continued in that position until 1792, when he was inducted into the Hollis professorship of divinity in Harvard college. He performed the duties of this office to universal acceptance, until his death, which occurred August 27, 1803.

Doctor Tappan's mind was active and vigorous; fertile in invention, and his command of language not often surpassed. As a preacher he was decidedly

13

evangelical. The peculiar contents of the gospel were the principal subjects of his discourses. He was not only doctrinal, but very practical in his religious lessons. Every gospel doctrine, he insisted, had its corresponding precept and duty. In piety, knowledge and Christian good he was exemplary; but his development of his principles was too candid and catholic, too characteristically Christian, to satisfy the lovers of ecclesiastical controversy. By these he was thought, in some instances, wanting in resolution and decision; as not sufficiently showing his esteem, for what they called "the distinguishing doctrines of the gospel;" as reluctant to suggest an opinion, which did not meet the approbation of others; and as too careful to accommodate himself to the opinions and prejudices which he disapproved and believed pernicious. But he was superior to all these considerations; he was ever anxious for the well-being of his fellow-creatures. His nature disposed him to sympathy, tenderness and charity. "He exemplified on every occasion," says this most appreciative biographer, "the temper, which he so impressively inculcated in doctrine, spirit and deportment, to be a constant recommendation and defence of Christianity, by exhibiting it in its native sweetness, sobriety and dignity."*

* See Quincy's History of Harvard University.

THE TREATY OF PEACE.

FRIENDS AND FELLOW-COUNTRYMEN, while I vent the fulness of my heart in the sincerest congratulations of you and myself, and our common country, on the arrival of the auspicious day, which gives confirmed sovereignty and independence to confederate America, and pours into her bosom the blessing of a safe, advantageous, honorable peace, the charms of which are vastly heightened and endeared to us by the horrid contrast of an eight years' cruel war. Permit me at the same time to remind you, that the professed design of this solemn assembly* should give a religious direction to our common joy, and consecrate it into the liveliest gratitude to that Supreme Power who at once styles himself a Man of War and the God of Peace. That the rapture of our hearts on so glorious an occasion may be thus guided into a holy channel, and elevated into a pious transport of God—exalting adoration and thanksgiving—let us turn our contemplations to a noble pattern of this kind in the grateful, exulting Jews, on their liberation from Babylonish captivity, as we have it exhibited in Psalm cxxvi., three first verses:

When the Lord turned again the captivity of Zion we were like them that dream. Then was our mouth filled with laughter, and our tongues with singing: then said they among the heathen, the Lord hath done great things for them. The Lord hath done great things for us, whereof we are glad.

As the deliverance here celebrated by the church

---

* This sermon was delivered at the Third Parish in Newbury, Mass., on the 1st of May, 1783, occasioned by the ratification of the treaty of peace between Great Britain and the United States of America.

of God was the most illustrious of any in the Old Testament annals, and a most remarkable type of our spiritual redemption by the Messiah; as many of its leading circumstances bear a striking similarity to those which have distinguished and dignified the salvation of united America; and as their sentiments upon it are such as remarkably suit and become every American heart and tongue on the present occasion—let us, therefore, run over the affecting picture which they themselves give of the matter, in the words now read, in which they relate, in *the first place*, the pleasing, overwhelming surprise that seized their minds on first receiving the glorious tidings. "When the Lord turned again the captivity of Zion, we were like them that dream." As if they had said: "The deliverance was so great and glorious in itself; so astonishing in its circumstances; so sudden in its accomplishment; so unexpected and improbable in every human view; so far above our highest ideas and hopes; so opposite to our just deserts and apprehensions—that we could scarce credit the testimony of our own senses, and were ready to imagine the news of liberty no better than the pleasing dream of a transported, deluded fancy, or the airy, baseless fabric of a midnight vision." So Peter, when a celestial messenger knocked off his prison chains, and brought him forth to liberty, was at first so surprised at the sudden, extraordinary deliverance, that he could not believe it to be a waking reality, but only a visionary picture painted on his imagination. And, doubtless, the first ideas and feelings of many an American heart, on the news of the equitable, liberal treaty of peace, ratified between Britain and these sovereign states, were nearly coincident with this description; for the improbability of the haughty monarch and court of Britain ever submitting (at least at present) to such *mortifying concessions—especially of their adopting so generous a system of policy, so contradictory to the narrow, deceitful, underhanded, cruel politics, which before they had uniformly pursued toward this country; the disappointment of our sanguine prospects of pacification in some former stages of this contest; the long continuance of our distresses; the visibly growing degeneracy and wickedness of America under the judgments of heaven, sent, and so long continued, for her correction and reformation—these, and many other discouraging ideas, combined their influence to render the glorious tidings of peace a very surprising, unexpected, overwhelming sound in the ears of many sober Americans—a sound too grand, good, joyful, to gain their ready, confident belief. "Their rapture seemed a pleasing dream, the grace appeared so great."

"Then was our mouth filled with laughter, and our tongue with singing." The surprise of such a deliverance produced an ecstasy of joy, so that we could scarce restrain our passions or our tongues within the bounds of decency or decorum. "Then said they among the heathen, The Lord hath done great things for them." Those heathen neighbors who had observed and insulted the distressed, abject state of these captive exiles, were now constrained to own the superintending, triumphant power, wisdom and goodness of Jehovah, in their surprising deliverances, in rescuing his feeble people Israel out of the hands of their mighty oppressors, when they were without friends, without resources, without any enlivening hope or spirit; in raising up for them in this situation, and affecting their instant deliverance by a most unlikely instrument, indeed; a pagan, idolatrous monarch, a stranger and an enemy, both by nation and religion; the king of that very empire which held them in servitude as its legal, conquered captives, and esteemed and treated them as the lowest dregs of mankind! that such a prince, without any human solicitation, without, yea, contrary to, any of the usual motives of human policy, should proclaim the remains of poor, oppressed Israel, a *free* and *independent* nation, and furnish them out of his own treasures, with every requisite for the re-establishment and secure enjoyment of their ancient privileges in their own land. This was such a spectacle of divine wonders in behalf of that people, as extorted a confession from the most stupid idolaters, that Jehovah, the God of Israel, was far superior to their idoldeities. Just as, my brethren, the successful struggles of oppressed America, at first a feeble, naked, friendless infant, against the gigantic power of Britain. a nation then respectable and terrible to all the world for military prowess, strength and glory, have displayed an august spectacle of divine manifestations in our favor, which commands the admiring attention of the world. All Europe, whether Popish or Protestant, Christian or infidel, has beheld the advancing stages of this contest with growing astonishment; and while our wonderful success has given a lustre and dignity to our national character in the eyes of mankind, I doubt not but all sober observers, and, one would think, all that are not abandoned atheists, are constrained to say:

The Lord hath done great things for America. Even the poor Indian savages around us could make this remark on some great victory or deliverance granted to our pious, praying fathers: "Your God must be a very great and good Spirit, to hear and answer your prayers in so surprising a manner!"

If, then, heathens, idolators and scoffers are compelled to own a Superior Hand in these great events, with what eager, grateful transport should those in whose behalf they are wrought reply, as in the next verse: "The Lord hath done great things for us, whereof we are glad?" He hath done great things *for us.* Our heathen neighbors are only cool spectators, but we are the feeling, happy subjects of the surprising mercy, "whereof we are glad;" our neighbors are struck with amazement, and some of them filled with rage and vexation, but we are filled with grateful joy—a joy proportioned to the greatness of the blessing, and the evidence we have that it flows from a God that is reconciled and in friendship with his now penitent, purified, reformed Israel. As I mean to make the pious ascription in this third verse the principal basis of the ensuing part of my discourse, I shall accordingly attempt to show—

First. When the interpositions of Jehovah in favor of his people may be styled *great*, or what it is that stamps them with this high character, which will naturally bring into view the principal events which have introduced and established the American revolution.

Secondly. Point out and enforce the manner in which the happy subjects of such great divine manifestations should entertain and improve them.

Respecting the *first head*, I would presume that

all the works of Jehovah are great, as being the prod-
ucts and displays of infinite perfection, and designed
and adapted to some very grand and excellent end :—
particularly, all his acts of kindness to any of our fallen
species, are the fruits of a benevolence infinitely great,
prompting and co-operating with equal knowledge and
power. But though all God's benevolent works are
in this respect equal, as proceeding from the same effi-
cient and impulsive cause, yet the effects hereof, as
terminating upon, and displaying the divine goodness
and other attributes to the view of the creature, are
almost infinitely diversified; and in this view, some
of the kind dispensations of Heaven are vastly, unspeakably greater than others. For instance, those
fruits of divine goodness, which have a very great intrinsic worth—which carry in them a deliverance, or
security from very great and terrible evils, and a complication of many positive blessings—which promise
very durable advantages, or draw after them a large
series of beneficial consequences—which embrace
great numbers of persons as joint-sharers in the important benefit—which triumph over mighty obstacles
that lie in their way—which are conferred in an uncommon, unexpected, sudden, improbable, or peculiarly seasonable manner; such operations or effects
of divine goodness may be styled *great* in an emphatical and most glorious sense.

There was a signal concurrence of many of these
heightening circumstances attending the liberation of
the Jewish captives celebrated in the text. But the
divine manifestations in favor of these United States,
in which we this day rejoice, are eminently marked
with *all* these dignifying characters. For the benefits

granted possess a vast *intrinsic value*, being no less than INDEPENDENT LIBERTY, both civil and religious—the confirmed power of choosing our own government and worship, of enacting our own laws, of acquiring and enjoying our own property, of regulating and extending our own commerce, and, in a word, of securely and peaceably enjoying the most valuable temporal blessings and spiritual privileges, in the greatest and best country in the world! Will any son or daughter of America, in view of these precious gifts, now ratified to us by Heaven, venture to speak in a contemptuous or murmuring tone, of the issue of our long struggle with tyranny, as if we had reaped no other harvest from it than the loss of a great deal of our choicest blood, and an insupportable weight of debt and of taxes for many years to come? But what, my friends, are these sacrifices and inconveniences compared with those *terrible evils* from which Heaven, by this conflict, has delivered and secured us?—compared with unconditional submission to a foreign legislature *in all cases whatsoever*, which was expressly demanded by the British Parliament, and attempted to be enforced by the whole military power of the nation—a demand which, at one stroke, annihilated the very foundation of liberty in this country, and placed her in the lowest, basest state of vassalage, without leaving to her the least right or property in any instance whatever! And as complete servitude must have been the immediate effect of a passive, non-resisting submission to this despotic claim, so, if Heaven had permitted them to seduce or conquer us into this subjection, after resisting them with our arms, the consequences must have been still more insupportably

13*

dreadful; for a conquest would at once have made the court of Britain both lords and landlords of this whole continent; and while our principal leaders, in the cabinet and field, would have been doomed to the block, or the gallows, the rest of us, with our children, down perhaps to late posterity, must have been humble, cringing tenants and slaves, hewers of wood and drawers of water to the haughty minions of British power!

Let us seriously contemplate, my brethren, those tremendous evils, which we had so much reason to fear, together with those we have actually felt, from the disappointed ambition and cruelty of our foes;— let our thoughts take a range through their polluted prison ships, and other murderous places of confinement, which have slain so many of our deserving sons —let us visit the many populous towns wantonly consumed, with the vast amount of property pillaged or destroyed by their hands, with the many other traces of a base, vindictive spirit, which has marked their conduct toward us;—let us cast a retrospective eye on the many awful scenes of blood and carnage, of havoc and depredation, with the long train of evils, both natural and moral, which compose war's gloomy retinue; and then say, whether that event which puts a period to all these distresses, perils, and fears, which anchors our political ship in the harbor of security and peace, after having so long encountered the rage of so tempestuous a sea, is not a very great and capital mercy of Heaven!—a mercy unspeakably enhanced and sweetened by the long and gloomy scenes of trouble which have preceded and introduced it! A mercy too of a very *complicated* kind, not only as it saves us from such a complication of evils, but as it carries in its bowels, or naturally draws after it, a long chain of important *positive* blessings, of *extensive* and *permanent* advantages.

For, besides the usual sweets and benefits of peace, accompanied with freedom—in the full scope and animating encouragement it gives to industry, to arts, to science, to every noble, advantageous employment, improvement, and gratification of life—besides these, the peaceful establishment of our liberty and independence opens to us far more extensive and glorious prospects; it presents us with a fair opportunity, with the noblest inducements and advantages, for converting this immense northern continent into a seat of knowledge and freedom, of agriculture and commerce, of useful arts and manufactures, of Christian piety and virtue; and thus making it an inviting and comfortable abode for many millions of the human species; an asylum for the injured and oppressed in all parts of the globe; the delight of God and good men; the joy and pride of the whole earth; soaring on the wings of literature, wealth, population, religion, virtue, and every thing that is excellent and happy, to a greater height of perfection and glory than the world has ever yet seen.

It likewise opens a door for an extensive commercial intercourse between us and all nations, and directly leads to a rapid increase of it among the various parts of the world; which is not only an inexhaustible source of wealth and opulence, but tends to expand the human mind; to introduce a reciprocation of good offices and benefits; "a general knowledge of wants, and the means of supplying them; an experimental acquaintance with the necessity and beauty of hospitality; an universal enlargement of the habits of thinking;" more rational ideas, and a more liberal administration of civil government; a better knowledge and relish of the sacred rights of humanity—all which directly conduce to humanize, refine, and exalt the human mind and manners, and carry forward mankind to a greater perfection and happiness than have yet been attained.

Our late convulsion, with its present happy termination, tends to wake up and encourage the dormant flame of liberty in all quarters of the earth—to rouse up an oppressed, enslaved world from that stupor which has so long benumbed it—to rouse it to a due inquiry into the natural rights of man, and its own disgraceful and wretched situation in tamely submitting to the deprivation of them—to open the eyes of kings and subjects to the true principles of liberty and justice, and to the absurdity and iniquity of tyranny and persecution in all their forms; and thus to lead mankind to a manly assertion, and a happy recovery and re-establishment of their civil and religious rights, and hereby open and prepare their minds for a more complete reception of the truth and grace of the gospel. Accordingly, every wheel of Providence seems to be now in motion to hasten on the downfall of tyranny, of popish superstition and bigotry, and promote the cause of freedom, knowledge, and truth.

The destruction of the whole order of Jesuits, who were the main prop of the papal power—the abolition of persecution in many European countries, particularly in France, where the present truly great and generous monarch has placed the Protestants on an equal footing with his other subjects—and in Germany, where true liberty of conscience is granted to all peaceable subjects of every denomination—the downfall of the hellish Inquisition in Spain, and the liberal institutions which begin to take place in that country, so remarkable hitherto for a blind, narrow, persecuting bigotry—the secret contempt in which almost all the learned and more knowing in popish countries are said to hold the absurdities and fooleries of that religion—the rapid progress of knowledge, and a spirit of free inquiry, of late years over the earth: these, and other similar events, form a grand chain of Providence, in which the American revolution is a principal link—a chain which is gradually drawing after it the most glorious consequences to mankind, which is hastening on the accomplishment of the Scripture prophecies relative to the millennial state, the golden age of the church and the world in the latter days. How magnificently great do the works of Jehovah toward America appear, when viewed in this light!—what complicated, extended, lasting advantages seem to be wrapped up in them, not only to many millions in this Western World, but to countless multitudes, as we trust, in various parts of the globe!

If we go on to apply the other characters or greatness enumerated above, relating to the manner in which divine favors are conferred, or deliverances wrought, we find them all emphatically verified in God's gracious manifestations toward America. For was it not a very uncommon, unexpected, unlikely spectacle, to see Heaven not only raise up and inspirit as it were an infant from its cradle, to encounter a mighty, armed giant, but to guide, aid and succeed its untaught feeble efforts, and infatuate, confound, baffle its boasting, terrible antagonist, in a manner almost unparalleled in the annals of the world? Was it not an extraordinary phenomenon in the political world, for so many distinct and distant states, so different in many respects in their education, laws, customs, manners, prejudices, and interests—not only to unite in one common cause, but to preserve and even strengthen their union amidst all the serpentine, unwearied artifices of a subtle enemy to divide them: insomuch that the very measures they took to disunite and destroy us, have uniformly operated to defeat their own designs and expectations.

Was it not a very unusual spectacle to see so young a country produce such a number of able, spirited statesmen and commanders, whose abilities and patriotism, whose equally judicious and vigorous measures, have at once saved their own country, and commanded the admiration and applause of the world?

The celebrated Lord Chatham, speaking of our first general Congress, gives them this very honorable testimony :—"I must declare and avow, that in all my reading and observation, for solidity of reasoning, force of sagacity, and wisdom of conclusion, no nation or body of men can stand in preference to the general Congress at Philadelphia." And if we turn our eyes from the cabinet to the camp, what an assemblage of wonders rises to view in our illustrious military CHIEF! A general destined by Heaven for just such a period, country, and cause as ours!—whose judiciously cautious, defensive, delaying mode of conducting this war has at once saved his own army and country, and weakened and worn down those of the enemy—a gen-

eral whose character combines all the different qualities of coolness and spirit, consummate prudence, and
proportionate vigor, the most generous tenderness and
compassion joined with the most firm, undaunted
heroism, the most patient, unshaken constancy under
heavy discouragements and sufferings, joined with a
noble spirit of enterprise on all proper occasions.

My friends, while we contemplate this great character, placed at the head of our inexperienced forces,
at such a critical, seasonable juncture—when we survey the bright constellation of heroes under him, the
subordinate officers and soldiers, whose hardships,
toils, dangers, battles, victories—whose triumphant
patience, courage, and perseverance, have instrument-
ally procured the blessings in which we now rejoice:
when we travel over the several bright stages of this
contest, from the bloody, yet victorious *Nineteenth of
April*, 1775, to the ever-memorable preservation of
our young troops, and destruction of the veteran foe,
at the battle of *Bunker-hill;* the brilliant magnificent
attacks and victories at *Trenton* and *Princeton;* the
glorious capture of two whole British armies at *Sara-
toga* and *Yorktown;* the very critical detection and
defeat of Arnold's black conspiracy, by a train of nice
and seemingly fortuitous incidents: when to all this
we add, the astonishing magnanimity, generosity and
fidelity of the king of France, the *Cyrus* of our Israel,
whose paternal, liberal, and effectual aid, afforded to
us in our low estate, so remarkably resembles the conduct of that ancient, noble prince, whom Heaven inspired, though an alien from their religion, to proclaim
and effect the great deliverance celebrated by God's
Israel in the text: when we further behold the top-

stone of this grand fabric laid, in the ratification of a
treaty of peace, which establishes our unconditional
independence, enlarges our territories, and gratifies
our highest expectations and wishes : and lastly, when
we reflect on the ill-deserving, provoking character of
the people, in a moral view, for whom Jehovah has
wrought all these wonders ; are we not constrained
to own, with raptures of grateful admiration, that the
Lord hath indeed done great things for us—that his
perfections have triumphed gloriously in our favor—
have triumphed not only over all the hostile attempts
of our foes, but over all our own increasing and crying guilt.

What then remains but that we suitably entertain
and improve these astonishing and endearing divine
manifestations in our favor? Which is the *second
thing* to be illustrated and enforced.

It becomes us then, in the first place, to ascribe the
whole glory of them to God, in imitation of the pious
pattern of the text. This is nothing more than rendering to Jehovah his due :—this is a debt, which
every sacred motive, every ingenuous principle, every
tie of gratitude, decency, and equity, forcibly urges
us to pay. For sound reason, as well as revelation,
teaches us, that all the abilities, prowess, conduct, and
success, which have guided and crowned our long
conflict, have been derived from above—from the
same Being, who raised up Moses to lead his Israel
from their *Egyptian* bondage, and Cyrus to emancipate them from their *Babylonian* servitude. It was
therefore a very foolish as well as impious speech of
an European commander in a former war, *that Providence always favors an hundred thousand men ;*

meaning, that notwithstanding the influence of Providence, the strongest army may be sure of success;—for there are a thousand contingencies, which essentially affect the health, supplies, counsels, courage, operations and success of an army, which no human sagacity can foresee, or human power control, but which are wholly determined by an omnipotent Providence. To the God of providence then let us consecrate the gladness of this day—let us return back to Him, in devout ascriptions of praise, that full tide of joy, which He is pouring into our hearts—let us say, in the language of inspiration: "I will sing unto the Lord, for he hath triumphed gloriously." "O sing unto the Lord a new song: for his right hand, and his holy arm hath gotten the victory." "The Lord reigneth: let America—let the earth rejoice: let the multitude of the isles be glad thereof."

But while we religiously adore the governing providence of Jehovah, and gratefully ascribe to him all those great events which swell our bosoms with joy, let us beware that we do not impute these signal divine appearances in our favor, to any peculiar excellence in our national character. Alas, sirs, the moral face of our country effectually confutes such a vainglorious sentiment. Crimes of the blackest hue—countless multitudes of abominations, mark the visible character of this great, this highly favored community, and still provoke the great displeasure of Heaven, while they serve as a foil to heighten and set off the triumphant freeness and riches of that goodness which has done such great things for so unworthy a people; as, on the other hand, the turpitude and guilt of our national provocations are exceedingly enhanced by those glorious manifestations of divine benevolence against which they are committed. The present occasion, then, loudly calls us to mingle the most humble penitence and contrition with our joyful gratitude and praise; and, indeed, there can be no truly grateful and holy joy in the goodness of God, without true humility, repentance and reformation, for its foundation, companion and fruit; for humble, godly sorrow and thankful joy, mutually beget, and strengthen, and keep pace with each other; and no people, however highly favored in external respects, have any sure ground or warrant, or, indeed, any present moral capacity or meetness for the exercise of true rejoicing in the divine goodness, while persisting in an impenitent course of rebellion against him.

These considerations call upon us to rejoice with trembling, with humility, with a sober, cautious, serious air, in opposition to all levity, pride, vainglory, sensuality, carnal confidence and security. While we rejoice in the divine beneficence, let us remember that for his own sake he hath done these great things; not for any righteousness in us; not merely that we might enjoy the exultation of victory and peace, or the pride of independence and empire; but that his own name may be exalted, that his own great designs, hinted above, of glorifying Himself, and extending the kingdom of His Son, may be carried into effect: and though he has been using us, in the late revolution, as instruments of carrying forward this glorious and benevolent plan, yet, if we ourselves *mean not so*—if in our hearts and practice we are opposed to his interests and glory—if we as a people continue to fight against Him, after such great displays as he has made of Himself before our eyes—if we abuse the blessings of returning peace and public felicity to greater wantoness in sin, to nourish a spirit of pride, ambition, luxury, dissipation, venality, infidelity, and other concomitant vices : in this case our very prosperity will finally destroy us in the most aggravated manner, and God will promote the designs of his glory in our exemplary ruin, as he has now been doing in our surprising salvation.

These ideas may well give a solemnity to our joy, and cause it to flow in the channel, and bring forth the fruits, of true holiness. Oh let us exhibit our praises, not in word only, but in deed and in truth; let us testify the cordial sincerity of our joys and thanksgiving on this occasion, by a practical, steady conformity and obedience to that great and good Being whom we profess to extol ; and, let me add, by generous testimonies of our esteem and gratitude for those whose toils, dangers, and suﬀerings have eminently contributed to our present security and happiness; let our grateful love to the infinite Author flow down and flow out, in suitable proportions, to the honored instruments of these inestimable benefits. Let those men who have stood forth in the foremost rank of danger, and made the greatest private sacrifices to the public cause, whether in the senate or in the field—whether at home or in foreign climes—let these live in our hearts; let their names and heroic deeds live and shine in our grateful annals, till time shall be swallowed up in eternity. Let us be eager to recompense their important labor of love for us and our children, and for the unborn millions of our future descendants. Let us welcome the suffering soldier to the bosom of a free and peaceful country, with tears of gratitude and smiles of applause—let us gladly divide with him those sweets of independence and wealth which his gallantry and wounds have secured to us. Let us fly to sooth the griefs and wipe away the tears of the many widows and orphans which this cruel war has made, and to relieve the mortifying distresses of poverty into which it has plunged many of our meritorious citizens.

Let us gladly contribute our share toward fulfilling the engagements of the public, to all that have credited or in any way assisted it, whether our own citizens or foreigners; and instead of complaining of the load of debt which lies upon us, let us bless God that the great object of our long struggle is obtained at so cheap a rate; that our burden, however pressing, is light, compared either with the value of the acquisition, or with the insupportable load which must have fallen upon us and crushed us into ruin had we been reunited to Great Britain; let us be willing to sacrifice the paltry yet expensive pleasures and parade of luxury, prodigality, vain magnificence, and other impoverishing though fashionable vices, and practise frugality, industry, humility, and moderation, with the whole train of private and patriotic virtues; then, by the blessing of God, we may hope that our country will ere long be delivered from every embarrassing difficulty which retards her progress toward the zenith of perfection, and will become an ample theatre for the last and most glorious displays of the divine benevolence to the human species. Who, that loves his country or mankind, can help exulting in so glorious a prospect, and wishing to see it speedily realized?

That it may be so, O thou great Arbiter of the nations, who hast done such great things for us, still guard, maintain, and perfect the magnificent structure which thine own hand hath reared in this western world! Grant that here may ever dwell the uncorrupted faith, the pure worship, the benevolent, peaceful virtues of primitive Christianity, extending their benign influences to the utmost bounds of this vast continent, and causing the wilderness and waste places of America to blossom like the rose, and flourish as the garden of God! May this infant empire, this new-born nation, live in thy sight! May it grow and flourish under thy almighty patronage, in every thing that is great, good, and happy, till all the states and empires of the world shall be absorbed in the everlasting kingdom of thy Son!

JOHN RODGERS, D. D.

Doctor Rodgers was born in Boston, Massachusetts, on the second day of August, 1727. At an early age, being a frequent listener to the eloquence of the pious Whitefield, his mind became impressed with the importance of religion, and he commenced his preparation for the duties of the Church. His teacher was the eminent Doctor Blair, one of the most learned, pious and venerable men of his day. Under his tuition, he was soon enabled to preach, and at twenty-two he was ordained at St. George's, Delaware, where he remained in the exercise of great usefulness until 1765. At that time he went to New York, and on the death of Doctor Bostwick he was called to fill his place in the Wall street Presbyterian Church. In this position he remained for many years. The sacred functions of his office were exercised with purity, simplicity and truth. Though he had not the aid of a collegiate education, which circumstance he often regretted, he possessed a rich vein of pulpit eloquence, accompanied with irresistible energy and pre-eminent zeal in the cause of Christianity, which placed him high on the list of the most distinguished ministers of his time.

Doctor Rodgers possessed a retentive memory, and

was a great textuarian. The strength of the solemn truths he wished to enforce were always supported with a torrent of scriptural testimony, which carried irresistible conviction to the minds of his hearers. The natural powers of his mind were only exceeded by his piety and zeal. Convinced of his piety toward God, and benevolence toward his fellow-men, he shone auspiciously in the general conduct of his life, and secured the warm affections of the church over which he presided, with the commanding dignity which the consciousness of the sacredness of his high charge naturally inspired.

He survived the greatest part of his usefulness, and, when his faculties had fallen into decay from the languor of age, humbly retired, impressed with the sense of duty, into the humble vale of private life.* He died on the seventh of May, 1811, universally beloved and respected by his fellow-citizens.

---

* *Public Advertiser*, May 9, 1811.

DIVINE GOODNESS DISPLAYED.*

The Lord hath done great things for us, whereof we are glad.

PSALM cxxvi. 3.

THE subject of this divine poem, from whence I have taken my text, not obscurely points us to the occasion on which it was penned. It was the return of the Jews from their captivity in Babylon. This is what is meant by "the captivity of Zion," in the first verse.

It is generally supposed, and with great probability, that the prophet Ezra was its inspired penman. The first verse expresses the effect this signal deliverance of his people had upon them: "When the Lord turned again the captivity of Zion, we were like unto men that dream."† It was so great and unexpected an event, that they could not, at first, believe it was real. But they soon found it was real, however great; and, in consequence thereof, were filled with the most sincere joy and gratitude to God. "Then was our mouth filled with laughter, and our tongue with singing."‡ Such was the nature of this deliverance, that the heathen nations around them took notice of it. "Then said they among the heathen, The Lord hath done great things for them."§ It is no uncommon thing for our God so to effect the salvation of his people, as to attract the attention and force the acknowledgments of

---

* "The Divine Goodness Displayed in the American Revolution;" a Sermon, preached in New York, December 11, 1780, appointed by Congress as a day of public thanksgiving throughout the United States.

† Verse 1.   ‡ Verse 2.   § Verse 2, latter part.

their enemies themselves. But, however they may treat it, those who are the subjects of God's delivering goodness, at any time or in any way, ought to notice it with care, and acknowledge his hand in it with gratitude of heart. Thus did the people of God of old, and thus are we taught to do in the words of our text: "The Lord hath done great things for us, whereof we are glad."

You will readily perceive, my brethren, with what ease and propriety the words of our text apply to the design and the duties of this day. They contain the very language the God of Providence has put into our mouths, and teach us that notice we are to take of the dealings of his gracious hand toward us.

If you will please to attend, I will

I. Point you to some of the great things our God has done for us; and for which we have cause to be glad this day.

II. Show how we ought to manifest this gladness.

I. Let us consider some of those great things our God has done for us; and which it becomes us to acknowledge this day.

These are different, according to the different points of view in which we consider ourselves: either as the creatures of his hand; as sinners, under a dispensation of grace; or as the members of society. But to enter into a particular consideration of each of these would be as vain as to attempt to count the stars in the firmament, or number the sands on the sea-shore. You will expect, therefore, but a very few of the numerous instances of the great things our Lord has done for us.

1. He has given us his son, Jesus Christ, to redeem

14

us from the curse of his broken law; and open the way for our return to the favor of heaven, which we had lost by sin. And who that attends to the inestimable value of this gift of God; the character of the persons for whom he was given; the nature of the work for which he gave him; and the rich and numerous benefits that flow to our race from God through him; but feels the force of the apostolic remark: "Herein is love; not that we loved God, but that he loved us, and sent his Son to be the propitiation for our sins."* Surely God has done great things for us in this unspeakable gift of a Saviour.

2. He has opened a treaty of peace with us through the mediation of this his incarnate son. He is "God in Christ, reconciling the world unto himself; not imputing their trespasses unto them."† This treaty he is negotiating in and by the ministry of the gospel; which is therefore styled: "The ministry of reconciliation."‡

I am well aware that the ministry of the gospel, however judiciously and faithfully discharged, is esteemed by many as the Israelites esteemed their manna of old; but as a light thing. They do not consider there is not a faithful minister of Christ, whatever may be his particular denomination, or wherever he may be employed, but his gifts and grace cost the Son of God his blood upon the cross; or a single gospel sermon they hear, or might hear and neglect, but what our Lord purchased with his expiring groans on Mount Calvary. And this is the reason why the ministry of the gospel is ranked, by

---

* 1 John iv. 10.   † 2 Cor. v. 19.   ‡ Verse 18.

the apostle of the gentiles, among the richest of our Lord's ascension gifts.*

Thus it appears, God does great things for a country or a people, when he blesses them with a judicious and faithful administration of his word, and ordinances; however the more ignorant, or profane part of mankind, may esteem it.

3. He gives us his Holy Spirit, for the rendering this word and these ordinances effectual, for the great purposes for which they are instituted. Thus they become. "the power of God, and the salvation of God, to them that believe." Such is the ignorance and depravity of human nature, that they will be all unavailing, unless rendered successful by this divine agent.

Hence we hear the evangelical prophet complaining, "Who hath believed our report, and to whom is the arm of the Lord revealed?"† And it is worthy of our notice, that our Lord himself, was far from being so successful in his ministry, as might have been expected, seeing, "he taught as man never taught." Multitudes who heard him, not only continued unbelieving, but blasphemed him and his doctrine. This was, no doubt, wisely ordered, for the support of his faithful ministers, in every age; who for reasons, worthy of God, though not known to us labor so much in vain.

But this serves to illustrate the necessity of the operations of the spirit of grace, for rendering the ordinances of the gospel successful; and at the same

---

* See Eph. iv. 8, 11, 12, comp.
† Is. liii. 1.

time highly illustrates, what great things God has done for us, by appointing him to this important office.

4. God does great things for his people, when his spirit applies the redemption of Christ to their precious souls. Then it is their sins are pardoned, and they receive a title to the inheritance of the saints in light. Then it is, they become "the children of God by faith in Christ Jesus."* Then it is, they are renewed in the spirit of their minds; and that good work begun in them that shall be perfected to the day of the Lord Jesus. "Happy is that people, that are in such a case; yea, happy is that people whose God is the Lord."†

But it is time I should proceed to observe, God has done great things for us, if we consider ourselves as members of society. This is one of the most interesting points of view in which man can be considered; and a point of view, in which much is required of us, and much is done for us. This is the point of view in which the Psalmist principally considers himself, and the church of Israel, when he exclaims exulting in the text : "The Lord hath done great things for us, whereof we are glad." And this is the point of view in which we are especially to consider ourselves this day. And were we to take a particular survey of what God has done for us, as members of society, we should be led to consider the many blessings, spiritual and temporal, we enjoy, either as the church of God, or as citizens of the state. But this would be a subject too copious for our time.

---

* Gal. iii. 26.   † Psalm cxliv. 15.

I shall call your attention, therefore, to those things only, which our God has done for us, as a people struggling for our inestimable privileges. This best accords to the design of the day.

And it may be truly said, the Lord has done great things for us, in this point of view; whether we consider the ends he has accomplished for us, or the means by which he has accomplished them.

I. Let us briefly consider the ends, the great ends, God has accomplished for us. He has graciously and fully defeated the designs the court of Britain had formed to deprive us of our liberties. They had laid their plans with such art as to deceive the nation into favorable sentiments of their measures, and thus led them to aid in the accomplishment of their purposes. I need not here repeat the measures pursued by them for this end. They are too recent to be forgotten by us.

The warding off this blow, was all we at first thought of. The redress of these grievances, which their unconstitutional acts of Parliament laid upon us, was the only object we had first in view. And oh, with what joy and gratitude of heart, would we have received this at their hands, any time before the beginning of the summer of 1776.

But this is not all heaven has done for us! He has broken our connection with that people, long practised in the arts of venality, and grown old in scenes of corruption. He has fully delivered us from all their unjust claims and future practices upon us; and given us a place among the kingdoms of the world. We have, under the auspices of his holy providence, risen into existence as a people, and taken our station among the nations and the empires of the earth!—an event of such magnitude, that it forms a new era in the history of mankind. And we have nothing to do now, but wisely improve this event, to render it a fruitful source of happiness to ourselves and millions yet unborn.

Little did we think of such an event as this, when we began the struggle for our invaded privileges. The growing injustice of the British administration; their accumulated injuries opened it upon us, and forced us into the measure, as the only alternative to save our oppressed land. It was this, or the most abject slavery! A dread alternative, indeed, at which every bosom, at first beat with terror; but which an all-governing Providence has wisely overruled for our salvation! Surely our God has done great things for us!

But this will appear still more clear, if,

II. We attend to some of the ways, the means, in and by which God has effected these great things for us.

But where shall I begin, or where shall I end here? The subject is so copious, that I can but barely glance at the few following particulars.

The early and just alarm our country took at the measures pursued by the British court toward us, strongly points us to the watchful care of a kind Providence over us. The unanimity in opposing these measures that prevailed among the then colonies, and among all ranks and degrees of their respective inhabitants, with a very few exceptions indeed, is another remarkable display of the kindness of heaven toward us.

It is true, both these were the native effects of the

unconcealed designs of the court of Britain upon our liberties, and the manifest injustice of their claims. But this strongly marks the hand of Heaven—that they should be left to act a part so undisguised and impolitic, and therefore so calculated to alarm, when they could have effected their purposes with unspeakably more ease, with less expense, and with a moral certainty of success, without giving any alarm at all, unless it had been to the sagacious few. And, as if the avowal of their designs was not sufficient to alarm and unite us, they did not hesitate to enforce these claims, by all the terrors of the sword. Thus we were called to resistance, and obliged to resistance, by the principles of self-preservation—that first law of nature. Their violence awakened those fears, and armed those resentments, that their artifice could not reach. Heaven designed our emancipation, and therefore left them to act the part best calculated to effect it.

Again, the appointment of proper men, by the then several colonies, to meet in Congress, to consult respecting the general interests and defence of the whole, was a measure of the highest importance. And the prudence and firmness of the measures pursued by them exhibit the fullest evidence of the wisdom of that august body, and the kindness of Providence in directing them thereto.

The military ardor, in defence of our privileges, that inspired all ranks, from the one end of the continent to the other, deserves our careful notice here. Into what but the hand of Heaven can we resolve that military enthusiasm that seized our country, and spread like a rolling flame from colony to colony?—bosom catching fire from bosom, and thus pouring forth an army, sufficient to make a most respectable resistance against the enemy (for so we must now call them through the remaining part of the war), wherever they came forth against us. In evidence of this, you will please to recollect the manly resistance they met with at Lexington, where the first American blood was shed in the controversy, April 19th, 1775—the well-fought battle of Bunker Hill, so fatal to the British troops, on the 17th of June following; and the confining their whole army within the town of Boston and its environs, for near a year from this time, by a set of raw, undisciplined men, till they were obliged to steal away, with precipitation and shame.

The northern expedition in the fall of this same year, under the brave General Montgomery—the taking St. John's, Chamblée, and Montreal—in a word, the over-running the whole province of Canada, and laying siege to the city of Quebec* itself, by this new raised army, exhibit another lively display of this military ardor.

Allow me to add, for the event is memorable, of the same kind is the gallant and successful defence of Fort Moultrie, on Sullivan's Island, in South Carolina, in the month of June, the following year. By this event, truly glorious to the American troops that defended it, and equally reproachful to the British forces that attacked that unfinished fortress, the town of Charlestown, and thus the whole state of South Carolina, were

---

* At this siege fell, greatly and deservedly lamented, the gallant Montgomery, his aide-de-camp, Major John Macpherson, a most amiable and accomplished young gentleman, and the brave Captain Cheeseman, of New York.

saved from falling into the enemy's hands. Had that southern expedition succeeded against us, that year, you will easily perceive the baleful influence it must have had upon our affairs, at that early period of the war.

The providing a proper person to take command of the American army, is none of the least of the displays of the goodness of God to us, in this struggle. How judicious, how heaven-directed the choice of Congress in this matter! You all know the illustrious Washington was the man on whom their unanimous choice fell—the man whom Heaven had raised up, for the great business of leading our armies, and saving his country—the man in whom all the states, and all ranks in these states, have so happily, and so justly reposed the most entire confidence. But the interest had by this great man, in the esteem and the confidence of those he commanded, through the course of the war, both Americans and foreigners, illustrates in a signal manner, the goodness of God to our country, in raising him to this elevated station; and at the same time illustrates his great personal merit. But, above all, the event demonstrates both these.

The kindness of Heaven also in providing officers of an inferior rank to command our armies in one department and another, deserves our grateful notice. We have had officers of different ranks who have highly merited of their country during the course of this severe and eventful war, and who stood justly entitled to their gratitude and their remembrance.*

---

* The early and active part which that illustrious young nobleman, the Marquis de Lafayette, took in our cause, and the eminent services he has rendered us, both with his court and nation, and in the field, justly entitle him to the warmest gratitude of every American.

14*

But this army, thus collected and thus commanded, had neither arms, ammunition, or military skill, to oppose the formidable enemy that came forth against us. But how conspicuous the hand of Heaven, in providing us with all these from time to time.

The contempt with which our enemies treated us in the beginning of this struggle, led them into a system of conduct ruinous to themselves, and at the same time greatly advantageous to us in all these several points of view. There are two things that deserve our notice upon this head—their making their first attack upon the Eastern colonies (for so they were at that time), instead of the Southern, and particularly their attacking the well-peopled and brave province of Massachusetts Bay. Had they gone with equal numbers against any of the three Southern colonies at that time, the events that afterward took place in the course of the war show with what ease they would have possessed themselves of them, and, at least, prevented their joining in the general union, and thus prevented their emancipation. To this I may add, the smallness of the army they at first sent out against us. They thought a few thousand men would effect their purpose; which gave us leisure, after the commencement of hostilities, to prepare, in all the above respects, for opposing and defeating them. They themselves contributed not a little, during this period, to teach us the art of war: and after we had taught them to fear us, and they had, in consequence of this fear, augmented their numbers to more than a sufficiency to crush us, their pusillanimous caution was, in the hand of Heaven, no small mean of our salvation. Witness their conduct during the summer and fall of 1776.

This system of pusillanimity, among many other instances of that campaign, was shamefully conspicuous, in their suffering the retreat of our army, not half their number, from Long Island, two nights after the battle of the twenty-seventh of August, that year. And while the secrecy and expedition with which this retreat was conducted, do the highest honor to the military talents of our great commander and his brave officers, its success, and the signal interpositions of Providence that contributed thereto, exhibit a most lively display of the guardianship of Heaven over us and our liberties.*

* This retreat was determined upon in a council of war, in the afternoon of the day before it took place; and the more effectually to cover the design from the army themselves, and the enemy, in case of information by deserters, the militia, then on the island, were ordered over immediately, as if to provide them with shelter in the city, from the heavy rains then falling, as they had no tents.

The embarkation of the troops was committed to Major-General M'Dougall, then a brigadier, who was upon the spot at Brooklyn ferry, at eight o'clock, the hour fixed upon for the commencement of this important movement; but, to his great mortification, he found the militia had not yet embarked. The getting them over protracted the time till between ten and eleven o'clock. In the mean time, about nine o'clock, or a little after, the tide of ebb made, and the wind blew strong at north-east, which, adding to the rapidity of the tide, rendered it impossible to effect the retreat in the course of the night, with the number of row-boats they could command, and the state of the wind and tide put it out of their power to make any use of their sail-boats. The brigadier sent Colonel Grayson, one of the commander-in-chief's aids, who attended him on that occasion, to report to his excellency their embarrassed situation, and gave it as his opinion that the retreat was impracticable that night. The colonel returned shortly after, not being able to find the commander-in-chief; on which, the brigadier went on with the embarkation under all these discouragements. But about eleven o'clock the wind died away, and soon after sprung up at south-west,

Who that reflects upon the dark scenes through which we passed, from the period now before us till the glorious battle of Trenton, December 26th following (and dark indeed they were)—who that considers the awful poise in which the fate of America then hung, destruction awaiting us on every side—and at the same time considers the complicated difficulties and hazards that attended that well-timed enterprise, with its signal success and extensive consequences—can help exclaiming, in the language of our text, "The Lord hath done great things for us?"

Think also, my brethren, of the masterly movement of our great general and his little army from the vicinity of Trenton a few nights after, by which he escaped the fangs of a greatly superior and enraged enemy. This grand military manœuvre, and the successful battle of Princeton next morning, which spread such dismay among the enemy, delivered the whole of West Jersey from their ravages, and drove them back with precipitation and terror to the banks of the

---

and blew fresh, which rendered the sail-boats of use, and at the same time, rendered the passage from the island to the city direct, easy and expeditious. By this means, the whole army, nine thousand in number, with all the field artillery and such heavy ordnance as was of most value, were got over safe by daylight, except the covering party; and not long after day broke, a heavy fog rose, and hovering over the heights of Brooklyn, concealed this party from the notice of the enemy, notwithstanding their vicinity to our works, by which means they also effected their retreat without interruption.

Had it not been for this providential shifting of the wind, not more than half the army could possibly have got over, and the remainder, with a number of the general officers and all the heavy ordnance, at least, must inevitably have fallen into the enemy's hands.

Raritan, to which they were confined, till they were obliged to abandon the state.*

The American army by a variety of casualties, during two campaigns, being now reduced to a shadow; the raising a new army; the making the necessary provision for the feeding, clothing and paying them; the keeping them together in the face of countless difficulties, with which both country and army had to struggle; the unexampled patience and perseverance of this patriot band, under every hardship, arising from cold and hunger, poverty, nakedness and neglect; and, above all, their astonishing success, from time to time; aided, indeed, by the brave militia of the country, ever ready when called upon, so clearly point us to the finger of God, that it would be unpardonable

---

* I need not inform those who are acquainted with the ground occupied by our army when this movement was determined upon, how perilous their situation! To all human appearance, they must have been completely taken, or cut to pieces before noon next day, had it not been effected. Which leads me to mention a providence that contributed to its accomplishment that deserves our notice. The weather had been very moist for some days, which rendered the ground so soft, and the roads and fields they had to pass so deep, that they were scarcely passable for the field-pieces and other carriages necessarily attendant upon the army, which must have rendered their march extremely difficult and slow, if at all practicable. But the weather cleared up in the evening, became very cold, and froze so severely, that the ground became sufficiently hard before the hour fixed upon to bear both men and carriages without the least inconveniency; and this gave a plausible pretext for that line of fires the commander-in-chief caused to be kindled soon after dark in the front of his army, the true design of which was to conceal him and his movements from the notice of the enemy, and induce them to believe he was still there waiting for them till morning. For this purpose, the men appointed to the business kept the fires in full blaze till break of day, and both these important ends were fully answered by the stratagem.

stupidity not to notice it and the basest ingratitude not to acknowledge it.

Think also this day, of the battle of Bennington, in the month of August, 1777, the first dawn of prosperity upon our affairs, in that quarter—and of the gallant and successful defence of Fort Schuyler. Think of the capture of General Burgoyne and his whole army, in the month of October, that same year. And the confining the British army within Philadelphia, during their possession of that city, notwithstanding their great superiority to our army in point of numbers, and their great advantages over them, in every other respect, save only in the goodness of their cause, and their military virtue. Think also of their evacuation of that city, unable to hold it full nine months, after all their immense expense of treasure and labor, and their no small loss of blood in taking it.* And of the battle of Monmouth, ten days after, by which they were driven back with disgrace, into this city. And "hath not the Lord done great things for us?"

I might here mention the evacuation of Rhode Island, in the month of October, 1779; by which they abandoned the conquest of the eastern states, as hopeless, at the end of four years and six months' fruitless toil for this purpose. And the severe repulse they met with, in their descent upon the eastern parts of New Jersey, in the summer of 1780; principally by the brave militia of that state. But our time does not admit of recounting all the various instances of success, with which Providence was pleased to bless

---

* Philadelphia was taken September 27th, 1777, and evacuated June 18th, 1778.

our arms, during this severe conflict; nor even of enumerating all his kind interpositions in our favor.

I may not, however, omit the providential discovery of that infernal plot, laid by the basest of traitors, for the delivering our strong-holds on the Hudson River, into the hands of the enemy, in the month of September of that year. This discovery was so seasonable, and even critical, and the evils from which our country was hereby saved, were so many and so great, that we may truly say: "The Lord hath done great things for us."

But it is time we should pass to the Southern states, whose deliverance out of the hands of our enemies, when so fully possessed by them, illustrates, in a striking manner, the great things our God has done for us. Here the American army, and the gallant militia of that country, exhibited the most astonishing examples of patience, perseverance and fortitude; and their success was the reward of their signal military virtue. Recollect here the battle of King's Mountain, September 1780, where Providence began to smile upon our arms in that quarter; the memorable victory of Morgan over Tarleton, at the Cowpens, January 17th, 1781; and his remarkable escape, with his prisoners, from the pursuing vengeance of Lord Cornwallis and his whole army.* Recollect, too, the

---

* Immediately after the battle was over, General Morgan, without loss of time, set out for North Carolina and Virginia, with his prisoners, to the number of five hundred, apprehensive that Lord Cornwallis, who lay with his army at no great distance, would attempt a rescue. In this he was not mistaken. His lordship, without delay, destroyed his heavy baggage, and pursued the fleeing victor. And being able to march with greater expedition than Morgan, encumbered with so many prisoners,

well-fought battles of Guilford Court-House, and the Eutaw Springs, with the delivery of the enemy's strong posts, in those states, into our hands, the one after the other, until the states themselves were totally and finally rescued from their domination. Can you review these scenes, to-day, and not acknowledge, with gratitude of heart, that "The Lord hath done great things for us?"

But one of the most signal displays of the great things our God did for us, in that quarter, is yet unnoticed. You will easily understand me as alluding to the capture of Lord Cornwallis and his army, in the month of October, 1781. There were so many events, the taking place of which, and the combination of which, were necessary to the accomplishment of this end; and these events so entirely dependent upon Providence—so wholly out of the reach of human wisdom to direct, or of human power to effect or combine, that the hand of the Lord was eminently conspicuous in them. Shall I mention the following, without enlarging? Lord Cornwallis taking post at York and Gloucester, the most favorable position in all that country for besieging him so as to secure him from escaping. The seasonable arrival of the French fleet commanded by the brave Count de

---

gained upon him. Morgan crossed the Catawba, if I am rightly informed, the evening of the second day; he passed it, however, without difficulty, and encamped on the north side of the river. A few hours after his lordship came to the river, and found it so swelled with rains that had fallen in the mountains, though they had none there, that he could not pass it. And being detained two days, notwithstanding all his efforts to get over, General Morgan, in the mean time, escaped with his prisoners out of his reach.

Grasse, so as to prevent his lordship's escape by sea, when he must have discovered he was the object of our illustrious commander's movements. The defeat of the British fleet on the fifth of September, off the mouth of the Chesapeake, when they attempted to throw in succors to his lordship's relief; or, it may be, take him off. The remarkably opportune arrival of the Count de Barras' squadron from Rhode Island, after having been in the utmost danger of falling in with the British fleet, and becoming a prey to their superior force. This gave the fleet of our allies so decided a superiority over the enemy as to cut off all hope of, relief from them. And, lastly, the safe arrival of General Washington, with the allied army under his command, after a march of five hundred miles in that hot season of the year, at the very juncture it was proper to commence their offensive operations. The entire harmony that existed in the allied army, notwithstanding their difference in language and manners, and what is more, their difference in religion, and their former national prejudices, is an event that also deserves our notice; especially considering the influence it must have had on the glorious issue of the campaign. And what was it our Lord did for us by all this? He hereby delivered into our hands an army of seven thousand two hundred and forty-seven chosen troops; the flower of the British army in America, and under the command of the most enterprising general they had upon the continent, with a large train of artillery, and all their military stores.

And what renders this Providence the more remarkable is, that it was the second British army God delivered into our hands during the war; an instance scarcely to be paralleled in history, that two whole armies, with all their military apparatus, should be thus completely taken in the course of four years. Thus it was God taught our enemies, that America was not to be conquered by the power of the sword: and hath not the Lord done great things for us?

It has been frequently remarked, and with great justice, that the goodness of God, in the great things he has done for us, has been not a little enhanced, by the seasonable manner in which he has often interposed in our behalf. When our affairs have worn the darkest aspect, then it was God has appeared for our relief." "In the mount of the Lord it has been often seen." Witness the winter of 1776, just before the memorable and critical battle of Trenton, already mentioned—the summer of 1777, just after the loss of Ticonderoga and its dependencies—and the winter of 1777, when Heaven provided the seasonable and powerful alliance with France, in our favor.

It also deserves our notice, that the means on which our enemies placed the highest dependence for accomplishing their purposes, had almost uniformly the directly contrary effect. This was remarkably the case respecting the cruelties exercised upon us, from time to time, in wantonly burning our towns; laying waste some of our richest frontier settlements, by the savages of the wilderness; murdering our citizens; burning and otherwise destroying so many of our churches, and the like.* They designed and expected by all these

* It is much to be lamented, that the troops of a nation that has been considered as one of the bulwarks of the reformation, should act as if

to break our spirits, and terrify us into submission, but their never-failing effect was, to rouse and animate the country into a more vigorous and determined opposition.

These addresses to our fears, as if we were capable of no more generous principle of action ; this treatment of us as slaves, excited our indignation and our contempt, as well as our resentment—our indignation at the insult hereby offered us ; and our contempt of the men who showed such ignorance of human nature, in its present state of improvement. They hereby taught us their utter incapacity to govern us, both in point of

---

they had waged war with the God whom Christians adore. They have, in the course of this war, utterly destroyed more than fifty places of public worship in these states. Most of these they burnt; others they leveled with the ground, and in some places left not a vestige of their former situation; while they have wantonly defaced, or rather destroyed others, by converting them into barracks, jails, hospitals, riding-schools, &c. Boston, Newport, Philadelphia, and Charlestown, all furnished melancholy instances of this prostitution and abuse of the houses of God. And of the nineteen places of public worship in New York, when the war began, there were but nine fit for use when the British troops left it. It is true, Trinity Church and the old Lutheran were destroyed by the fire that laid waste so great a part of the city a few nights after the enemy took possession of it: and therefore they are not charged with *designedly* burning them, though they were the occasion of it; for there can be no doubt, after all that malice has said to the contrary, but the fire was occasioned by the carelessness of their people, and they prevented its more speedy extinguishment. But the ruinous situation in which they left two of the Low Dutch Reformed Churches, the three Presbyterian Churches, the French Protestant Church, the Anabaptist Church, and the Friends' new meeting-house, was the effect of design, and strongly marks their enmity to those societies. It will cost many thousand pounds sterling to put them in the repair they were when the war commenced. They were all neat buildings, and some of them elegant.

wisdom and virtue; for all this was no doubt done by order of their rulers. And thus they taught us, too, the necessity of maintaining our independence, or perishing in the struggle.

I have only to remark farther here, that the successes of our enemies, have, in more instances than one, proved the very snares in which they have afterward been taken. Of this their taking Ticonderoga, in July, 1777, just noticed; and their boasted victory at Guilford Court-House, North Carolina, March 15th, 1781, are illustrious instances.

Again, the formation and completion of that social compact among these states, which is usually styled the Confederation, is another instance of the great things our God has done for us. This is that which gives us a national existence and character. Previous to this great event, we had no permanent union among ourselves; nor were we considered by the other powers of the earth, as a people, a nation, distinct from that from which we had so lately separated. By this event the THIRTEEN UNITED STATES, though so different in situation, customs and manners, and, in many respects local interests, became *one people*. Their interests, however different, are hereby united and consolidated into *one common interest;* and they stand jointly and severally pledged to each other, for the united defence of the respected rights of every distinct state, and the common rights and privileges of the whole body. And this teaches us, by the way, the *sacred* obligation each state is under, and every individual in each state, to support and strengthen this federal bond, and to give it energy and efficiency, to the utmost of his power. Our ALL, under Providence, depends upon this.

Once more, God's raising us up such powerful friends among the nations of the earth, who have so generously espoused our cause, is another instance of the great things he hath done for us, during the late war. I need not remind you here, how unable we were, in every point of view, to contend with the mighty nation that had made war upon us. But so had the God of providence ordered matters in the course of events, that it was the decided interest of the great nation who first took us by the hand, and indeed of all the maritime powers of Europe, to favor our cause. They, it is true, acted upon the principles of human policy; but that God whose kingdom rules over all, was hereby accomplishing his own great and gracious purposes, respecting these states.

Another instance of the divine goodness to us, and which we may not pass unnoticed, is, his providing us in New York with so good a constitution, for the securing our inestimable rights and privileges. I do not say it has not its imperfections; but it is upon the the whole, equalled by few, and surpassed by none of the constitutions of the sister states, in wisdom, justice, and sound policy. The rights of conscience both in faith and worship, are fully secured to every denomination of Christians. No one denomination in the state, or in any of the states, have it in their power to oppress another. They all stand upon the same common level in point of religious privileges. Nor is this confined to Christians only. The Jews, also, which is their undoubted right, have the liberty of worshiping God in that way they think most acceptable to him. No man is excluded from the rights of citizenship on account of his religious profession. Nor ought he to be.

What great things has the God of Providence done for our race! By the revolution we this day celebrate, he has provided an asylum for the oppressed, in all the nations of the earth, whatever may be the nature of the oppression. And that, while he is hereby accomplishing these great things, that are opening the way for the more general spread of the gospel in its purity and power; and in due time, the universal establishment of the Messiah's kingdom in all its benign efficacy in the hearts and lives of men. Interesting events that lie before us, in the grand system of Providence! How glorious the prospects which these scenes open upon human nature! But our time forbids the pursuing them.

Lastly, God has done great things for us, by that *honorable* and I may add *glorious peace*, by which he has terminated the late unnatural war. In whatever point of view we consider this event, it is all as important as we now represent it. It has closed a truly tragic scene in our country. It has secured to us *all* we have ever claimed or contended for in any stage of the war. *The fullest possession of absolute sovereignty, independent of the crown and people of Great Britain ; or any other power upon earth.*

We are hereby put in possession of a most extensive and fertile territory, abounding with every article necessary for the support or convenience of its inhabitants; a territory that furnishes the richest plenty of materials for every kind of the mechanic arts; and all the various articles necessary for the most extended commerce with all the nations of the earth.

The exhausted state in which this great event found our country, and the short time in which God has effected all this for us, not a little enhance the mercy. Not quite eight years, if we compute the time from the first commencement of hostilities between Britain and us, to the ratifying of the provisional treaty. This is a less time than that in which the states of Holland, in their glorious struggle with Spain, dared so much as lay claim to independence.

There is not an instance in history, within my recollection, of so great a revolution being effected in so short a time, and with so little loss of lives and property, as that in which we this day rejoice.

It is true it has cost us both blood and treasure; but if you consider the magnitude of the object for which we have been contending, the unequal terms on which we commenced and pursued the contest, and its glorious issues, now fully secured to us by the definitive treaty, these are less, much less, than we had a right to expect.

There is one circumstance that has had no small influence on the speedy accomplishment of this happy event, that must not be omitted; I mean the impoverished state of Britain, *as a nation*, notwithstanding her great resources, and the princely wealth of many of her subjects. Her national debt had grown to so enormous a height, that all the revenues of the kingdom, though improved by the highest arts of financing, are scarcely equal to the discharge of the annual interest, and the charges of collecting them.

Had it not been for this enormous, and this accumulating debt, which shook their national credit, they would not have so readily listened to terms of pacification with us, much less would they have given us the advantageous and honorable terms we have obtained.

Thus, that God whose kingdom rules over all, has been laying the foundation of this empire ever since the days of the illustrious William III.; for it was in his reign the foundation of this ruinous debt was laid, and laid by the friends of liberty in that day.

And now, my brethren, put all these things together, and may we not say with the greatest propriety : "The Lord hath done great things for us, whereof we are glad ?" Which leads me to

II. Show you how we ought to manifest this gladness of heart for all the great things our God has done for us. And here we must necessarily be very brief.

1. By a careful notice of them.

Not to notice these interesting events, and especially not to mark the hand of the Lord in them, would be both stupidity and ingratitude. They address us in the following language of inspiration : "The Lord reigneth, let the earth rejoice; let the multitude of the isles be glad thereof. Clouds and darkness are round about him; righteousness and judgment are the habitation of his throne."* This is one of the most instructive ways by which the Lord Jehovah is teaching us his being and perfections, his character and government.

2. By recounting them before God with joy and gratitude of heart. This was the frequent and instructive practice of the inspired Psalmist, respecting the deliverance of the people of Israel out of Egypt, and their peaceful settlement in the land of Canaan. You have repeated instances of this in the Book of

---

* Psalm xcvii. 1, 2.

Psalms. The song of Moses at the Red Sea is another instance of the same kind. And this leads me to remark the propriety of setting apart particular times and seasons for this important business—the Christian's setting apart seasons for it in private, and thus making it a part of the devotions of the closet. And it is admirably calculated to raise and promote a spirit of truly Christian devotion. And communities setting apart particular days, on proper occasions, for the same purpose. Of this kind is the day we now celebrate. They are tokens of national gratitude, and no improper way of expressing it.

3. By psalms and songs of praise to God for all these great things. The expressing our gratitude to God for his goodness, by songs of praise, is a natural and an ancient custom that has the sanction of divine authority. It was this gave rise to many of those divine poems called the Psalms of David. That from which we have taken our text is an instance of this kind, with many others. This, too, is the divine command: "Is any merry, let him sing psalms."

4. By testifying a benevolent and kind disposition one toward another. The Divine beneficence, in all the great things he has done for us, is designed and calculated to form us to a similar temper and conduct toward our brethren of the human race. Many of them indeed may be unworthy of it; but, you will please to recollect, that our unworthiness does not preclude us from the beneficence of Heaven, otherwise he had not effected this glorious revolution for us. This is, in no instance, the rule of his conduct toward

---

* James, v. 13.

15

us; neither ought we to make it the rule of our conduct toward our fellow-creatures in the duty before us.

You should especially beware of indulging a spirit of resentment and revenge on this occasion. True greatness of mind guards us against this evil. The decision of Unerring Wisdom and Truth is, " He that is slow to anger is better than the mighty, and he that ruleth his spirit than he that taketh a city."* Nor can any thing be more opposed to that benevolence which the religion of Jesus so strongly breathes, so warmly enjoins, and with which it never fails to inspire its genuine votaries.

This benevolence ought in an especial manner to manifest itself with respect to those religious distinctions that unavoidably take place among the disciples of our common Lord in the present state of imperfection. It is not to be expected that we should all be united in opinion, and it is best, for the more general exercise and improvement of the Christian temper, that we should not; but we may be all united in affection. And this is what I most devoutly recommend. And where we cannot agree to agree, let us agree to differ. Love is the peculiar characteristic of the religion of Jesus. Hark, in what affectionate language our Lord himself addresses us on this subject: " A new commandment I give unto you, that ye love one another; as I have loved you, that ye also love one another. By this shall all men know that ye are my disciples, if ye love one another." †

But I may not dismiss this improvement of the great things our God has done for us, without remind-

---

* Prov., xvi. 32   † John, xiii. 34, 35.

ing you of the case of those deserving citizens, who have lost their all, by this struggle, some in one way and some in another; and that, with many of them, while they have been hazarding their lives, in the high places of the field, in the defence of their country. To which I may add, the more piteous case of those, who have become widows and fatherless, by this great contest. My heart bleeds for them. Could the tears of sympathy supply their wants, or repair their losses, it should soon be done. I most affectionately recommend them to the notice and the friendship of their more opulent fellow-citizens, and the attention of the public; not upon the score of charity, but of justice. Can no plans be fallen upon, for employing such deserving members of the community, which is the best method of providing for them? And can luxury and dissipation, those awkward vices in our present situation (to give them the softest name), can they spare nothing for the supply of the more indigent among them? The approaching winter enforces the duty before us, with an energy that language fails to express.

5. We ought carefully to manifest our joy in God, and gratitude to him, on this occasion, by a wise improvement of the great things he has done for us—he has, by the revolution we this day celebrate, put all the blessings of liberty, civil and religious, within our reach. Perhaps there never was a nation that had the fair opportunity of becoming the happiest people upon earth, that we now have. But misery, as well as happiness, lies before us (and both in the extreme), unless the present state of things is wisely improved by us. They are both at our option. And heaven

and earth are looking with eager expectation, to see which we shall choose. The eyes of those ministers of Providence, the angels of God, who have so often aided us in this glorious struggle for liberty; the eyes of the nations of the earth, and particularly the eyes of all Europe, are upon these states, to see what use they will make of the great things God has done for us. How dignified, how interesting the situation! But, however solemn and interesting, the path is plain before us. Would you reap the fruits of your toils, your losses and your blood; it is indispensably necessary that the federal Union of these states be cemented and strengthened—that the honor of the great council of the nation be supported, and its salutary measures carried into execution, with unanimity and dispatch, without regard to partial views, or local interests—that the credit of this new empire be established, on the principles of the strictest justice—and its faith maintained sacred and inviolable, in whatever way, or to whatever description of persons it has been pledged, or may at any time be pledged. Alas! that its glory has suffered so much already, by the failure of our currency.

Let us carefully repair this waste of honor, if we cannot repair the waste of property, by the most sacred adherence to our engagements, in all future time. Among the virtues necessary to be attended to for the accomplishment of these great ends, industry and frugality are of the highest moment.*

---

* The following extract from my first sermon, after the evacuation of the city by the British troops, I take the liberty to annex, as not improper in this place :—

"Thus it appears we have been deeper and longer in the furnace

It is of the last importance, too, that you make the constitution and laws of our country the great rule of your political and civil conduct. Be pleased to remember here, that the government to which I recommend your reverence and obedience is a government of your own framing—and a government for which we have fought and bled; and, blessed be God, have fought and bled with success; and that the magistrates by whom this government is administered are the men of your own choice—the magistrates of your own appointing. Thus it becomes both your duty and your interest to strengthen the hands of government and its ministers, as the sure path to national happiness in all future time.

And would you know the influence this line of conduct will have upon your reputation as a people, recollect the ever-memorable 25th of November (the last month), the day when the deliverance of these states was completed, by the evacuation of New York. The order, decorum and dignity with which the change

---

of affliction than our brethren and sisters in the other states of the Union; we should therefore come forth more refined by our trials. This will be justly expected of us by our God and by our country.

"I particularly beseech you to beware of that pride and vanity, that dissipation and luxury, that so soon disgraced most of the cities and towns in the neighboring states, on their deliverance from the hands of the common enemy. These are evils at all times displeasing in the sight of a holy God, but especially so when under his correcting hand, or rejoicing in his delivering goodness. They will in our case and situation be an offence against all the laws of sound policy as well as true religion. Let patriotism and piety, therefore, unite their efforts in guarding you against these destructive evils, and engaging you in the practice of the contrary and important virtues of humility and temperance, industry and economy."

of government was introduced on that happy day, and which have ever since reigned in our city, do the highest honor to our cause, our citizens, and our army. They have attracted the notice, excited the admiration, and forced the acknowledgments of our enemies themselves, in favor of our virtue, and regard to order and good government; while they will greatly enhance the pleasure and esteem of every friend of the revolution throughout the Union.

6. And lastly, God calls us to testify our joy in him and gratitude to him, by lives devoted to his fear and service. This is the most acceptable manner in which we can express our thankfulness to God for any favor, spiritual or temporal. One of the great ends, for which he pours his goodness upon us, in such rich plenty and variety, is to lead us to repentance, for our manifold transgresssions against him. Every instance of his beneficence, is a cord of love thrown over our souls, to allure us to himself. To offer praise to God, to glorify him, and to order our conversation aright, are used by the Holy Spirit himself, as phrases of the same import, in the following words: "Whoso offereth praise, glorifieth me, and to him that ordereth his conversation aright, will I show the salvation of God."

You will please to remember, farther, that the virtue I recommend, both political and moral, is essential to the preservation of the dear-earned privileges in which we rejoice this day. This is especially the case in a democratic government, and the more democratic the government, the more necessary. Prevailing vice will assuredly sap the foundation of our privileges sooner or later; nor is any great length of time necessary for this fatal purpose.

I only add, once more, that the sons of profaneness cannot now sin at the cheap rate, in point of criminality, they were wont to do. Your guilt is greater, in your neglect of God, and contempt of his Son Christ; in your profane cursing and swearing; your drunkenness, reveling and uncleanness; your sabbath-breaking, gaming and dishonesty in dealing; in a word, in your every species of impiety, than in years past, in proportion to the great things God has done for us, as a people. I beseech you, then, my dear brethren, by all these mercies of God, in addition to all the grace of the gospel of his Son Christ, that you break off your sins by repentance, and study to walk before him as it becometh those for whom the Lord hath done such great things. Which may God of his infinite mercy grant you may be enabled to do, for Jesus' sake. Amen and Amen.

THIS distinguished and successful preacher was born in the month of October, 1732. He was educated for the ministry, and first settled at Carlisle, Pennsylvania. There he labored with all his energy. His natural abilities and energies enabled him not only to attend to the duties of his own church, but he was continually visiting and doing his good work among the people of the neighboring districts. These circumstances marked him out as one properly and peculiarly qualified for organizing churches, in places destitute of the regular administration of the gospel ordinances. To this important business he was therefore called and appointed, and in company with the missionary Charles Beatty, he passed a year in visiting the western frontiers, preaching to the Indians, and "those who were perishing for lack of knowledge," and forming them into congregations.

From Carlisle Doctor Duffield removed to Philadelphia, and entered upon the duties of pastor of the Third Presbyterian Church in that place. There he remained until his death, which took place on the 2d of February, 1790. His lifelong career in that position was one of constant devotion. His eulogist, in recounting this portion of his life to the congregation which he had so long directed, says: "Here, my brethren, you have been witnesses both of his respectability and fidelity in his sacred office. You have seen him possess a distinguished weight and influence in all the judicatures of the church to which he belonged. You have seen him happily unite the wisdom of the serpent with the harmlessness of the dove in the management of all its concerns and interests. You have seen him called by the Congress to officiate as one of their chaplains during the whole of their residence in Philadelphia. But what he was more solicitous about than for all earthly honors— you have seen him, 'instant in season and out of season,' to promote your spiritual and eternal welfare. It was his zeal to do good."

Doctor Duffield possessed an active, vigorous mind and a benevolent disposition. Quick in thought and prompt in utterance, he was enabled to preach with a freedom and frequency which few divines attain. These qualities gave him a great consequence and utility in deliberative bodies. The firmness of his mind was a leading trait, a prominent feature of his whole character. To the opinions which he formed he adhered with steadiness. He was neither frightened from them by the number of his opponents, nor soothed by the respectability of their characters.

As a scholar he was considerably distinguished. He early discovered a thirst for knowledge, which led him to the pursuit of liberal science. His knowledge was of the more solid, than of the ornamental or

15*

polished kind. He was accurate in the classics, and loved philosophy in all its branches. In the common walks of life he was eminent for public spirit, the love of liberty, and for the promotion of any design which had for its object the general welfare. No one was a more zealous and active patriot than he ; or, in the lesser divisions of society, more sincerely endeavored to do service to the community. In the revolution he was an early, a decided, and a uniform friend to his country, and after the peace he was equally assiduous in using all his influence to advance the public interest and tranquillity. This peculiarity of character is forcibly illustrated in the sermon which succeeds this sketch.

He was indefatigable and evangelical as a preacher. In the early part of his ministry he was remarkably animated in his public addresses, and acquired a high popularity. An intimation that he was to preach, was the sure promise of a crowded auditory. His manner was always warm and forcible, and his instructions always practical. He had a talent of touching the conscience almost peculiar to himself. He dwelt with emphasis and strength on the plain and essential truths of the gospel ; yet he was master of a singularly happy method of explaining the Scriptures, which, in later life he frequently practised.

As a Christian, Doctor Duffield lived the religion which he professed. The spirit of the gospel seemed to have tinctured his whole mind, and to possess a constant and powerful influence on his heart. He was truly and remarkably an example of the life of God in the soul of man. His "fellowship with the Father of his spirit," and his "conversation with heaven," appeared to be almost uninterrupted. Nor was he less distinguished in active duty. He sought all occasions of serving his Lord. Of him it may be said with truth, that he "went about doing good."*

DECLARATION OF PEACE.†

An event of such magnitude and importance as that which has occasioned our convening to-day, accomplished in so short a space of time, and with so small a share of difficulty in comparison with what might have been expected, is one of those occurrences in the kingdom of Providence that command the admiration of every observer. And while it affords an irrefragable argument (to convince even an Atheist) that the Most High ruleth over the affairs of men, and raiseth up and casteth down at his pleasure, demands also our warmest gratitude to that God who has done great things for us, whereof we are glad.

With a view, therefore, to assist in this delightful service, permit me to invite your attention to these emphatical words of the prophet Isaiah, lxvi. 8:

---

* See Rev. Ashbel Green's sermon on the death of Dr. Duffield.

† This sermon was preached in the Third Presbyterian Church, in Philadelphia, on the 11th of December, 1783.

Who hath heard such a thing? Who hath seen such things? Shall the earth be made to bring forth in one day? Shall a nation be born at once? For as soon as Zion travailed she brought forth her children.

This passage, it must be confessed, has a manifest respect to that happy period generally termed the latter-day glory, when the various nations of the earth, formerly styled Gentiles, and yet in darkness, shall, in a sudden and surprising manner, be converted to the knowledge and obedience of Christ, and the Jews, so long rejected of God, shall, by an admirable display of Divine power and grace, be gathered home from their dispersion as in one day, and being formed into a people in their own land, shall become the most remarkable and leading part of the Christian Church in activity and zeal for their God, and for *Jesus the Saviour*, their then acknowledged *Messiah*.

The former of these events appears designed, by the earth bringing forth in a day; and the latter, by a nation, viz., the Jewish, being born to God at once : both which, taken together, will constitute that joyous state of affairs which the apostle terms life from the dead. But, as the prophet has evidently in view to awaken our attention to the hand of God in his works of wonder among the children of men, and it is not without example in sacred record to accommodate passages to similar events, the importance of that event we celebrate to-day ; and the remarkable interposition of the providence of God, so manifestly displayed therein, will, I trust, sufficiently justify my applying the passage before us to the present occasion, to which also it appears with peculiar propriety adapted ; for who indeed hath heard such a thing?—who, but a few years back, would have believed the report,

had a prophet himself declared it? (his credentials, at
least, and marks of authority, had first been carefully
scanned with a critical eye)—who, since time began,
hath seen such events take place so soon? The earth
has indeed brought forth in a day. A nation indeed
has been born as at once. It has not been Israel's forty
years of tedious wilderness-journey; nor Rome's, nor
the united Belgic provinces' long-continued scene of
arduous, dubious struggle; but almost as soon as our
American Zion began to travail, and without experi-
encing the pangs and pains which apprehensive fear
expected, she brought forth her children, more numerous than the tribes of Jacob, to possess the land
from the north to the south, and from the east to the
yet unexplored, far distant west; that with great propriety may we hail every friend of liberty on this auspicious day, in the language nearly following our text.
Rejoice ye with America, and be glad with her, all
ye that love her; rejoice for joy with her, all ye that
mourned for her: "for thus saith the Lord, Behold, I
will extend peace to her like a river, and glory like a
flowing stream." Here, then, as from one of those
hills from whence the tents of Jacob were viewed
of old, let us look back on what God hath done, and
contemplate the prospect he opens before us, and may
He (in whose hands are the hearts of the children of
men) inspire every breast with a grateful sense of his
goodness, so liberally bestowed through the whole.

The British monarch had formed a design (for
actions speak louder than words) to reduce these
states, then British colonies, into absolute vassalage.
A venal Parliament had approved the unrighteous
purpose, and passed a decree to bind us in all cases,

both civil and religious, to the obedience of such laws as they might deem meet to enact. Some have ascribed this extravagant conduct to the same spirit of jealousy which once influenced the councils of Egypt against the house of Joseph; lest, waxing too powerful, they might break off their connection, and pursue a separate interest of their own. Pharaoh, indeed, might have reason to fear, because Israel was an entirely different people; and in their religion and manners separated far from the people of the land. But in the present case, though the court of Great Britain appear carefully to have copied the Egyptian model, and their measures have produced a similar event, yet, as the people of these states were the same as the people of Britain, their religion and manners the same, and no disposition to separate from them had ever appeared—but an attachment, even to enthusiastic fondness, had always obtained, it must have required an exorbitant share of infatuation to have raised a suspicion so high as to have produced the spirit and zeal that directed the British cabinet.

To raise a revenue, and bring America to bear her proportion of the national debt, has been assigned as the motive. America, by centring her trade in Britain, contributed her liberal share, nor had she ever withheld her blood or her treasure when requisitions were made; that even malevolence itself had been nonplussed from thence to derive a plea, unless through a mad desire to take by compulsion what would otherwise be cheerfully given. It seems, therefore, most probable his Britannic majesty wished to increase the power of the crown, so as to wrest the very shadow of liberty out of the hands of all his subjects, and reign an absolute monarch; and for this end began where he hoped, by bribes and craft, to cloak his design under the cover of parliamentary sanction. It may be, he desired to urge America to arms, that, being vanquished (which seems to have been taken as a granted point), and her principal men, and all who should dare to oppose his aims, having either fallen in the field, or been executed as traitors, or constrained to fly to some foreign land, the whole of the country, with the subdued, dastardly inhabitants that remained, might revert to the crown. This, with its native consequences of American lords and vassals, all at the monarch's pleasure, must soon have weighed down the liberties of Britain.

Or, perhaps he expected to intimidate into submission, by the appearance of determined military force. This charity would fondly persuade us to admit, as being the least wicked of the two. And in that case, an host of place-men and pensioners, with their influence among a people destitute of spirit and subdued by threats, though not so suddenly, would yet as certainly have produced the desired effect, and finally imposed the same humiliating terms on Britain herself. But whatever might have been the motive, America was marked out for servile submission or severe subjugation, and the power of Britain employed to accomplish the end.

. A day now arose, lowering thick with dark and heavy clouds. A scene was opened painful to the mind only to review. On the one hand to resign every dear birthright privilege and bow down unconditionally to foreign masters, from whom we had nothing to expect but sovereign contempt and heavy

burdens imposed; who, by their remote situation could
neither see our calamity nor partake in our sufferings.
On the other hand to wage war with the most formidable power on earth, that had been for ages a terror to
the nations, and had lately risen into a state of gran-
deur and glory far surpassing all her former greatness.
A nation long inured to war; her fleets commanding
the ocean; her troops numerous and veteran, and in
martial deeds famed as inferior to none; her wealth
immense; her resources many, and her pride and mistaken sense of honor prompting her to exert every
nerve, to secure a compliance with her claims and demands. Hard alternative! to resign liberty, or wage
this hazardous war; and yet none other remained.

America had her numerous husbandmen, her merchants and mechanics; her sons of the learned professions, and students in every science; her inhabitants were many; but untaught in the policy of courts
and cabinets; strangers to the art of war, and divided
into different colonies, under different forms of government, had scarce ever communicated sentiments on a
single point. Armies she had none, nor a single ship
of war to protect her coast. Arms and ammunition
had never been her care; and her money scarce sufficient for common occasions. Resources 'tis true there
were; but as the precious metal lies hid in the un-
sought-for ore, they remained unexplored and unknown. In this situation shall she dare to provoke the
vengeance of Britain! A stoical observer would have
pronounced it madness. But LIBERTY was the prize.
She chose "*Freedom or Death*" as her motto, and
nobly resolved on war with all its horrors; that at least
her last expiring groan might breathe forth FREEDOM.

Already had Britain planted her baleful banner on our coast, and her proud, insulting flag had possessed our harbors. Her oppressive edicts had gone forth; and her naval and military strength were combined to enforce obedience. As the careful mariner watches the heavy gathering cloud and dreads the approaching storm, America with anxiety beheld, and waited the event. Prudence would have seemed to dictate an early resistance to manifest hostile designs; nor suffer an avowed enemy to every privilege to intrench in quiet, and strengthen themselves in a capital town.* Nor was America blind to the measure; but that God who so early espoused her cause, that her innocence in the case, and her reluctance to arms, might be evident to all, withheld her from the deed, and left Britain, on LEXINGTON's ever-memorable day, to open the scene of war.

Quick as the flash of lightning glares from pole to pole; so sudden did a military spirit pervade those then limited colonies; but now, blessed be God, confederated, established states. The peaceful husbandman forsook his farm, the merchant relinquished his trade; the learned in the law dismissed their clients; the compassionate physician forgot his daily round; the mariner laid aside his compass and quadrant; the mechanic resigned his implements of employment; the sons of science ceased their philosophic pursuits, and even the miser half neglected, for a time, his gold and his gain; and the griping landlord his rents. All prepared for war, and eagerly flew to the field. The delicate female herself forgot her timidity, and, glowing

---

* Boston.

with patriot zeal, prompted the tardy to arms; and despised and reproached the lingerer that meanly loitered behind. Nor were those of the sacred order wanting to their country, when her civil and religious liberties were all at stake. But, as became faithful watchmen, they blew the trumpet on the walls of our Zion, and sounded an alarm for defence.

From then, standard was pitched against standard, and the battle was fought with varied success, from the east to the west, and from the north to the south; and the field and the forest, the hills and the valleys, the shore and the inland parts, have all heard the shoutings of the warrior, the clang of arms, and seen garments rolled in blood, and summer's scorching heat and winter's parching cold borne testimony to American perseverance and valor.

Nor was military prowess only given. He that put off the spirit of Moses on the elders of Israel, raised up senators, and guided them in council, to conduct the affairs of his chosen American tribes;* and though, like the Jewish congregation of old, language of murmur and complaint has been heard in our land, and we have had our *Korahs* and *Dathans*, whose endeavors have been to weaken the hands of our rulers, depreciate their merit and lessen their esteem in the eyes of the people, yet (I hesitate not to pronounce it) generations yet unborn will look back with wonder, and venerate the memories and long perpetuate the names of those who guided the helm through the storm, nor sunk dismayed while so furious a *Euroclydon* of innumerable difficulties lashed so sore and lay

---

* The Continental Congress.

so long upon us; but have at length, by the good hand of our God upon them, brought the billow-beaten vessel of public affairs safe into harbor. These posterity will admire and revere, and wish to have seen the day when those men lived upon the earth—a day which commanded the attention of states and kingdoms, far and wide. And as Joshua's day arrested the sun in its course, the nations stood still in silent surprise, to see the balance of war so nearly poised between contending parties so unequal. Fondly would the spark of humanity within have led them to aid the American cause. Their wish was all they durst give, for they dreaded the omnipotent arm of Great Britain, nor dared to awaken her resentment.

The monarch of France alone was found, whose zeal for the rights of humanity inspired him beyond the power of any meaner consideration. Solemn ties had bound him to consult the good of the people over whom he was placed. Nor could he have answered to his God, his conscience, or his kingdom, to have involved the nation in the calamities of an arduous, hazardous war, had no prospect of advantage risen into view. God, who had early designed him for distinguished honor, and raised him to the throne to establish his name and his glory as lasting as the annals of time, as the *protector of the rights of mankind*, had therefore, by a firm decree, united the interest of America and France; that his majesty might be just to his conscience, his people and his God, while indulging the ardent glow of his magnanimous breast, in affording to the distressed a vigorous aid. And his fleets and his armies were embarked in our cause. Let detraction, therefore, be silent, nor object the in-

fluence of interest to sully the generous deed. God
has connected duty and interest by indissoluble bonds;
nor may either, of right, assume the name alone.

Ancient prejudices, instilled by Britain, seemed to
forbid connection with a nation we had long been
taught to consider faithless, pusillanimous and cruel.
The generosity of France recovered the mind to judge
by a candid scale. And as a mutual intercourse increased our acquaintance, the scales of ignorance fell
from our eyes, the mist of prejudice vanished, and
America found herself united to the most enlightened
civilized nation on earth, and rejoiced in an alliance
cemented, not by interest only, but by the strong
additional bonds of cordial affection. An alliance
which, may that God whose watchful eye guards the
affairs of men, perpetuate unimpaired, while sun and
moon endure.

The citizens and subjects of both nations embraced
as brethren, and fought side by side, with united hearts
and hands, in the then made common cause. Their
only strife was, who should display the noblest deeds,
and render themselves worthy each other's esteem.
America's day, the morning of which had lowered
with heavy clouds, began to brighten apace, and its
hurrying hours hastened their way to a noontide glow.
The justice of her cause, the influence of her great
ally, and the insults and injuries experienced by other
nations, from British arrogance, procured her still
further support; and narrowed the distance to the
object of her wish. Britain saw with indignation,
and in firm alliance with every infernal power (for
from heaven she dared not expect, nor would any on
earth, Hesse, Anspach, and savages excepted, afford

her aid) she resolved on the utmost vengeance, and as a tiger in the forest, taken in the toils, exerted her every effort. Nor need I here recount Monmouth, Cowpens by Catawba, or Eutaw, with the many sore-fought days on the land, or the briny ocean, repeatedly stained with the generous blood of war; or the ravages which desolated the south; or the devastation and ruin that ranged along our coast; whilst their ruthless savage allies, to the eternal infamy of those who employed them, drenched the wide frontier with the warless blood of helpless women and babes. These deeds of Britain are written with the pen of remembrance on the minds of all. They are engraved as with the point of a diamond on a rock, on the pillars of time; and, handed down in the faithful historic page, shall long be read by ages yet to come. Nor shall Carolina or Georgia, New York or Virginia, Philadelphia, Rhode Island or Boston, be named, but grateful acknowledgments shall rise of the kind deliverance afforded. And oft shall the traveller turn aside to survey the seat of Gloucester and York in Virginia, and view the spot ever to be remembered, where the great decisive event took place; and shall read inscribed on the memorative marble,* the important victory there obtained. The inhabitant, instructed from father to son, shall bear him company, and recount the various parts of the scene. "On this point the *blood-stained* British general, Lord Cornwallis, held his garrison. Yonder the great Washington and illustrious Rochambeau, made their first approach. Across that rivulet and through that valley,

---

* A marble pillar ordered by Congress to be erected there.

ran their first parallel; and where now that range of
buildings stands, they drew their second.   There stood
a redoubt carried by cool, determined Gallic bravery;
and there the Americans stormed and conquered.
Here, encaved in the brow of the bank, the Britons
met to hold their dark and gloomy councils; in that
part of the river the Charon was set on fire; and yonder, across the water, the Generals Weeden and Chois-
sey hemmed in the imprisoned British ranks.   There
the French and American troops formed a glittering
lane; and on yonder plain the numerous garrison piled
their arms."

The listening child, led forth in his father's hand,
shall hear him relate, and repeat it over again to his
little companions.   And they also shall rejoice in that
great event, which struck Britain with terror and despair, and led on to that happy restoration of peace
for which, to-day, we give thanks to our God.   For,
according to this time, shall it be said of these United
States, What hath God wrought for them?   Great indeed, is the salvation he hath shown! and great the
obligations we are under to praise!   For had we
failed in our just attempt to secure our invaluable
rights, America's choicest blood had flowed in liberal
streams, and her most valuable citizens, throughout
the states, had expired by halters, and on gibbets.
The daring patriot, whose zeal for his country had led
him, with his life in his hand, to take a seat in the
great council of the states, or in legislation, or in ad-
ministering justice; or who had led in the field in his
country's cause—these had been led forth the first, in
haughty triumph, amidst ten thousand insulting scoffs,
as the victims of insatiable vengeance.   Nor only

these—but all who had dared to follow their councils, and abet the cause for which they contended; nor a single character worth notice left remaining, that dared to breathe the language of freedom. The paths of life had now been thin of the many virtuous citizens convened to-day, throughout these states, to give thanks on this happy occasion. America had been enriched, indeed, and her soil made fat with the blood of her children. Made fat—not for the rightful owners, but to pamper the lusts of tyrannical lords, sharing the country among themselves; the surviving former possessors only vassals at pleasure, and slaves to their lordly masters.

This, my friends, is not a flight of fancy, or apprehensive imagination run wild. It is founded in just observation, and what bitter experience would have taught but too late, had our enemy prevailed. But, blessed be God, with Israel of old we may take up. our song: "Blessed be the Lord, who gave us not as a prey to their teeth. Blessed be the Lord, the snare is broken, and we are escaped." We cried unto him in the day of our distress. He heard our entreaties, and hath brought us forth into a large place, and established our rights, and opened before us a glorious prospect. May wisdom be given to esteem, and improve the invaluable blessing. Here has our God erected a banner of civil and religious liberty,* and

---

* Religious liberty is a foundation principle in the constitutions of the respective states, distinguishing America from any nation in Europe; and resting religion on its proper basis, as supported by its own evidence and the almighty care of its divine Author, without the aid of the feeble angry arm of civil power, which serves only to disgrace the name and religion of Jesus, by violating the rights of conscience.

prepared an asylum for the poor and oppressed from every part of the earth. Here, if wisdom guides our affairs, shall a happy equality reign, and joyous freedom bless the inhabitants wide and far, from age to age. Here, far removed from the noise and tumult of contending kingdoms and empires—far from the wars of Europe and Asia, and the barbarous African coast—here shall the husbandman enjoy the fruits of his labor; the merchant trade secure of his gain; the mechanic indulge his inventive genius; and the sons of science pursue their delightful employment, till the light of knowledge pervade yonder yet uncultivated western wilds, and form the savage inhabitants into men. Here, also, shall our Jesus go forth conquering and to conquer, and the heathen be given him for an inheritance, and these uttermost parts for a possession. Zion shall here lengthen her cords and strengthen her stakes; and the mountain of the house of the Lord be gloriously exalted on high. Here shall the religion of Jesus—not that falsely so called, which consists in empty words and forms, and spends its unhallowed zeal in party names and distinctions, and traducing and reviling each other—but the pure and undefiled religion of our blessed Redeemer; here shall it reign in triumph, over all opposition. Vice and immorality shall yet here become ashamed and banished; and love to God and benevolence to man, rule the hearts and regulate the lives of men. Justice and truth shall here yet meet together, and righteousness and peace embrace each other; and the wilderness blossom as the rose and the desert rejoice and sing. And here shall the various ancient promises of rich and glorious grace begin their complete divine fulfilment;

and the light of divine revelation diffuse its beneficent rays, till the gospel of Christ has accomplished
its day, from east to west around the world—a day
whose evening shall not terminate in night, but introduce that joyful period when the outcasts of Israel
and the despised of Judah, shall be restored; and
with them the fulness of the Gentile world shall flow
. to the standard of redeeming love; and the nations
of the earth become the kingdom of our Lord and
Saviour, under whose auspicious reign holiness shall
universally prevail, and the noise and alarm of war
be heard no more. Nor shall there be any thing to
hurt or destroy or interrupt the tranquillity of men,
through all the wide dominions of this glorious Prince
of peace.

How pleasing the scene! How transporting the
prospect! And how thrice happy they whom God
has honored as instruments in the great work now
brought to pass, subservient to these important events.
May the blessing of Heaven surround them, and the
honor and esteem of a grateful country attend them
through life. May the names and memories of those,
O my country! who have planned your measures
and guided your councils through a wilderness of in-
surmountable difficulties, and brought your affairs,
by the blessing of God, to a happy conclusion, may
they ever be had in kind remembrance. Errors and
mistakes may have been; but it is matter of wonder
and praise, that whilst treading an unknown, a difficult and dangerous path, their mistakes and errors
have been so few.

Surely the hand of God was in it, to guide and
guard their way. And let THE ILLUSTRIOUS WASHING-

16

TON, the Joshua of the day and admiration of the age, who, inspired from above with every military endowment to command the American armies, and great in the field beyond example, retires still greater to the humble character of a private citizen among the citizens of the states; let him live perpetual in the minds and the praises of all. Aid here, ye his highly-honored fellow-citizens, aid feeble fame with her hundred wings and tongues to proclaim his worth; and let Time, on his full and ever-willing stream, convey down through every age, the unsullied remembrance of the patriot, the hero, and the citizen combined, and deliver his name to the unbounded ocean of immortal esteem. And, from the commander-in-chief down to the faithful sentinel, let the officer and soldier who have bravely offered their lives and have nobly dared death and danger in the bloody field, on the horrid edge of the ranks of war, be remembered with kindness. Let their services of hardship, toil, and danger be never forgotten; but may they ever experience a kind attention from their fellow-citizens, and a faithful reward from their country, whose rights they have so firmly defended. Let their military garb and character ever command esteem. Let their wounds and their scars plead their cause and extenuate their foibles, and the residue of their exhausted days be crowned with honor and ease.

With these let also be joined in never-dying remembrance, a *Warren*, a *Montgomery*, a *Biddle*, embraced by the briny waves, a *MacPherson*, and a *Laurens*, in the bloom of youth, fallen in the bloody field in their country's cause; with the countless train of MARTYRS for American freedom, who, from the ocean

and the land, from prison-ships and jails, have sealed
with their lives their attachment to her cause—these,
these—number them not of the dead, they are enrolled
in the list of glory and of fame, and shall live immortal beyond the power of death and the grave. Bind
their brows, O ye American daughters; haste ye!
haste ye! bind their brows with never-fading laurels
and glittering crimson wreaths; and let the evening
song and noon-day recital perpetuate their deeds and
their fame, while the silent tear stealing from the
eye shall testify how dear their memory and how high
their esteem. And whilst the curse of Meroz remains
on lasting record for those who withheld their aid, let
the blessings of all rest on every friend of liberty, who
willingly offered himself, when his country's necessity
called him to the field, and on all who have cheerfully
borne and suffered in its cause.

Nor let our great and generous ally, who offered
an early and a vigorous aid, be forgotten. But let
every American lip pronounce a "*Vive le Roi*," and
every heart conspire "long may his most Christian
majesty Louis the Sixteenth," long may he live, a
blessing and blessed on earth, and late resign an
earthly crown, to shine in brighter glory, and wear a
crown immortal, among the blessed above. And may
his subjects ever be embraced as brethren and dearest
friends, who have fought in our battles and bled in our
cause; and partiality here held worthy of praise.

Nor may a due esteem ever be wanting to the
United Netherland States, whose heart and endeavors
were with us; or to the court of Spain, for assistance
afforded, but be generously paid to all who have aided
to secure our rights. And whilst with a grateful sense

of their services done, we pay deserved honors to those whom God has honored to bear a part in the great work performed, let every heart adore the God of goodness in all, and every lip and every life proclaim his praise. 'Tis he, the sovereign-disposer of all events, hath wrought for us, and brought the whole to pass. It was he who led his Israel of old, by the pillar and the cloud, through their wilderness journey ; wherein they also had their wanderings ; 'twas he, the same, presided over our affairs, directed our councils, and guided our senators by the way. 'Twas he who raised a Joshua to lead the tribes of Israel in the field of bat- tle ; raised and formed a Washington to lead on the troops of his chosen states, to final conquest, and im- bued him with all his military patience, perseverance, prowess and skill ; and admirably preserved his life and health, through all the danger and toil. 'Twas he who, in Barak's day, spread the spirit of war, in every breast, to shake off the Canaanitish yoke ; and inspired thy inhabitants, O America, with an ardent glow through every rank, to assert the cause of free- dom ; and led forth the husbandman and mechanic, with those of every class, to offer themselves undaunt- ed in the daring conflict. It was he who hid fear from their eyes of either the superior numbers or skill of the powerful foe they rose to withstand ; and from him came down that firmness and fortitude that raised American officers, and soldiers, beyond all former example, through hunger, nakedness and cold, to fight the battles of their country, and never forsake its standard. It was he breathed from above, and fired their bosoms in the hour of action, to crop the laurels of triumph, or, having dearly sold their precious lives,

to embrace death, in all his glory, on the bloody field!
And he only inspired our generous seamen with invincible firmness to endure the horrors of prison-ships and jails, and expire by famine and British barbarity, rather than renounce the virtuous cause in which they embarked. It was he who raised up Cyrus, to break the Assyrian force, and say: "Let Israel be free," endued the monarch of France with an angel's mind, to assert and secure the freedom of his United American States. And by him were the hearts of other nations disposed to our aid. And he, and he alone, who saith to the proud waves of the sea: "Hitherto shall ye come, but no farther," restrained the councils and arms of Britain from improving against us many opportunities and advantages which evidently lay within the line of their power.

Who can recollect the critical night of retreat from Long Island; the scene of retiring from New York; the day of Brandywine; or the endangered situation of the arms of America on Trenton's ever-memorable night—and not be constrained to say: "If it had not been the Lord who was on our side, our enemy had swallowed us up; the waters had overwhelmed us; the proud stream had swept us away!" But, blessed be his name, our help was found in him who made the heavens and the earth.

It was God who blasted the secret designs of enemies and traitors against us; and, by an admirable interposition, brought forth into light the dark and deep-stained villany of an *Arnold*, cursed and detested of God and men.* And converted our repeated

---

* Deuteronomy, xxvii. 25.

misfortunes, and even mistakes, into singular mercies
and peculiar advantages, that not more manifest was
his voice on Sinai, or his hand in his affairs of his
Israel of old, than we have seen the wisdom, the
power, and the goodness of our God displayed through
the whole of our arduous contest, from its earliest period down. We may, with emphatical propriety, say: It is He, the ALMIGHTY GOD, has accomplished the whole in every part, and by his kind care
and omnipotent arm has wrought out our deliverance;
cast forth our enemy; bestowed upon us a wide, extended, fruitful country; and blessed us with a safe
and honorable peace; and has brought the whole to
pass in so short a space of time, and with so few difficulties attending, in comparison with what we had
reason to expect, that the establishment of these
United States in the peaceful possession of their rights
and privileges, stands, an instance of divine favor, unexampled in the records of time.

Who does not remember the general language when
the war commenced? *Cheerfully to pay one half our
property to secure our rights.* But far from even the
half of this has been required. Individuals, it is true,
and those amongst the most virtuous of the community, have suffered—have sorely suffered—by specu-
lative miscreants, and a depreciating currency; their
confidence in the public faith has proved the temporal
ruin of many; and widows and helpless orphans been
made a prey—many of whose sufferings might yet
still be greatly alleviated by a due attention, and a
sacred regard to justice and good conscience in directing affairs; which must, also, sooner or later take
place—or the righteous God, who hates injustice, op-

pression and fraud, be highly displeased, and his judgments be yet poured out on our land, as he afflicted Israel of old for unredressed injuries to the Gibeonites among them. His justice and his power are still the same.

But the price of our peace, taken on a national scale, compared with the advantages gained, and the number by whom to be paid, scarce deserves a name.

In whatever point of light we view this great event we are constrained to say : " It is the doing of the Lord, and marvellous in our eyes," and to him be rendered the thanks and the praise. " *Not unto us, not unto us, but unto thy name, O Lord, be the glory;*" for thine is the power, and the victory, and the greatness ; both success and safety come of thee, and thou reignest over all, and hast wrought all our works in us and for us.

PRAISE, THEREFORE, THY GOD, O AMERICA ; PRAISE THE LORD, YE HIS HIGHLY-FAVORED UNITED STATES. Nor let it rest in the fleeting language of the lip, or the formal thanksgiving of a day ; but let every heart glow with gratitude, and every life, by a devout regard to his holy law, proclaim his praise. It is this our God requires, as that wherein our personal and national good, and the glory of his great name consist, and without which all our professions will be but an empty name.

It is that we love the Lord our God, to walk in his ways and keep his commandments, to observe his statutes and his judgments—that a sacred regard be maintained to righteousness and truth—that we do justice, love mercy, and walk humbly with our God— then shall God delight to dwell amongst us, and these

United States shall long remain a great, a glorious, and a happy people. Which may God, of his infinite mercy, grant! Amen.

THE END.

wedding parties, sleigh-rides, the Whigs tarred and feathered by the Tories, and *vice versa;* fox-hunts by the officers of the British army; surprises, birth-day celebrations, practical jokes by men whom we have been taught to believe were of the most serious natural disposition; patriotic songs and ballads; horse-races, games, masquerades, reviews; anecdotes of the most celebrated men and women, popular merriments and usages, and the celebrations of national festivities.

The work carries the reader back into the homes, upon the very hearthstones, the highways and battle-fields of the Revolution, and lets him hear the Whigs and Tories lampoon and abuse each other, and see the armies fight in their own way.

Among the numerous letters and notices recommendatory of the work, are the following:

From Hon. CHARLES KING, LL. D., *President Columbia College, N. Y.*

President's Room, Columbia College, NEW YORK, 1859.

"I have looked, with some care and more interest, over your 'Diary of the American Revolution,' etc. Its plan makes it a popular as well as instructive publication. Made up mainly of the contemporaneous utterances of the daily press of all shades of opinion, it is like listening, as we read, to the voices of the actors in the great struggle for independence.

"The press, which has now grown up into an all-pervading and powerful agency in our polity, had even as far back as your Diary begins, a most important influence in moulding public opinion. Through its columns burst forth on the one hand in all their fiery freshness the daring language and schemes of the Sons of Liberty, and on the other were more craftily insinuated or boldly avowed the cautious doubts and timid counsels or unhesitating loyalty, of those who yet clung to the mother country.

"It is for us, who stand in the light of posterity to the men of those days, to judge with impartial serenity their deeds and their motives, and in your Diary the very best of means of judging correctly are furnished, since both sides are heard in their own language.

3

"As an occasional student of our earlier annals, I thank you for the undertaking."

Believe me, truly yours,
CHARLES KING.

From Hon. MILLARD FILLMORE.

BUFFALO, Nov. 28, 1859.

FRANK MOORE, Esq.

Dear Sir:—"I have found your Diary of the Revolution very interesting. The thought of giving the events of that period in the form of a Diary is a most happy one, and has only its equal in the famous travels of Anacharsis the younger, through Greece. I anticipate both pleasure and profit in a further perusal of it."

Truly yours,
MILLARD FILLMORE.

From E. B. O'CALLAGHAN, Esq., *author "Documentary History of N. Y.*

STATE HALL, Albany, Dec. 26, 1859.

My Dear Sir:—I have enjoyed much pleasure and information from your 'Diary of the American Revolution.'

"The histories hitherto published of that great epoch, were necessarily restricted to the principal events and actors, as they appeared on the stage.

"Your work admits us behind the scenes; where we are afforded an opportunity of seeing many things of which we have been hitherto ignorant.

"Here men, some already known, many long since forgotten, but all active partisans on either side, give unreserved vent to their patriotism or passion, their temporary fears or lofty aspirations, their individual sufferings, and private misfortunes.

"It is, indeed, the Domestic History of the Revolution, which all will do well to study."

Yours, very sincerely,
E. B. O'CALLAGHAN.

From W. B. SPRAGUE, D. D.

ALBANY, N. Y., Jan. 17, 1860.

My Dear Sir:—"I must tell you how much I have been gratified by your recent work, 'Diary of the American Revolution.' The conception was certainly a most felicitous one, and the execution in every way worthy of it. While it contains a vast amount of valuable information, much of which could not be reached through any other channel, you have contrived, by the manner in which you have presented it, to invest sober facts with the attraction of romance.

"I congratulate you sincerely, upon having made a book upon

the Revolution at this late period, that must take its place among the most interesting and valuable works on that subject that have ever been written."

I am, my dear sir,
with great regard,
faithfully yours,
W. B. SPRAGUE.

From Hon. JARED SPARKS, D. D., LL. D.

CAMBRIDGE, Feb. 20, 1860.

Dear Sir:—"I have perused the two volumes of the 'Diary of the Revolution' with much satisfaction and profit. The selections, taken as they are from various sources, show the spirit of the times in a very remarkable degree, and exhibit in a strong light the exciting topics which agitated the public mind from day to day during the eventful period of the Revolution. Thus they become the interpreters of history, and you may well congratulate yourself upon the success of your labors in having made a valuable contribution to the accessible aids for the reader who would acquire a complete and accurate knowledge of the great national struggle for achieving independence."

Respectfully and truly yours,
JARED SPARKS.

From HORACE WEBSTER, LL. D., *Pres. New York Free Academy.*

NEW YORK, Jan. 9, 1860.

FRANK MOORE, Esq.

Dear Sir:—"I have read and re-read, with increased interest at each perusal, your 'Diary of the Revolution.' The contents being made up of the incidents of the Revolution, the accounts of which were published at the time of their occurrence by the parties engaged in the contest, give the present generation of readers a truer insight into the then condition of things, the spirit and nature of the war waged, than can be obtained by reading the more elaborate histories of that eventful period. These circumstances give great value to your publication.

"No intelligent American who takes an interest in the history of his country, or in the perpetuity of its institutions, can afford to do without it, as it contains very peculiar and valuable information found in no other publication with which I am acquainted.

Very respectfully,
HORACE WEBSTER.

From the London Saturday Review.

These volumes are a sort of substitute for the *Memoires pour servir* which are so fruitful a mine to the student who is exploring the history of an older nation. It would be vain to look for diaries and autobiographies from combatants in a war of inde-

pendence. Such struggles are too stern and too engrossing to
leave the actors in them much leisure for catering gossip and
piquant anecdotes for the entertainment of posterity. Mr. Moore
has supplied their place by reprinting a laborious selection from
the fugitive literature of the moment. He seeks his material in
the lampoons and libels which the animosity of both sides furnished in abundance, in newspaper articles, and sometimes in un-
published letters. . . . There never was a contest in which
the premium upon lying was so large. The Americans were fighting against a great empire, without any certain supply of men,
money, or munitions. To make good this deficiency involved a
constant and exhausting drain upon the mass of the peaceable inhabitants, which not only deprived them of the comforts, but often
of the barest necessaries of life. Such sacrifices could not but
have had a damping effect upon an enthusiasm which, to a large
number, must have seemed absolutely theoretic. The pressure
of hardship, mutual jealousy, the apparent hopelessness of success, the certain disastrousness of failure, were always tempting
the Americans to sluggishness, if not to desertion. In such a state
of popular feeling victory became a matter of prestige. It was
almost of more importance to be thought triumphant than to be
so. The representations of newspapers, the manipulation of intelligence, became a warlike weapon of the most deadly efficacy.
The fortunes of the struggle depended in no small degree on the
false fears or the false hopes that could be instilled into the American population. Accordingly, the journals published in America
during the war became about as careful of the truth of their information as the *Moniteur* during a Napoleonic campaign. The
wildest *canards* were circulated without scruple; the most liberal
accusations of the foulest atrocities were bandied freely from side
to side; and the most conflicting narratives were solemnly attested
on each side concerning every one of the innumerable petty engagements of which the war was made up. The historical in-
quirer will see in these pages an accurate and most mournful picture of the fiendish passions which can be roused between kindred
races by a petty cause of quarrel, and he may make a fair collection of tolerably clever parodies and pasquinades.

The feeling with which most Englishmen will rise from the
perusal of this work will be one of sorrowful but profound contempt for the government under which their ancestors flourished
in the good old days. Nobody, except perhaps Washington, appears in very noble colors; but the only actors who make a
thoroughly despicable figure are the English ministers and their
favorite generals. It was not that they committed here and there
an isolated mistake—the demon of blundering possessed them
from the very first measure to the very last of the twenty years'
struggle. Without subscribing to all the imputations of tyranny
in which the Americans vented the discontent that had been accumulating for many years, no one doubts that the taxation of so

powerful a colony was, as a mere matter of statecraft, a mistake. If not a crime, it was certainly a blunder. The military operations, too, of the war on the English side are sufficiently infamous. No commander, probably, throughout the whole course of the warlike history of England has surpassed Howe and Clinton in inefficiency, with the single exception of General Whitelocke, whose sinister fame is linked to the same fatal soil. But these errors hardly equalled the folly of the policy which was pursued between the first outbreak of discontent and the time when the armed conflict was commenced in earnest. It was not the policy of statesmen, but the policy which a spiteful woman pursues to obtain a household victory. The English government would not yield, and they either could not or would not take the steps necessary to conquer; and so they adopted a middle course, which conveniently combined the expenses of the one with the humiliation of the other. They did nothing to enforce obedience, but they did every thing to tease, to irritate, to exasperate. The shutting up of the port of Boston was not likely to cow the resistance or allay the resentment of a high-spirited people. The closing of the fisheries of Newfoundland to American enterprise had the effect of depriving numbers of their bread, and making it their interest to dare the utmost for the overthrow of the power that was ruining them; but it did not deprive the rebels of a single resource, or win back to loyalty a single wavering heart. The campaigns of many of the English commanders were carried on in the same spirit. They made war on peaceful industry, on defenceless commercial towns, on public buildings, on every thing except armed men. They undertook scarcely any great military enterprises, and generally contented themselves with sitting down in some seaport town until they were driven out of it; but to make amends, they destroyed every sort of property that they could reach without fighting a battle. Even before the Declaration of Independence had been made, they went on the principle that whatever was loss to America was gain to England; and, consequently, they conducted war on a system even more barbarous than is commonly adopted in contending with an alien nation. Having command of the sea, they bombarded and burnt petty seaport towns, which could not have been troublesome if they had wished. They forged imitation Congress notes and circulated them by thousands, in order to depreciate the American currency. And General Gage even went so far as to transport to this country all the title-deeds on which the New York proprietors depended for the possession of their estates—though, happily for our credit, his proceedings were not supported by the authorities at home. The tales of plunder, of cruelty, and of maltreatment of prisoners, with which the American papers, and even the Congress reports, are rife, it is, of course, impossible to test. But their complaints are pitched in a tone, and repeated with a perseverance, to which Davoust's campaigns in Northern Germany furnish the nearest parallel. Throughout this disgraceful war, the maximum of mischief with the minimum of risk appears to have been the object of the English soldiery.

This was not the way to reconquer alienated affections. When Lord Cornwallis had taken Charleston, and found that none, even of those who submitted and stayed in the town, would speak to his officers, he is reported to have said, that, even if they should succeed in conquering the men, the heavier task would still remain of conquering the women. And one of the most striking features in this 'Diary of the Revolution,' and the strongest proof of the exasperation that prevailed, is the prominent share taken by the women. They were all Joans of Arc or Maids of Saragossa in their way. In one place, we find an association of young ladies formed on the basis of refusing every lover who had not taken an active part in the revolutionary campaigns. In another, a "Tory," who, finding himself in exclusively feminine society, thinks that he can parade his sentiments with impunity, is set upon by the incensed Amazons, stripped incontinently to the waist, and tarred and feathered on the spot. In a third place, a party of ladies, equally patriotic, hearing that an unworthy member of the sex had baptized her child by a Tory name—baptisms were a great subject for party demonstrations—marched up to her with the intention of visiting her with the same sort of summary justice; but, in this case, the victim had timely warning, and made off. And many other similar demonstrations of female patriotism are recorded in this book. But this exasperation of the enemies of England was not the only evil effect of the atrocities that disgraced the English arms. They had a direct tendency to alienate her friends. For the English ministers—and it is one of the circumstances that deepens the ignominy of their failure—had at first a very large support in native American opinion. Throughout the Diary we find the rebels very much more afraid of "Tories" than of British soldiers. In many States they attempted counter memorials and organizations. In North Carolina, a refugee Jacobite at the head of the Tories, appeared in the field against the troops of Congress; and Long Island was so completely and inveterately Tory, that it was found necessary to make a descent upon it from the mainland, and instil a wholesome Liberalism by force of arms. The passionate appeal at page 168, vol. 2, for an extension of this system of proselytism, which has always been popular in America, will give an idea of the extent to which the Tories might have been made available for the English cause, if common vigor or common temper had existed in the councils of the king.

From the Philadelphia Bulletin.

"A really original work on our Revolution is, of course, a surprise. The facts are all so well known that it would seem impossible to impart to them an air of novelty. But Mr. Frank Moore has presented a most fresh and vivid picture of the whole course of events, from the beginning of 1775 till the close of the war. The plan adopted has been to take the accounts of newspapers of the time, both Whig and Tory, and such private diaries and correspondence as were within his reach, and to arrange all these in the form of a diary. The skilful execution of this design has given us one of the most readable and impartial narratives of our struggle for independence that has ever been produced. *The events seem to pass before the reader's immediate vision, and to be reported by him while the impression they produce on his mind is entirely fresh.*"

From the New York Evening Post.

"Mr. Moore has happily executed a happy thought: he has written a history of the most important events of the last century in the very words of its contemporaries.

"It would be impossible for any historian who merely writes after authorities to impart so vivid an impression of the occurrences of the period. All the great characters of the war, who are now so venerable in our estimation that they seem rather demi-gods than men, pass before us as they lived, and are seen as they were seen by their contemporaries.

"Washington presents himself, not merely as the noble and successful leader of a great people struggling for their rights, but as the *rebel and the partisan*, having many and bitter enemies, who were capable of covering his name with the filth of their abuse."

From the Philadelphia North American.

"The work is novel, curious, interesting, and valuable in a very high degree. Its effect is, to transport us back into the time of the Revolution in a more '*realizing*' manner than ever known before; so that we seem ourselves to be a living, moving portion of the great panorama."

From the N. Y. Herald.

"We have been so accustomed to read American history through the medium of rhetorical periods, better adapted to Fourth of July orations than to the calm and impartial investigation of past occurrences, that it is refreshing to meet with a book in which the exact color of events is preserved, and the individuality of the author lost. Every page of the work teems with facts gathered from the daily life of the Revolution, and thus, without the intervention of modern speculation, we have brought before us not merely the actors in the great drama of the Revolution, but their actual thoughts, feelings, and emotions.

From the Independent.

"There is not—we speak advisedly and deliberately—in the

whole range of volumes and libraries upon American history, there is not to be found any *single* contribution toward that history of such value as that contained in these two volumes. The author has made no attempt to write a history, nor does he indulge in comment or criticism upon the materials which he has so laboriously brought together; BUT HE HAS REPRODUCED, AS BY THE PHOTOGRAPHIC ART, THE VERY TIMES AND SCENES OF THE AMERICAN REVOLUTION AS THEY WERE TO THE MEN WHO MOVED IN THE MIDST OF THEM. From the newspapers of that period, papers of every shade of political opinion, he has carefully and conscientiously culled the facts and incidents of the hour, with the notes and comments of those who recorded them;—these he has arranged in chronological order, and then has classified them in a complete and elaborate index. The labor of such a work is immense; its value is incalculable: the reader will find in it much to amuse and instruct him upon many incidental topics, and a perfect mirror of the Revolutionary era."

From the Christian Enquirer.

" 'The Diary of the Revolution' marks a new era in the literature of the American Revolution. It presents no opinions and no comments, but reproduces, with the naturalness of a daguerreotype, the thoughts, feelings, aspirations, hopes, misgivings—in one word, all the conflicting emotions which stirred the minds of men during the exciting period of our War of Independence. Here we have, for the first time, history untainted and unsophisticated by the individuality and the fancy of the writer—history stripped of all its meretricious adornments of style and criticism —undefiled, genuine history, based upon facts squeezed out from the newspapers of the times, and bearing upon their face the marks of their truthfulness and stern reality. In pondering over Frank Moore's unpretending but instructive pages, we become, as it were, for the first time, aware that our Revolution was not due to a few ambitious leaders, but that hundreds and hundreds of anonymous writers all over the country sounded its tocsin, and prepared the explosion of public opinion which found its climax in the Declaration of Independence.

" The Diary is animated by a more truthful appreciation of our national character than all the emanations of rhetorical historians. The Toms, Dicks and Harrys whose communications he introduces for the first time before the public, are much more sturdy specimens of the spirit of the universal Yankee nation than the stilted heroes of their imaginations. Far from us the desire of detracting either from the patriotic glory of the venerated founders of our Republic, or from the literary laurels of their eulogists and chroniclers; but Frank Moore demonstrates the truth which the latter have failed to establish.

"His 'Diary' shows that the leaders of our Revolution acted in obedience to the public sentiment, and tells us, by its copious and sagacious newspaper extracts, how this public sentiment was formed by those anonymous writers, whom we are obliged to designate by the general name of *people*, because we do not know their real name, and because their name was legion.

"In this respect, then, the 'Diary' has struck an entirely new chord. Our eminent writers bring before our eyes the stage of history with the masterly skill of experienced dramatists, but the editor of this work leads us behind the curtain. The heroes of the former are few in number, but are made to dazzle the sight by the splendor of their appearance. The 'Diary,' however, teaches us to understand the tricks or mysteries of the stage, and points good-naturedly to the pile of dusty papers in the green-room, and to the voice of the prompter, who whispers to the actors the words of the play, but whose name is never mentioned.

"While our rhetorical historians crown the actors with laurels, and are greeted with enthusiastic applause by the audience, Frank Moore labors faithfully at the dusty papers behind the curtain, and gradually, after some sixteen years of persistent toil, it oozes out that those much-bepraised actors were only the agents, and that they were roused to action by the omnipotent voice of public opinion, as it thundered through the pages of those dusty journals which this 'Diary of the American Revolution' has saved from oblivion."

From the *Philadelphia Evening Journal*.

"The 'Diary of the Revolution' is a photograph of the times, and is a graphic delineation of the manners, the customs, the whole social life of the country in an era of distinguished men, and which was fruitful of great events. We know of no work which gives us so vivid a picture of the days which tried men's souls as the interesting volumes which are now presented to the American public."

From the *New York Express*.

"By this work we are taken behind the scenes; we are introduced to the actors; we talk with them and listen to them; we feel with or against them; we believe in their motives. We are not reading a calm statement, but receiving an animated defence or attack. We laugh or are indignant; we blush or are angered at what we see or hear. We gain all sorts of odd information; out of the way news comes straight to us. We form a more correct and better idea of the times and the men than from reading a hundred measured tomes."

From the *Philadelphia Press*.

"The peculiar feature in this work which distinguishes it from all other historical collections is that the conflicting views of persons and events, as produced by writers on both sides of the question

—the whigs favoring independence, and the tories desirous of keeping the United Provinces under the harsh dominion of George the Third—are here related with great tact, blended with surprising felicity, and dovetailed together with remarkable success. Of all the historical works treating of our great revolutionary struggle, there is not one so full of varied interest as this. Open either volume where you may, and something amusing or instructive strikes the eye.

" It may be said that this 'Diary' is the apotheosis of journalism, for it is principally composed of newspaper accounts, for and against, of the incidents, great and small, of the War of Independence."

This work is sold by Subscription only, at Five Dollars per Set, in Cloth; or in Sheep Library Style, $6 50; in Half Turkey Morocco, $7 50; in Half Calf Extra, or Antique, $8 00; in Turkey Morocco, $12 00.

CHARLES SCRIBNER, Publisher,

124 Grand Street, New York.

NOTICE.

An earlier series of this work, embracing the newspaper history of the American colonies, from the year 1750 until the commencement of 1775, is in course of preparation, and will be published, BY SUBSCRIPTION ONLY, at an early day. Subscriptions, *payable on delivery of the work*, are received by mail or otherwise, by the Editor. at New York City.

PRICE PER VOLUME, 575 PAGES, TWO DOLLARS AND FIFTY CENTS.